FROM GOODS TO A GOOD LIFE

MADHAVI SUNDER

From Goods to a Good Life

INTELLECTUAL PROPERTY AND GLOBAL JUSTICE

Yale UNIVERSITY PRESS

NEW HAVEN AND LONDON

Yale University Press books may be purchased in quantity for educational, business, or promotional use. For information, please e-mail sales.press@yale.edu (U.S. office) or sales @yaleup.co.uk (U.K. office).

Set in FontShop Scala types by Duke & Company, Devon, Pennsylvania.
Printed in the United States of America.

Library of Congress Cataloging-in-Publication Data
Sunder, Madhavi.
From goods to a good life : intellectual property and global justice / Madhavi Sunder.
    p.   cm.
Includes bibliographical references and index.
ISBN 978-0-300-14671-4 (hardcover : alk. paper) 1. Intellectual property. 2. Justice. 3. Law and globalization. 4. International law—Philosophy. I. Title.
K1401.S86 2012
346.04'8—dc23
2011045974

A catalogue record for this book is available from the British Library.
This paper meets the requirements of ANSI/NISO Z39.48-1992 (Permanence of Paper).

10 9 8 7 6 5 4 3 2 1

For Anoushka and Milan

CONTENTS

INTRODUCTION: CULTURE AND FREEDOM

FROM BARBIE TO HARRY POTTER, the Beatles to Beyoncé, Hollywood
to Bollywood, and Viagra to life-saving AIDS medications, intellectual
property now dominates our culture and rules our economy and welfare.
Our children grow up in a world of copyrighted characters surrounded
by trademarked goods. With the advent of the World Trade Organization
and its legal obligations, intellectual property also increasingly affects
people across the globe, from Brazil to Bangladesh. Yet the full cultural
and economic consequences of intellectual property policies are often
hidden. We focus instead on the fruits of innovation—more iPods, more
bestsellers, more blockbuster drugs—without concern for what is being
produced, by whom, and for whose benefit.

But make no mistake: intellectual property laws have profound effects
on human capabilities, what Amartya Sen and Martha Nussbaum define
as what people "are actually able to do and be."[1] The most obvious example
is law's regulation of access to basic necessities, such as textbooks and essential medicines. But the connections run deeper still. Intellectual property incentivizes pharmaceutical companies to innovate drugs that *sell*—
hence we are flooded with cures for erectile dysfunction and baldness, but
still have no cure for the diseases that afflict millions of the poor, from malaria to tuberculosis, because these people are too poor to save their lives.
Intellectual property laws affect our ability to think, learn, share, sing,

dance, tell stories, joke, borrow ideas, inspire and be inspired, reply, critique, and pay homage. In short, intellectual property laws do much more than "incentivize innovation," as the common perception goes. Intellectual property bears fundamentally on the basic activities that make for a full and joyful life. Furthermore, in a global Knowledge Economy, intellectual property distributes wealth and power and affects global justice.

Take the example of one Solomon Linda. A black migrant worker living in a squalid Johannesburg hostel in 1939, Linda composed a song based on his own childhood experiences protecting cattle from lions in the jungle. The song borrowed the syncopation of American jazz from across the Atlantic and mixed it with an a cappella melody to create what would become Africa's first recorded pop hit. Linda's song soon crossed the Atlantic and was reborn, first as "Wimoweh" and later as "The Lion Sleeps Tonight." It would go on to be recorded over 170 times, eventually finding its way into Disney's immensely popular film and Broadway production *The Lion King*. But while the song eventually produced millions of dollars for Disney and others, Linda died destitute, suffering from a curable kidney disease at the age of fifty-three. One of Linda's children died of malnutrition and another died of AIDS.

Linda's story illustrates how intellectual property laws have effects that extend well beyond incentives for creation. Law regulates recognition (or here, misrecognition) of the contributions of diverse people to our global culture, and distributes the material rewards of innovation. A misrecognition of Linda's contribution led to his inability to pay for food and drugs that could have saved his and his children's lives; conversely, recognizing Linda's cultural contribution would have given him the agency to provide for himself and his family. Intellectual property governs the flow of *free* culture, allowing Solomon to remix American jazz with his own South African music, and yet also raises issues of *fair* culture. Solomon's creation was left to the laws of the jungle, free to be exploited by Westerners with more knowledge and power. Finally, Linda's song reveals the power of culture as a vehicle for mutual understanding, shared meaning, and sociability. "The Lion Sleeps Tonight" is praised as a song "the whole world knows."[2]

This book highlights the broad social and economic dimensions of innovation and cultural exchange in a global context of sharp inequalities in power and knowledge. I argue that law must facilitate the ability of all citizens, rich or poor, brown or white, man or woman, straight or gay, to participate in making knowledge of our world and to benefit materially from their cultural production. Democratic cultural production promotes not only economic development from market exchanges in a Knowledge Age, but also *human* development. Enhancing one's capacity to participate in cultural production and critique engenders autonomy and equality, learning, critical thinking, sharing, sociability, and mutual recognition and understanding. This book is a call for intellectual property law and legal decision makers to expressly recognize and contend with the plural values at stake in cultural production and exchange.

FROM GOODS TO A GOOD LIFE

In this book I will show that intellectual property laws shaped only by the narrow economic view that predominates today results in a crabbed understanding of culture and law's role in promoting culture. Current law takes as its mandate the production of more cultural goods, from R2D2 to iPads, to be exchanged in the global marketplace. To date, even the most trenchant critiques of the excesses of this law take this normative goal as given. The influential "public domain movement" led by scholars critiquing the exponential growth of intellectual property laws at the turn of the century focused their ire on the counterproductive effects of too much property on this ultimate goal—intellectual productivity. Too many property rights, they argued, will more likely stifle innovation than promote it.

But copyright and patent laws do more than incentivize the creation of more goods. They fundamentally affect human capabilities and the ability to live *a good life*. As we will see, the impact of these laws goes far beyond gross domestic product. At the start of the twenty-first century, the legal regime of intellectual property has insinuated itself more deeply into our lives and more deeply into the framework of international law than at any other period of time in history, affecting our ability to do a broad range of activities, including to create and contest culture and to produce and distribute life-saving drugs. Indeed, now that full compliance with the Trade Related Aspects of Intellectual Property Rights (TRIPS) Agreement is required in all but the world's very least developed countries, intellectual property has become literally a question of life or death.

Intellectual property's march into all corners of our lives and to the most destitute corners of the world has paradoxically exposed the fragility of its economic foundations while amplifying its social and cultural effects. Global actors have responded to these effects. During the Doha Round of World Trade Organization (WTO) negotiations in 2001, the WTO declared that intellectual property, while important, should not stand in the way of "WTO members' right to protect public health and, in particular, to promote access to medicines for all."[3] The World Intellectual Property Organization (WIPO) responded to the dramatic social and economic effects of intellectual property on developing countries, in particular, by adopting in 2007 a "development agenda" that would reorient the organization's policymaking from promoting efficiency to "development." The WIPO pledged "to approach intellectual property enforcement in the context of broader societal interests and especially development-oriented concerns," stating that intellectual property law and policy must be created and carried out in "a manner conducive to social and economic welfare."[4]

Despite these real-world changes, in the United States, intellectual property scholars insist on explaining this field only through the narrow lens of a particular economic vision. Giving evidence to Amartya Sen's observation that "[t]heories have lives of their own, quite defiantly of the phenomenal world that can be actually observed," by and large, American legal scholars continue to understand intellectual property solely as a tool to solve an economic "public goods" problem: nonrivalrous and nonexcludable goods such as music and scientific knowledge will be too easy to copy and share—and thus there will not be an incentive to create them in the first place—without a monopoly right in these creations for a limited period of time.[5]

But intellectual property today is more than simply a tool for incentivizing creative production. Intellectual property laws bear considerably on central features of human flourishing, from the developing world's access to food, textbooks, and essential medicines; to the ability of citizens everywhere to participate democratically in political and cultural discourse; to the capacity to earn a livelihood from one's intellectual contributions to our global culture. This book calls for a deeper understanding of intellectual property and its broader social, cultural, and economic effects, one that acknowledges that regulation of cultural production and exchange has a profound impact on human freedom.

In the pages that follow, I argue that we must recognize culture not just as *products,* but as critical *processes* of creative and social interaction that promote our humanity. Cultural participation is an end in itself and cultural participation has intrinsic value. Singing, dancing, and sharing stories together; utilizing our intellect to make new knowledge of the world—these are fundamentally what human freedom is *for.* At the same time, cultural participation is a critical *means* for fostering cultural change and exchange. Individuals take values, norms, images, and ideas from the world around them—near and far, past and present—and recast them to tell their own stories and remake culture. Yet a decade on into the twenty-first century, much of the cultural forms that are familiar and dear to us are in private hands, wrapped up as intellectual property in the form of copyrights (in books, music, art, and film), patents (in scientific innovation), and trademarks (in commercial brands). The law of intellectual property—what it allows; what it prevents; who makes the decisions; and crucially, who pays or receives the money—thus is central to our ability to talk back to or talk through our culture. Cultural exchanges cultivate humanity in other important ways. Exchanging stories and knowledge with one another both confers recognition on diverse others and fosters mutual understanding.

Today we readily understand how ownership of property in land is central to our ability to control our own destinies; at the same time, we regulate property relations to reflect the kinds of interactions we deem just. Modern property law "governs human interaction to ensure that people relate to each other with respect and dignity,"[6] for example, by implying into every leasehold a warranty of habitability, prohibiting racially restrictive covenants, and guaranteeing equal access to places of public accommodation. As Joseph Singer reminds us, real property law both reflects and shapes our free and democratic society.[7]

This book seeks to bring our attention to the increasingly important ways that intellectual property law frames a free and democratic society and just global social relations. As I will show, intellectual property laws that regulate the ability to produce, share, and enjoy culture are central to our ability to cultivate ourselves and our communities.

THREE VIEWS OF CULTURE

"Culture" is a word on everybody's lips in intellectual property scholarship. James Boyle has spurred a "cultural environmentalism" movement to counter the privatization of our intellectual heritage. Larry Lessig has warned that legal code and computer code together are morphing our once "free culture" into a "permission culture." Yochai Benkler has explored how commons-based methods of production "provide more opportunities for participating in the creation of culture." And Jack Balkin has said that interpreters of the First Amendment and intellectual property ought to be concerned with "cultural democracy." All of these scholars seek to protect our cultural commons and the processes of cultural innovation. Yet there is resistance in the academy to the elaboration of a cultural theory of intellectual property that would stand beside and help illuminate the dominant economic account of our law, and none of these theorists has offered such an account. This book takes up that task.

Before elaborating, I should briefly distinguish my view of culture from two common perceptions of culture: culture as tradition and culture as commodity. (I consider these distinctions in detail in Chapter 2.) For well over a century the dominant anthropological conception of culture was of static *tradition* handed down from above, rotely reproduced from generation to generation. Culture as tradition takes, in Michel Foucault's words, "the spectator's posture" toward the present—that of "the *flâneur*, the idle . . . satisfied to . . . build up a storehouse of memories."[8] But this view of culture has been rejected both positively and normatively by modern theorists from fields as wide-ranging as anthropology to philosophy.

The view of culture as *commodity* has particular resonance in intellectual property law. On the one hand, mass culture has a democratizing effect, increasing access to cultural works by the public. At the same time, however, architectures of commodity culture, from technology to law, have enforced autocratic cultural authority. As told in Jürgen Habermas's influential account *The Structural Transformation of the Public Sphere,* culture by the end of the twentieth century was transformed into static commodities handed down to the masses with little if any opportunity to meaningfully engage with the imposed culture. During the late twentieth century, social theorists from Habermas to Foucault came to focus on the constraints of culture on human freedom.

In short, neither the tradition nor commodity views of culture, which conceive culture as something that is given and passively consumed, are fully in tune with modern Enlightenment values, which emphasize innovation as critical thinking and engagement, not mere passive enjoyment of goods handed down by others.

This book begins the project of developing a third theory of culture that would better reflect and shape a free and democratic society and the demands of global justice. Anthropology, cultural studies, philosophy, and development economics offer rich views of culture and its effects on human freedom and development. Notably these views are influencing, and are being influenced by, transnational actors working on intellectual property issues, from multilateral agencies such as WIPO, the WTO, and the World Health Organization (WHO) to a civil society movement for "Access to Knowledge." Yet they have not fully challenged the dominance of the single-minded economic account of this law at home in the United States.

The capabilities approach associated with Amartya Sen and Martha Nussbaum supplies the normative vision animating this book. I rely on both Nussbaum's elaboration of a list of central human capabilities that law should promote, as well as Sen's description of development as freedom, to elaborate the plural values at stake in modern intellectual property conflicts.

Today there is growing recognition that culture is a key component of human development. Surely this includes the production and just distribution of essential cultural goods, from medicines to biotechnology to educational materials, art, and literature. All of these are critical to enabling a fulfilling life, bearing direct relation to what Nussbaum identifies as "central human capabilities," from the capability to live "a human life of normal length," to "being able to use the senses, to imagine, think, and reason . . . in a 'truly human' way . . . cultivated by adequate education."[9] In adapting Nussbaum's capabilities approach to intellectual property law, I seek to elaborate the connections between the cultural sphere, intellectual property, and the expansion of human capabilities. Where traditional intellectual property scholarship focuses on knowledge products, a cultural approach takes a broader view of cultural freedom and equality as vital to promoting not only health and education, but also a whole host of central human capabilities, including:

- Being able to use imagination and thought in connection with experiencing and producing works and events of one's own choice (religious, literary, musical, and so forth)
- Supporting forms of human association that can be shown to be crucial in the development of emotions
- Being able to form a conception of the good and to engage in critical reflection about the planning of one's life
- Being able to engage in various forms of social interaction
- Being able to laugh, play, and enjoy recreational activities
- Being able to hold property, and having property rights on an equal basis with others
- In work, being able to work as a human being exercising practical reason, and to enter into meaningful relationships of mutual recognition with other workers.[10]

Margaret Jane Radin brought theories of human flourishing to bear on real property law (including Nussbaum's own theories), highlighting this law's role in promoting personhood. Today, Nussbaum and Sen's theory of human capabilities may usefully help us begin to reorient *intellectual property* law, as well.

In these pages, I suggest that culture is better understood by considering three central features: *participation, livelihood,* and *shared meaning.* This view of *culture as a participatory community* is more in line with the values of a free a democratic society and, as I shall argue, is the view of culture that modern intellectual property laws ought to promote.

Participation

What Foucault famously described as the "author-function" describes how power and knowledge are controlled by a select few. The juridical category of "author" serves to legitimate and insulate cultural authority from the proliferation of alternate meanings.[11] But today this vision of cultural authority is yielding to a more dialogic process, in which ordinary individuals wield the power and claim the authority to produce knowledge of the world, from journalism to music, art, and science. This democratization is taking place through a confluence of innovations, from blogs to customer reviews; to YouTube, MySpace, and peer-to-peer file sharing; to open-source collaboration. Participatory culture democratizes cultural meaning-making: cultural meaning derives less exclusively from traditional authorities and more from the people themselves. And as examples from Ethiopia to India to South Africa in the proceeding pages illustrate, participatory culture extends well beyond the United States. More and more, individuals and communities around the world seek to engage in global processes of meaning-making.

Of course, the rise of participatory culture does not mean that we should reorient law to promote it. There are certainly normative benefits to stable cultural meaning and authority. Trademark law is built on this premise, reasoning that without stable meanings, marks would lose their ability to signal to consumers the source of the product. Copyright and patent, too, are premised on the notion that protecting authors and inventors produces better art and science. Indeed, in a recent book, *The Cult of the Amateur,* Andrew Keen suggests that by embracing cultural democracy we would be giving up on cultural quality.[12]

But while we have elaborated reasons for privileging stable cultural meanings, the case for cultural democracy—that is, dissent and change *within* culture—has been more elusive. This book begins to elaborate the benefits of democratic culture, a culture in which all people have the capacity to participate. I use the phrase *working through culture* to describe the myriad ways in which individuals exercise their human capabilities—from critical thinking to learning, sharing, playing, and engaging in meaningful work—*within* the cultural domain, and not just outside of it. The normative benefits of active engagement in rather than passive acceptance of culture are legion: from producing greater and more diverse cultural content, to fostering engaged democratic citizens, to promoting learning through emulation and pretend play, to engendering mutual recognition and understanding among diverse peoples. In addition, participatory culture has significant economic value, especially for marginalized communities historically left out of the processes of cultural production.

Livelihood

A twenty-first-century theory of culture cannot ignore the important issues of development and global justice. Culture plays a critical role in development, in particular in countries' ability to meet the U.N. Millennium Development Goals, which include the eradication of global poverty, universal education, gender equality, child and maternal health, progress in fighting HIV/AIDS, and environmental sustainability.

To promote *development as freedom,* in Sen's words, intellectual property law should seek to enhance people's capacity to participate in cultural production and shared communities of meaning. Furthermore, we must recognize that cultural production is both an end and a means of development. Recognition of Australian aboriginal artists, African musicians, and Ethiopian farmers as producers of cultural meaning, for example, could potentially direct significant revenues into these countries. As Sen has written, "cultural liberty is important not only in the cultural sphere, but in the successes and failures in social, political, and economic spheres. The different dimensions of human life have strong interrelations."[13] Here, *working through culture* has yet another meaning. In the Knowledge Age, cultural work is a promising means of economic development. Concerns about the commodification of culture notwithstanding, working through culture can offer an antidote to alienation by providing recognition and remuneration for meaningful work.

Shared Meaning

Finally, growth and diversification in cultural production may promote mutual recognition and understanding across diverse cultures. As media scholars observe, the phenomenally popular new websites of the early part of this new century, from Facebook to YouTube to Flickr, are not necessarily about high-quality content but "social connections."[14] Shared meaning goes to the very heart of what makes culture tick; culture evokes communal responses to and affection for common musical and literary referents. The communal nature of the new Participation Age cannot be overstated. As President Obama stated in his Inaugural Address, today's electronic networks not only "feed our commerce," but also "bind us together."[15]

Put simply, a global culture in which all peoples have an opportunity to be creators is surely a means to economic development, but it is also much more. The cultural sphere of life encompasses those joys that make a human life truly worth living. As child psychologists observe, "When young children are free from illness, malnutrition, neglect, and abuse, they turn their considerable energies to play."[16] This is the crux of Sen's insight that economic development goals must go beyond raising GDP to ask what is required to ensure that people can live fulfilling lives.

Cultural exchanges are not merely monetary transactions involving static goods. Individuals make cultural goods to share with others parts of themselves—their history, their music, their stories. Cultural activity promotes self-development and mutual understanding, potentially realizing G. W. F. Hegel's twin goals of "individual self-realization and reciprocal recognition." Serious study of the processes of cultural production and exchange governed by modern intellectual property laws must recognize the special ways in which culture can promote mutual recognition and understanding. As John Dewey eloquently put it, "the art characteristic of a civilization is the means for entering sympathetically into the deepest elements in the experience of remote and foreign civilizations."[17] By pointing out the common human characteristics that bind us all, culture promotes shared meaning not only among those who look and think alike, but also among far-flung peoples.

BEYOND EFFICIENCY

Intellectual property scholars today focus on a single goal: efficiency. But in this book, I elaborate the connections between cultural production and plural values, from freedom to equality, democracy, development, and mutual recognition and understanding. Freedom to participate in cultural life stands at the very core of *liberty*. As Salman Rushdie has stated, "Those who do not have power over the story that dominates their lives, power to retell it, rethink it, deconstruct it, joke about it, and change it as times change, truly are powerless, because they cannot think new thoughts."[18] Cultural liberty also has important implications for *equality*. The liberty to contest hegemonic discourses has particularly profound possibilities for women and other minorities who have not traditionally had power over the stories that dominate their lives. Drawing on the insights of Charles Taylor's "politics of recognition," I will show with various real-world examples how democratizing the capacity to make and contest culture can distribute power to shape meaning and enhance the capacity to contest hegemonic meanings—so long as copyright and trademark laws do not stand in the way.

Active engagement in the cultural sphere can also be a school for engendering the central traits of democratic citizenship, from *critical thinking* to *creativity* to *sharing* and *sociability*. I have already alluded to how democratic participation in making culture is linked to *economic develop-*

ment; I will also consider how recognizing diverse others as authors and inventors promotes *mutual recognition* and *mutual understanding.*

THE PUBLIC DOMAIN

This book affirms the important observation of scholars of the public domain that creativity is a social and reiterative process. I elaborate on their descriptive claims for a robust public domain by developing further the normative importance of cultural participation. Cultural sharing promotes our humanity.

At the same time, some public domain advocates may find discomforting my calls to democratize who we recognize as authors and inventors. In subsequent chapters, I argue that histories of colonialism and cultural and racial stereotypes have often led us to overlook the knowledge contributions of the poor. While I do not advocate for new sui generis intellectual property rights for indigenous peoples or the poor, I point out how poor people's knowledge—even when qualifying as novel and nonobvious, or as original and fixed—often gets freely appropriated by creators in the developed world because the works are presumed to be ancient or folk culture. I argue that a more democratic culture, that is, one in which more and more of the world's people are engaged in cultural production and exchange, requires first the simple recognition that each of us has a story to tell and knowledge to share.

THE LADY WITH A MOUSE

I write this book about culture and freedom at a moment of profound cultural change around the world. While culture has always been something invented rather than discovered, cultural reform until now has largely been the work of artists or an elite vanguard. Today the tools for authoring our own lives and creating our own communities are increasingly coming into the ordinary person's grasp, and on a truly global scale.

Immanuel Kant iterated his Enlightenment imperative "Sapere Aude!" (Think for oneself!)[19] long before the emergence of the Internet and the tools of digital technology known as "Web 2.0" dramatically enhanced our ability to rip, mix, and contest our given culture from the bottom up. By and large, late into the twentieth century, Enlightenment, where it emerged at all, had come mostly to the political sphere. The cultural sphere, in contrast, remained largely in the control of traditional authorities, from media moguls to religious mullahs, backed by the force of law, if not God. Indeed, while much of the world embraced democracy in the political realm, the cultural sphere grew less democratic. As told in Habermas's foundational work *The Structural Transformation of the Public Sphere,* culture by the end of the twentieth century was transformed into static commodities handed down to the masses with little if any opportunity to meaningfully engage with them.

But today we see signs that Enlightenment may finally go the next mile, as social movements and new technologies usher in critical modes of being *within* culture. The twenty-first century has ushered in a Participation Age that is turning on their head our centuries-old conceptions of culture as tradition or as static, canned commodities. The convergence of social movements with digital technology and the Internet has enabled the rise of a democratic culture in which more and more people claim a right and ability to participate not just in the political sphere, but in the domains of culture as well. Individuals, traditionally the consumers of "take-it-or-leave it" culture, make "bespoke" culture—that is, a culture tailored for their own use. On the Internet, Netizens are a part of not only the Information Age—in which consumers passively receive culture protected by intellectual property—but also a Participation Age of remix culture, YouTube, MySpace, blogs, podcasts, wikis, and peer-to-peer file sharing.

This new generation views intellectual properties as the raw materials for its own creative acts, blurring the lines that have long separated producers from consumers. Witness a disc jockey named "Dangermouse" who mashes up the Beatles' *White Album* and hip-hop artist Jay-Z's *Black Album* to create the award-winning *Grey Album*. Witness girl fans of Harry Potter who post stories at www.fanfiction.net to retell life at Hogwarts from Hermione's perspective. Witness Nintendo's Wii game console, which allows players to personalize their "Mii" avatars—from gender and skin color down to the shape of their eyes—before setting off on their adventures. The enhanced ability to write oneself into the traditional script offers a powerful new take on Legos and action figures. Our children now have the virtual building blocks to render cultural universes their own.

Indeed, the whimsical painting *Lady with a Mouse* may serve as a useful allegory for modern culture. Rendered by the Indian artist Mohan Sivanand, it depicts a slender Indian woman sitting at a computer.

While the image of an "Indian woman" has typically been used in art as a standard-bearer of tradition, the presence of the computer in the image reminds us that the rise of YouTube, MySpace, and a read-write culture forces a reconsideration of such old notions. The "lady" in the painting is no passive receptacle of tradition. Far from it, in this context, with technology as a leitmotif of modernity, she is poised with the power to make culture herself. Is she writing a blog? Posting a video to YouTube? Connecting with a virtual community on Facebook? The *Lady with a Mouse* reminds us that culture is made, not inherited. We are moving away from culture as Mickey Mouse—the immutable, prefab product of a corporation—to culture empowered by a computer mouse.

REDUCTIONISM, FACTIONALISM, NARCISSISM

Talk of inventing oneself, if taken literally, can surely give pause. As Zadie Smith warns: "When a human being becomes a set of data on a website like Facebook, he or she is reduced. Everything shrinks. Individual character. Friendships. Language. Sensibility."[20] The fear is that "inventing ourselves" may indeed produce a society of products, but not people.

Others such as Cass Sunstein lament that the Internet is leading to communities that are highly factionalized and offer little exposure to opposing viewpoints.[21] In a related point, Andrew Keen argues that the world of participatory culture on YouTube and Facebook is atomistic and narcissistic.[22]

These are important concerns, and I agree we must protect against reductionism, factionalism, and narcissism. At the same time, I am emboldened by examples as far-flung as open-source collaboration, fan fiction, and YouTube, which show us that what we are witnessing is often not a rejection of culture and community by individuals sloughing off their communal skins, but rather the emergence of *autonomous and democratic participation within communities of shared meaning*. Despite their affiliation and shared norms, robust debate within cultural communities remains, especially on the Internet, where, as the media critic of the *New York Times* observes, "the only authentic response to a YouTube video is another YouTube video."[23] Shared meaning does not imply obedient acceptance of cultural traditions. Much of the cultural creativity on YouTube and the Internet I will describe reveals individuals not as subjects but as citizens, taking up their responsibility to participate and engage in reasoned argument and critique within cultural domains.

Lady with a Mouse—painting by Mohan Sivanand, photograph by Sam Sellers.
(Courtesy of Mohan Sivanand)

INTELLECTUAL PROPERTY AS A TOOL, NOT A RIGHT

Let me clarify that in my view, intellectual property remains a tool, not a right. Mine is a complex consequentialist approach that seeks to expand the purpose of this law beyond incentives and efficiency to promoting the broad range of values we hold dear in the twenty-first century. As mentioned earlier, my book dovetails with the broad contemporary movement in international intellectual property circles to reconsider this law as a tool for promoting human development and not GDP or efficiency alone. But my goals are also fundamentally connected to our own domestic law. If the goal of American utilitarian intellectual property law is to promote culture, we must pay heed to what vision of culture we are promoting.

An important question arises: if intellectual property remains a tool, is it too blunt a tool to promote the broad canvas of values we place under the rubric of human development? Henry Smith's persuasive query to scholars advocating a social relations approach to property law applies well in the intellectual property context, too. Perhaps, as Smith suggests, "talking about ultimate ends is more glamorous than asking the more engineering-like question of how to serve them."[24] But to this I reply that the simple elegance of economic analysis has both masked problematic assumptions behind its numbers and failed to give clear empirical support for current laws—a point that, as I show in the next chapter, even the father of economic analysis of law, Richard Posner, concedes.

FROM IP TO iP

"IP" is the well-recognized shorthand for an intellectual property law focused on the production of *culture as stuff,* whereas "iP" is a shorthand for a new vision of culture that recognizes *culture as a community* that individuals make together, if not brick by brick, then video by video. The interdisciplinary, pluralist vision of intellectual property developed herein prioritizes people and participation in creative global markets and recognizes that intellectual property laws affect human capability, distributive justice, and global social relations. My reinterpretation of intellectual property applies to suburban American fan-fiction authors and African coffee farmers alike: all seek a greater capacity for accessing and crafting new knowledge of the world. In turn, these cultural capabilities structure our social relations, as new creators seek to access global markets to attain recognition for their creativity, share meaning with others, and ultimately to be fairly remunerated for their contributions to our global culture.

TOWARD A MORE COMPREHENSIVE, INTERDISCIPLINARY APPROACH

In Chapter 1, "Beyond Incentives," I present the limits of the current incentives approach as a comprehensive theory of intellectual property. I show that the narrow economic account of intellectual property can neither fully explain nor guide resolution of some of the most troubling intellectual property conflicts of our day, from the rise of user-generated content on the Internet, to biopiracy, to the expansion of intellectual property rights to the developing world. This chapter calls for a reorientation in intellectual property law and policy away from a singular focus on ex ante incentives to a consideration of law's broad social and economic effects.

The next two chapters begin to theorize a cultural approach to intellectual property that would stand beside and complement the current economic approach. Chapter 2, "Bespoke Culture," compares two conceptions of culture, *culture as tradition* and *culture as commodity*, with a new vision of *culture as participatory community* emergent in the new millennium. Liberal democratic theory has largely ignored the cultural sphere, privileging freedom and equality in the political sphere but allowing for fewer rights to contest or remake cultural norms and community. In this chapter I pull from interdisciplinary theory—from the cultural theory of Pierre Bourdieu, to the philosophy of Habermas and Foucault, to the art criticism of Dewey—to highlight the effect of freedom in the cultural sphere on society, politics, and the economy. Our vision of culture matters. Armed with a fuller understanding of the descriptive and prescriptive superiority of a participatory vision of culture, we may more profitably critique and remake intellectual property law with careful attention to just what kind of culture this law ought to promote.

I turn to the links between cultural democracy and development in Chapter 3, "Fair Culture." At the turn of the millennium, the Participation Age and the goal of poverty eradication have dovetailed. As a recent U.N. Human Development Report has noted, in a Knowledge Age in which wealth derives from cultural production and exchange in global markets, "cultural freedom is not just a human right, but also a key to development."[25] The concept of fair culture yokes together meaning and livelihood. But in this chapter I consider the impediments to cultural participation by the poor, which range from unequal capacity and lack of capital to stereotypes and biases that lead to misrecognition and exploitation. This chapter considers strategies for stimulating cultural production in the developing world, and for recognizing the ongoing innovation and authorship of those in the developing world, from coffee farmers in Ethiopia to the auteurs of Bollywood films.

Chapter 4, "Everyone's a Superhero," elaborates the connections among culture, freedom, and equality through a close study of fan-fiction communities on the Internet. The stereotypes of popular culture insinuate themselves deeply into our lives, coloring our views on occupations and roles. From stories featuring Hermione Granger as the lead heroine, to *Harry Potter in Kolkata,* to Star Trek same-sex romances, fan-created fiction reimagines our cultural landscape, granting liberty and agency to those denied it in the popular mythology. Lacking the global distribution channels of traditional media, diverse authors now find an alternative in the World Wide Web, which brings their work to the world. I argue that fan fiction that challenges the hegemony of the original ought to be considered fair use where the writer is commenting on either the absence or negative portrayal of girls, women, or minorities in the original work. Alice Randall's unauthorized parody of Margaret Mitchell's *Gone with the Wind*—cheekily titled *The Wind Done Gone*—is a case in point. Randall's book, which retells the story of the Civil War from the perspective of a black slave woman on Scarlett O'Hara's plantation, seeks to upend the highly influential yet racist portrayals of blacks in Mitchell's iconic work. Scholars raise three principal critiques to such unlicensed use: (1) Why not write your own story rather than borrowing another's? (2) Even if you must borrow, why not license it? and (3) Won't recoding popular icons destabilize culture? Relying on a cultural theory that prizes participation in, rather than separation from, culture as a response to cultural hegemony, I reply to these objections.

I turn from the local to the global in Chapter 5, asking, "Can Intellectual Property Help the Poor?" Many have critiqued the rapid expansion of intellectual property rights into the developing world as impediments to development, and in Chapter 7 I explore the pernicious effects of strong intellectual property rights on access to life-saving medicines for the global poor. In this chapter, however, I ask whether intellectual property law must do more to recognize the innovations of the poor. While the poor are often presumed to be the bearers of "traditional knowledge" rather than the innovations that are the subject of modern patents and trademarks, I argue that poor people's knowledge is much more dynamic than the term traditional knowledge recognizes. I consider the impediments to our understanding poor people's knowledge (a term I prefer to traditional knowledge) as creative work deserving of ex ante intellectual property rights, and argue that the poor wish to be seen as creators of their own destiny and to be treated fairly in world trade.

I turn from innovators to authors in Chapter 6, "Bollywood/Hollywood," where I consider cultural exchanges involving films between the East and West. Acknowledging that a free flow of culture is not always a fair flow of culture, I consider a recent spate of copyright suits by Hollywood against Bollywood that accuse the latter of ruthlessly copying movie themes and scenes from American films. But claims of cultural appropriation go far back, and travel in multiple directions. The revered American director Steven Spielberg has been accused of copying the idea for *E.T.: The Extra-Terrestrial* from legendary Indian filmmaker Satyajit Ray's 1962 script for *The Alien*. Disney's *The Lion King* bears striking similarities to Osamu Tezuka's Japanese anime series, *Kimba the White Lion*. Neither Ray nor Tezuka's studio sued the American filmmakers, and this chapter is by no means an attempt to rekindle any particular legal case. Rather, I use these examples to consider copyright's role in promoting cultural exchange, mutual recognition among global authors, and mutual understanding through the sharing of diverse cultural works.

The final chapter, "An Issue of Life or Death," reiterates that there is much more at stake in intellectual property law than the production of more technological gadgets or literary characters. Life itself hangs in the balance, and the example of AIDS patients in sub-Saharan Africa drives home the point that the simplistic incentives/access trope that dominates contemporary intellectual property analysis is an inadequate framework for addressing local and global intellectual property conflicts in the twenty-first century. The problem of poor people's access to medicines is a prime example of the failure of the narrow incentives model, since patents provide little incentive for the production of medicines that would treat the poor. In this chapter, I propose that just as the New Jersey Supreme Court in *State v. Shack* declared that "property rights promote human values," *intellectual property rights* should give way to the human values of freedom and equality as well. While this subject may seem distant from the topic of cultural participation addressed in earlier chapters, the connection between the ability to live a full and healthy life and cultural participation is far from tangential. Intellectual property rights and the freedoms they can promote are interrelated—patents govern the ability to live a healthy life, which in turn enables human beings to fully contribute to making our culture.

Today intellectual property law has grown and expanded to every corner of the earth. The law has come of age, but we will need a social enlightenment in intellectual property law similar to the one we witnessed in real property law during the last century in order to recognize the plural social, cultural, and economic effects of a legal regime that governs the global production, enjoyment, and exchange of culture. Intellectual property laws affect fundamental values, from freedom to efficiency, from democracy to development, from dignity to distributive justice. Our laws ought to promote these plural values, including but beyond efficiency alone.

If intellectual property is to serve humankind, we need to better understand the process of cultural creation. Economists point out that these processes may be impeded by too little or too much property. Social and cultural theory can illuminate how individuals and society grow and change through cultural exchanges. In sum, this is not just the domain of economists who study innovation; it has long been the domain of musicologists, anthropologists, sociologists, literary critics, philosophers, and others in the cultural study business. This book makes the case for broadening our methodological approaches to intellectual property to include perspectives from fields including but beyond economics, such as development economics, anthropology, cultural studies, and philosophy. In the pages that follow, I elaborate how these fields can enrich our understanding of the deep connections between culture and human freedom.

While specific doctrinal reforms may follow from my critique, that is not my project here. In these pages I urge a broader vision of law's effects on culture and freedom. But I believe that a radical revision of the law is not necessary to effectuate the plural values at stake in cultural production, for two reasons. First, intellectual property law has historically incorporated plural values—from fairness to free speech to the importance of promoting diverse speakers and creators. But these plural values have increasingly been swallowed up by a single-minded law and economic rhetoric focused on efficiency alone. In part, my project is to resurrect these plural values. Even so, my theory is also surely influenced by new normative visions of equality, development, and human capability—understandings that have not yet fully influenced intellectual property law.

In short, where traditional accounts of intellectual property understand this law as a mere instrument to incentivize efficient production, this book maps a network of cultural, social, and technological regimes that are making and remaking intellectual property law in the new century. Indeed, the *New York Times* writes that conflicts around intellectual property just may well be "the first new social movement of the century."[26] Call it the ripping, mixing, and burning of *law*.

MODERN MAN INVENTS HIMSELF

Born in India in the 1920s, my grandmother Sita was the youngest of five sisters. All of her elder sisters married in their teens; none was educated beyond secondary school. But by the time my grandmother came of age, her father saw that her possibilities could be far greater. A visionary in his own right, my great-grandfather encouraged my grandmother to seek an education. Sita attended St. Mary's College in Madras, where she was elected student body president and became a champion tennis player. Later, she was accepted to Banaras Hindu University, often called the "Harvard of India," where she earned a master's degree in physics. When her peers were willingly led into arranged marriages, Sita defied one of the most entrenched of Indian cultural traditions and married for love. Later in life, my grandmother, who would eventually become a professor of physics and mother of six, would quip: "In this dynamic world, one cannot be static."

This is a book about intellectual property. But I do not share this story because my grandmother, a professor of physics, was an inventor of things—that is, the traditional subject of intellectual property. Rather, I share it because my grandmother was the inventor of her own life. To paraphrase Foucault, modern man invents himself.[27] My grandmother was born two decades before Indian Independence, as ideas of freedom, democracy, and equality were taking root, challenging traditional culture and customs. While the masses may have believed that culture was composed of fixed traditions to be passed down, unchanged, from generation to generation, reformers like my grandmother saw culture as something invented by individuals themselves. She saw diverse options within Indian culture and chose for herself the path she would take. In the modern parlance, she did not take culture as given, but "ripped and mixed" it to create something new.

Intellectual property is the law of innovation, both in science and in the arts. But it is not only about authoring books or inventing tools. Intellectual property law is also about authoring our own lives and inventing our own communities. The capacity to critically engage "given" cultural norms lies at the heart of social change and freedom itself. This book functions both as critique and as foundation. It critiques the dominant modern understanding of intellectual property, a view that portrays innovation as a simple function of monetary reward, and specifies the goal as the creation of more—more products, more movies, more books—in an effort to offer a foundation for a broader vision of intellectual property's role in society. Intellectual property is the law not only of innovation, but also of culture, and its change and exchange. An intellectual property law befitting this new participatory century, then, must lift its gaze beyond the narrow goal of incentivizing the creation of more intellectual products to facilitating critical and autonomous participation in the cultural sphere. Modernity is not simply technology. A modern intellectual property law must promote our capacity to author our own lives.

CHAPTER ONE

Beyond Incentives

MORE THAN A QUARTER-CENTURY AGO, property scholars inter-
rupted the hegemony of a law and economics discourse focused exclusively on efficiency to introduce broader theories about property and social relations. As the New Jersey Supreme Court declared in 1971 in the
historic case of *State v. Shack,* "[p]roperty rights serve human values."
Modern property law was to balance plural values beyond efficiency to
consider personhood, health, dignity, liberty, equality, and distributive
justice.

In contrast, at the start of the twenty-first century *intellectual property*
scholarship remains moored to a singular economic account. In the modern day, intellectual property is understood almost exclusively as being
about *incentives.*[1] Its theory is utilitarian, but with the maximand simply
creative output: law's goal is to promote the invention of more machines,
from the Blackberry to the iPod, and more intellectual products, from
Mickey Mouse to R2D2. Scholars and legislators struggle to calibrate
the optimal length of copyright and patent terms to promote efficient innovation. Even critiques of the recent expansion of intellectual property
law's breadth, scope, and duration adopt the same language. Progressive
law and economics scholars argue that too much intellectual property
law can impede innovation, locking up the building blocks necessary for
further innovation.

We did not always understand copyrights, patents, trademarks, and trade secrets this way. Copyright law emerged out of the Enlightenment in England in the early eighteenth century, when the granting of limited rights to authors broke the perpetual monopoly in intellectual works held by printers, encouraging the creation of new works and their broad dissemination to a more democratically engaged public. Patent law has always sought to encourage access to knowledge, requiring owners to share knowledge of their inventions in exchange for limited monopoly rights, rather than protecting the knowledge as a trade secret. And trademark law originated in theories of unfair competition and consumer protection, not property law.

But over the last few decades law and economics scholars have reimagined intellectual property law, portraying it as solely an instrumental mechanism to incentivize creativity (copyright), invention (patents), and industry (trademarks). Because information is assumed by its nature to be nonrivalrous and nonexcludable, the concern is that free-riding will eliminate any incentive to produce information. The insertion of property rights, the theory goes, incentivizes the production of information, which will then inure to society's benefit through the market mechanism, with those willing and able to pay being permitted to consume the information. Others might free ride, but only where high transaction costs would make marketplace exchanges unlikely. In short, market failure is cited as the raison d'être for intellectual property, explaining copyright, patent, and even trademark.

But intellectual property today is more than simply a tool for incentivizing creative production in the form of more things, from Bratz dolls to PCs. Intellectual property laws bear considerably on the ability of humankind to flourish, affecting everything from the developing world's access to food, textbooks, and essential medicines, to the ability of citizens everywhere to democratically participate in political and cultural discourse, to the equal opportunity to earn a livelihood from one's intellectual contributions toward making a better world. Today, the legal regime of intellectual property has inserted itself more deeply into our lives and more deeply into the framework of international law.

Despite these real-world changes, intellectual property scholars continue to understand intellectual property solely as a tool to solve an economic "public goods" problem: nonrivalrous and nonexcludable goods such as music and scientific knowledge will be too easy to copy and share—thus wiping out any incentive to create them in the first place—unless a monopoly right in the ideas is provided for a limited period of time. The dominance of this singular, narrow economic discourse has rarely been challenged.

Yet in case after case today, we see that traditional law and economic analyses fail to capture fully the struggles at the heart of local and global intellectual property law conflicts. In the handful of cases that follow—ranging from high technology to low, from first world to third—we will see that the proponents of that school have failed to persuade the U.S. Supreme Court, let alone activists in the developing world. Indeed perhaps one of the most remarkable facts about William Landes's and Richard Posner's seminal text *The Economic Structure of Intellectual Property Law,* hailed as "the most important book ever written about intellectual property," is that it finds that much of intellectual property law's expansion at the end of the last century *cannot be justified by economic reasoning.* They conclude devastatingly that "no public-interest explanation for the evolution of intellectual property law over this period seems plausible."[2] Their book is as much of a wake-up call for reform of intellectual property law as it is a massive undertaking to rationalize this law within an economic framework.

But where Posner and Landes would correct the descriptive disconnect by mooring intellectual property law more firmly to economic analysis, I argue that a more multidimensional account of this law is necessary. Pundits declare that "[i]ntellectual property has come of age,"[3] but it is increasingly apparent that current intellectual property law is not mature enough to face the diverse and changing world in which we now live. I offer three critiques of the narrow intellectual-property-as-incentives understanding: (1) it fails descriptively as a comprehensive account of extant legal doctrine, (2) it fails prescriptively as the exclusive basis for deciding the important intellectual property conflicts of the day, and (3) it fails to capture fully the dynamics of cultural creation and circulation.

One prominent example of the disconnect between intellectual property theory and practice is *Eldred v. Ashcroft,* the first copyright case to go before the Supreme Court in the new century. At issue in *Eldred* was the constitutionality of the Sonny Bono Copyright Term Extension Act of

1998, in which Congress extended the already lengthy copyright term by another twenty years. The first copyright term established in 1790 lasted fourteen years from the time of publication, with the option to renew for another fourteen years. In contrast, with the 1998 extension, the copyright term was extended to last for the life of the author plus seventy years. Thus today copyright in a work will often last well over a century. Consumer rights advocates argued that the extension was unconstitutional, violating the U.S. Copyright Clause's provision that copyrights last "for limited times," and that the extension trampled on First Amendment rights to use cultural works in speech. But the Supreme Court approved the extension over these objections. Notably, the Court reached this conclusion despite the objections of illustrious economists, including five Nobel laureates, who wrote as *amici curiae* that "[t]he term extension for existing works *makes no significant contribution to an author's economic incentive to create.*"[4] The Court upheld the act nonetheless, citing fairness and cultural restoration explanations.

Economic analysis also did not fare well in the other recent, landmark copyright case to come before the Court, *Metro-Goldwyn-Mayer Studios Inc. v. Grokster.*[5] In that case, the Court considered whether the makers of a peer-to-peer file-sharing software could be held secondarily liable for copyright infringement. Again, the Supreme Court refused an invitation to rewrite copyright law according to popular law and economic rationales. Consider the backdrop against which the Court decided the case: a brief of illustrious law professors and economists—including, in a rare moment of agreement, Nobel laureates Kenneth Arrow and Gary Becker—urged a purely economic approach. In answering whether peer-to-peer file-sharing services such as Grokster should be secondarily liable for copyright infringement committed by users of its software, *amici* sought to make trial courts economic cost accountants, imposing liability on the basis of whether the intellectual property holder or the alleged secondary infringer is the cheaper enforcer of the intellectual property holder's rights. Arrow and company urged that the Court adopt a test inquiring "whether the indirectly liable party at low cost could have discouraged the infringing uses, and whether the complaining copyright holder at low cost could have pursued the direct infringers rather than litigating on indirect liability theories."[6]

But where the law and economics scholars argued in favor of imposing liability on Grokster on the basis of efficiency, the Supreme Court
chose to impose liability for what it saw as *moral* wrongdoing. Justice
Souter's opinion for a unanimous Court adopted the common law approach to fault-based liability, which turns not on cost-benefit analysis
but on the basic principle of fair business practices. The Court ultimately
held that Grokster could be accountable because it had demonstrated a
bad intent to encourage and profit from illicit copying by users. The Court
cited common law precedent, concluding that "[t]here is a definite ten-
dency to impose greater responsibility upon a defendant whose conduct
was intended to do harm, or was morally wrong." The Court adopted
an inducement theory that ultimately premised liability on "purposeful,
culpable expression and conduct." Where an economic approach might
predicate liability on least-cost avoiders or on the effects of infringement
on creators' incentives—but certainly not on the bad mind of the actors—
the Court focused on moral culpability.

A brief in favor of Grokster written by Harvard law professors would
have simply reaffirmed the prevailing secondary liability approach articulated in *Sony Corp. of America v. Universal City Studios, Inc.* In *Sony*,
the Court refused to impose secondary liability on the makers of the
VCR, worried that liability would harm the incentives for innovation. That
standard, the Harvard professors argued, "has proven to be an effective
means of balancing the interests of copyright owners with the equally
important need to preserve incentives for technological innovation."[7] The
Harvard brief pressed the Court to conclude that since Grokster's technology permitted "substantial non-infringing uses," it should be immune
from secondary liability.

But the Court declined to ground its ruling on either economic theory.
It acknowledged the validity of both economic approaches, recognizing
indirect liability as a practical option when direct enforcement is infeasible
and recognizing the need to limit liability so as to not thwart future innovation. But the Court decided this momentous case on other grounds,
invoking morality and fairness. To be sure, the Court in *Grokster* ignored
many other cultural values at stake in the case. Lacking a language for
recognizing participatory culture, for example, the Court failed to note
the social benefits of peer-to-peer file-sharing technology, which allows

individuals to share information widely without paying for server space or high bandwidth connections. But simply by embracing basic values of morality and fairness, the Court offers an analysis that suggests that for all of its uniqueness, intellectual property law is also *common* law, teeming with plural values including, but not limited to, incentives. Indeed, a recent article in the *Harvard Law Review* puts further into question the centrality of the incentives rationale in copyright law. In the article, Shyam Balganesh shows that despite copyright's lip service to incentives, *not a single doctrine in this law actually focuses on the way in which market incentives influence creators.*[8]

The problem of overreaching rights is by no means limited to copyright. In the patent field there has been uproar over the introduction of patents on methods for doing business in cyberspace—for example, Amazon.com's infamous "One-Click" patent. For decades courts had been reluctant to recognize patents in "business methods" such as the use of grocery carts at supermarkets; the natural competitive advantage of introducing better business methods was considered enough incentive —a patent, overkill. But in 1998 in the case of *State Street Bank v. Signature Financial Group,*[9] the U.S. Court of Appeals for the Federal Circuit clearly embraced such patents, opening the floodgates to business-method patents related to e-commerce in particular. These patents are controversial, because many find it hard to justify a twenty-year exclusive monopoly as necessary to incentivize improvements in means for servicing e-commerce consumers. Yet as recently as 2010 the Supreme Court affirmed the continued availability of business method patents in *Bilski v. Kappos.*[10]

Another important patent case of the twenty-first century, *eBay v. MercExchange,* involved the question of whether injunctions should automatically issue in the face of patent infringement.[11] The main argument for automatic injunctions turned on the idea of "patent exceptionalism"; although injunctions are equitable remedies that generally require careful weighing of the equities, some argued that this familiar consideration was not required in patent cases. The Court in *eBay* rejected this notion, not merely on grounds of efficiency but rather, by acknowledging the need to take the basic value of fairness into consideration in patent cases. The Court affirmed that the equitable standards that apply elsewhere in the law apply in patent law, too. In short, despite its preeminent position in legal scholarship, the narrow understanding of *intellectual property as incentives* is not, in fact, driving the most important legal decisions in the field.

Meanwhile, rapid-fire technological advances and new forms of creative output, from YouTube and MySpace to the advent of open-source collaborative networks, garage bands, remix culture, and the World Wide Web itself, undermine utilitarian intellectual property law's very premise: that intellectual property rights are necessary to incentivize creation.[12] Indeed, there is a growing body of literature focused on explaining the existence of "IP without IP"—that is, intellectual production in the absence of intellectual property rights, from the innovation of French chefs to the creativity of stand-up comedians and fashion houses.[13]

There are normative concerns as well. The dominant law-and-economics approach in this field would rely on the market to spur creation—but this leads to the appalling conclusion that drugs for baldness must be more important than drugs for malaria because the former enjoy a multi-billion-dollar market, while those who need the latter are too poor to offer much to save their own lives. Understanding intellectual property as incentive-to-create reduces to the claim that the ability to pay, as evidenced in the marketplace, should determine the production and distribution of knowledge and culture. A central feature of this account as it has taken hold in intellectual property law is its focus on the market as the vehicle for solving distributional problems. Willingness to pay determines access to the fruits of this information regime. After the property right is established, the government's role is limited to protecting that property right, and to intervening only in cases of further market failures.

A central failure of intellectual property as incentives is its neglect of distribution. As I have argued, utility in the intellectual property context is defined simply as the maximization of creative output. The goal then becomes creating the greatest number of cultural artifacts to be trickled down to the greatest number of people. The utilitarian approach to intellectual property does not ask: Who makes the goods? Who profits, and at whose expense? Is high-tech production up in India but without significant benefit to women or the poor? Martha Nussbaum describes this as "the problem of respect for the separate person." A utilitarian calculus that presumes overall welfare in the aggregate "doesn't tell us where the top and the bottom are," Nussbaum observes. "[I]t doesn't tell us 'who has got the money, and whether any of it is mine.'" Analyses based on the well-being of the aggregate do not confront distinctions between the developed and developing worlds, the urban and the rural, and women and men, or among blacks, Asians, Latinos, and whites.

To be sure, this account in *legal* scholarship differs from the understanding of utilitarianism among moral philosophers and even among economists themselves. Rather than presuming the goodness of maximizing creative output, utilitarians would begin with individual preferences and build the theory from there. Focusing on individual preferences would require us to consider impacts on people who have no ability to pay for intellectual goods. But given that my goal is to reinterpret intellectual property law, I will concentrate my energies on the utilitarianism expressed by today's intellectual property scholars.

Before I turn to my cultural critique, it may be useful to review the existing critical intellectual property landscape. To date, most intellectual property scholars have sought to rationalize intellectual property law within the framework of economics. Some, let us call them Intellectual Property Originalists, argue that intellectual property was narrowly construed at the time of the nation's founding as an instrumental tool, grudgingly accepted as necessary for incentivizing innovation. They are Originalists in the sense that they are elaborating their understanding of the founders' constitutional mandate in the domain described by the phrase "To promote the Progress of Science and useful Arts." Scholars such as James Boyle, Mark Lemley, and Larry Lessig read this clause as limiting copyright and patent to the narrow goal of incentivizing production.[14] By confining intellectual property to this goal, they hope to fight its creeping extension. Boyle and Lessig's nonprofit organization, the Creative Commons, even offers a Founders' Copyright—a license for fourteen years with a one-time option to renew.[15]

Originalists emphasize an "incentives/access tradeoff" at the core of intellectual property law. Intellectual property rights are necessary incentives to promote creative activity, but if they go too far they may impede access to knowledge. For most critics of intellectual property law today, these two values—incentives and access—are the two that matter; other values are typically subsumed by these two broad categories of intellectual property law's central values. Questions about productivity implicate "incentives," while concerns as diverse as the fair use of copyrighted materials to the distribution of drugs to the poor are issues of "access." In sum, the prevailing vision is an incentive vision. Intellectual property is to conform to this single purpose. For some, like the Originalists, this leads to a narrow view of the extent of intellectual property rights. They worry that broader rights harm downstream production. New innovation always occurs on the back of older innovation. Thus the focus of contemporary scholars is the length of the copyright or patent term and the scope of these rights, to be determined entirely on the basis of incentives for present and future innovation. Others see the incentive theory as justifying broad intellectual property rights. The intellectual property holder of a broader right can always negotiate with downstream users, at least in the absence of overwhelming transaction costs, which presumably have been reduced because of technology. By and large, the fight is over the proper economic analysis to incentivize production or sometimes more broadly, as in the work of Landes and Posner, to correct market failure in information production.[16]

My goal here is to move intellectual property beyond this struggle. This is not to say that getting the economics of innovation right is not important. But it is not *all* that is important in setting the metes and bounds of intellectual property. The fight over intellectual property should consider values beyond simply the value of incentivizing production. While many will view this as radical, upsetting the simple elegance of a single-minded legal domain, I am far from the first to propose a broader account of intellectual property. Neil Netanel, Jack Balkin, and David Lange would have us keep First Amendment values foremost in mind when analyzing intellectual property conflicts. Richard Epstein has argued for intellectual property scholars to consider more closely this law's similarities to real property law. And William Fisher more than a decade ago made the prescient call for reorienting intellectual property law to promote a good life.[17]

I suggest that intellectual property law must adopt broader social and cultural analysis. The fundamental failure in the economic story of intellectual property has to do with information's role in cultural life and human flourishing. It is odd that the area of law most closely focused on Dickens, Rowling, *Star Trek, Lost,* Gershwin, and Prince is indifferent to understanding these creative works and their relationship to society, and to that part of the academy that seeks to understand these relations. The disciplines of cultural studies, sociology, science and technology studies, and development studies offer theories of cultural production and human flourishing, but their insights have been largely ignored for the elegant simplicity of the economic narrative.[18] In this chapter and throughout this book, I will try to bring development and cultural theory to bear on local and global conflicts related to intellectual property. Culture is not just a set of "inputs" necessary for further innovation. Culture is the sphere in which individuals participate, create, share ideas, and enjoy life with others. Cultural works engender empathy for the other and foster mutual understanding. In short, culture plays a critical—and in the Knowledge Age, an increasingly important—role in promoting freedom in the social, political, and economic spheres of life. Thus rather than narrowly viewing intellectual property as incentives-for-creation—that is, as merely economic or technology policy—we must understand intellectual property as social and cultural policy. Increasingly in the Knowledge Age, intellectual property laws come to bear on giant-sized values, from democracy and development to freedom and equality.

I want to be careful to avoid falling prey to Hume's is-ought fallacy. In the examples that follow, I show the complexity of values that appear to be at stake in local and global intellectual property conflicts, and seek to demonstrate the inadequacy of the utilitarian intellectual property story as a descriptive matter. This alone does not tell us what our normative values should be, yet in discussing these cases, we can begin to see that the very recognition of the disparate social and cultural effects of our global intellectual property policy becomes a rallying cry to take these effects into account.

Before proceeding let me clarify that my critique, which among other ideas builds on Amartya Sen's broad conception of development as freedom, does not reject economics. Far from it, it adopts a broad economic view that recognizes more fully the rich interconnections between economics and culture, and the effect of freedom in the cultural domain on overall individual well-being.

FROM YOUTUBE TO FANDOM TO REMIX: WORKING
THROUGH CULTURE

The Harry Potter stories have captivated the world, even reviving interest in reading. Penned by J. K. Rowling, they glorify the exploits of an English boy who is to save humanity and the enchanted world—with a little help from his friends. In the offline world, Rowling's multipart series has come to an end, but the familiar characters of Harry, Ron, Hermione, and their gang live on in the ether, where young and old recast familiar people and places from this lore to tell new stories. A thirteen-year-old, Heather Lawver, began editing an online, real-world version of the fictional *Daily Prophet* newspaper for the wizarding world in the Harry Potter series. Many girl fans bring Harry's sidekick, Hermione, to the front and center of the action in their own stories. In India an author penned *Harry Potter in Kolkata,* turning his own street corner into a site of magic. The book was quickly pulled after Indian lawyers for Rowling and Warner Bros. (producer of the Harry Potter films) issued a cease-and-desist letter to the work's Indian publisher. Meanwhile, Rowling has abided literally hundreds of thousands of other fan-fiction stories based on her characters.

Current copyright theory takes a narrow view of fair use. From YouTube videos to fan works to digital mash-ups of music, the dominant approach of the last quarter century focuses on *market failure.* Law views unauthorized imitations of original copyrighted expression—from songs to characters, settings, and plots—as theft. In the absence of an express license for use, statutorily authorized fair use is limited to a narrow set of circumstances where market failure prohibits private bargains from being struck. A classic case for fair use under this rationale is parody of the copyrighted work. Consider the case of the rap group 2 Live Crew, which sought a license from Roy Orbison to lampoon his song "Oh, Pretty Woman" with the lyrics "bald headed woman" and other insulting phrases. Not surprisingly, Orbison denied permission. The group 2 Live Crew went ahead and made their song anyway, and Orbison's publisher brought suit. The U.S. Supreme Court held that the rap group's version was a fair use because it parodied Orbison's song. Although there are many reasons for privileging parody as fair use[19]—the First Amendment comes immediately to mind—many legal scholars have explained the Court's rationale in terms of market failure.[20] In Posner's words, "negotiating for a parody license" is a "high-transaction-cost negotiation." The logic is simple: few are ready to license a right to be made fun of. Posner contrasts parody, where the copyrighted work is "the target not the weapon" of the infringing use, with satire, where the copyrighted work is the weapon, used to make fun of some other thing—society, or a politician. In the heat of the U.S. presidential election during summer 2008, for example, John McCain used in a campaign ad—without permission—the Frankie Valli song "Can't Take My Eyes Off of You" to make fun of the press's infatuation·with his rival Barack Obama. Few would argue that the McCain ad is less socially valuable than 2 Live Crew's spoof. But under the market failure rationale for fair use, social value is not the key determinant. As Posner asks, if the copyrighted work is not the butt of the joke, "why should the owner of the original be reluctant to license the parody?"[21] "Only if the parodist is seeking to ridicule the original work," Posner reasons, "is a market transaction infeasible and an involuntary taking therefore justifiable."[22]

To be sure, fair use is a flexible doctrine that requires careful weighing of many factors on a case-by-case basis. But by and large, this view of thinking about fair use as justified only in instances of market failure has prevailed in theory and practice, and serves as the current backdrop against which users nevertheless continue to interact with copyrighted materials on and off the Internet, often at their own peril. The fact is, even though much user-generated content is noncommercial, and consciously so, it may be illegal under current copyright law and policy, where the default rule is to get a license. Girls writing themselves into the Potter stories are "pirates" taking the property of Rowling and Warner Bros., unwelcome in copyright law's fair use "safe harbor."

In his important book *Convergence Culture*, Henry Jenkins calls it a "paradoxical result" where "works that are hostile to the original creators . . . can be read more explicitly as making critiques of the source material," thus "having greater freedom from copyright enforcement than works that embrace the ideas behind the original work and simply seek to extend them in new directions."[23] Furthermore, Jenkins laments today's effects of a fair-use law developed in a bygone era of unidirectional media, where professionals created content largely for the static consumption of the masses. Today's technology, in contrast, emboldens citizen participation in cultural works and cultural production like never before. Yet copyright fair-use analyses have been slow to recognize the rise of participatory culture. As Jenkins writes:

> Current copyright law simply doesn't have a category for dealing with amateur creative expression. Where there has been "public interest" factored into the legal definition of fair use—such as the desire to protect the rights of libraries to circulate books or journalists to quote or academics to cite other researchers—it has been advanced in terms of legitimated classes of users and not a generalized public right to cultural participation. Our current notion of fair use is an artifact of an era when few people had access to the marketplace of ideas, and those who did fell into certain professional classes. It surely demands reconsideration as we develop technologies that broaden who may produce and circulate cultural materials.[24]

The result? Heather Lawver and other kids who inhabit the Potter universe, developing their own critical reading, writing, and thinking skills through it, are left in a legal grey zone. Indeed, rather than parody, many user-created YouTube videos and other fan works shared on the Internet are better understood as paying homage to the original works and their creators.

The critique here is twofold: first, current visions of fair use driven by market failure analysis show little understanding of the benefits of *working through culture*—that is, playing, learning, and creating through the cultural objects given to us. Law privileges only a narrow form of working through culture—parody—not because of its normative benefits, but because a license for parodies may be difficult. This leaves a host of socially and culturally worthwhile activities in a legal grey zone. Second, the narrow market failure analysis of fair use does not acknowledge the ways in which the culture concept today is radically changing. Increasingly, culture is no longer a static object handed down by cultural authorities. Changing technologies and social mores have made culture more interactive and participatory. But this paradoxically puts more ordinary people at risk of committing copyright infringement.

One of the most famous mash-ups of recent years, which I mentioned briefly in the Introduction, offers an illustration. Turning the tables on the traditional modalities of cultural production and reception, one disc jockey known as "Dangermouse" digitally mashed The Beatles' *The White Album* with hip-hop artist Jay-Z's *The Black Album* to create *The Grey Album*. Dangermouse celebrated his copying, boldly declaring on his website that his album "uses the full vocal content of Jay-Z's *Black Album*" and that "[e]very kick, snare, and chord is taken from the Beatles *White Album* and is in their original recording somewhere."[25] Despite its pointedly derivative nature, the album drew critical acclaim. Culling from the past, DJ Dangermouse created music that *Rolling Stone* hailed as "ahead of its time."

In the hip-hop music world, this modus operandi is not new. Indeed, Jay-Z had intentionally facilitated mash-ups by releasing an a cappella version of *The Black Album*. The owners of copyrights in The Beatles catalog, in contrast, had long resisted licensing these works. Publishing house EMI, which claims ownership in *The White Album,* issued a cease-and-desist letter to Dangermouse, to which he quickly complied, removing *The Grey Album* from his website. But by then the cat was out of the bag. The work quickly became a cult hit in underground hip-hop clubs, exchanged via peer-to-peer file-sharing services and other Internet-based protocols. On a single day declared "Grey Tuesday," more than a hundred websites distributed 100,000 copies of the work, making *The Grey Album*, "if only for a day, the #1 release in the country."[26] Grey Tuesday was widely reported as a coordinated act of civil disobedience against an excessively restrictive copyright law. Suddenly, the copyright law of the last century appeared too obedient to traditional cultural, technical, and legal authorities.

Technically, sampling is "a digital process in which pre-recorded sounds are incorporated into the sonic fabric of a new song." Socially, sampling is homage: new creators use the technique to represent themselves historically within a lineage of earlier creators and traditions. The popular practice of digital sampling in hip-hop and rap exemplifies this approach of working through culture. Sampling reveals its social side in precisely its reiterations of tradition. Far from simple mimesis, rappers practice an art that cultural theorists call signification: the exercise of cultural agency within a context of discursive hegemony.[27] Individuals express themselves through critique, comment, or parody of cultural authorities, all the while seeking to represent themselves within a culture that had previously overlooked, or even worse, oppressed them. Stated differently, the mash-up is often a form of cultural dissent. The sample is used to evoke the past and to create a lineage between authors, thus claiming a place for oneself within a culture's historical narrative. Sampling signals that an artist is working within a tradition, not without it. At the same time, as Walter Benjamin has described, the proliferation of copies contributes to the "shattering of tradition"; it debunks the mythical cult of the original, questioning the very existence of a singular text or cultural authority. The Age of Mechanical Reproduction is yielding to the Age of Electronic Participation. To unmask cultural autocracy is to make way for cultural democracy.

But while private arrangements may sometimes strike in favor of these new auteurs, the default rules themselves offer little predictability or comfort for those fan creators who express themselves by *inhabiting*, or working through, the canon, without necessarily critiquing or writing against the original. The current legal regime would either chill such creative efforts or drive cultural democracy and equality underground. Hence Jenkins calls for rewriting the law of fair use to cover "legitimate grassroots, not-for-profit circulation of critical essays and stories that comment on the content of mass media."[28]

The economic theory of fair use as market failure in fact has an underlying *cultural* theory—even if it is an accidental one. The market failure approach privileges creative work developed wholly outside popular culture (hailed as "original") or that goes against culture (understood as parody, or critique), but it does not recognize activity *working through culture*. This view of fair use, and of culture, is too narrow. In contrast, where Posner would allow a free ride for a "take off" on an original copyrighted work, I would emphasize the importance of a "take on" an original copyrighted work.[29]

My analysis is both descriptive and prescriptive. The current market failure approach misrecognizes how individuals actually participate in culture. I use the phrase "working through culture" to describe what contemporary cultural theorists from Bourdieu to Foucault to Habermas recognize about how modern subjects engage the world (I develop this theory further in Chapter 2). Foucault, for example, describes authorship not as the search for an original subject, but rather as the quest to "grasp the subject's points of *insertion,* modes of functioning, and system of dependencies" on existing discourses.[30] As I show in the next chapter, cultural theory elaborates the view that the modern subject is situated within contemporary discourses, and yet is not fully defined by them.

It is true that, by and large, the Enlightenment understood freedom and equality as developed in *opposition* to culture. The Romantic Movement exalted the artist above others as someone who created truth and meaning for him- or herself, unlike those for whom knowledge came from religious and cultural authorities from above. Recall this was the first time we saw use of the word "creator" with a little "c"—until then, only God was endowed with the gift of Creation.[31] But the proliferation of authorship *alongside* cultural rights at the turn of the century has confounded expectations that Enlightenment would triumph over culture. Increasingly, we now understand that we develop our autonomous selves through and within a cultural discourse, inhabiting tradition, not just resisting it.

In the next chapter, I elaborate normative arguments for freedom within culture. These range from liberty to "think for oneself," to the use of rational argument to seek equality and liberation from oppressive culture, to the ethical responsibility to critique unjust traditions.[32] There are still other reasons. According to Habermas, communicative action is the process through which people form their identities, transmit and renew cultural knowledge, and achieve mutual understanding.[33] I consider, as well, how active participation within the cultural sphere promotes learning and qualities central to a well-functioning democracy, especially critical thinking and communal engagement. In short, rather than focusing on market failure and building the theory from there, I argue that we must first recognize the social value of working through culture, from autobiographical storytelling through YouTube videos; to empowerment by making oneself the superhero in the story; to satire, homage, and sharing as ways of connecting with others for mutual understanding.

A libertarian may argue that we may find more freedom by exiting restrictive cultures rather than remaining within them. Indeed, this notion underlies traditional copyright law, which envisions creativity as taking place either against culture or outside of it. But this traditional binary option of culture (on the terms of the powerful) or freedom (without culture) is less and less satisfactory today. In the modern world, individuals want both: they demand freedom, but often within the cultural communities in which we live and grow.

The law and economic scholar of intellectual property will reply that intellectual property law should address not just market failure, but also incentives. The concern is that a rule broadening fair use will not promote innovation as well as a rule focused on originality would. The conceit is that fan fiction and mash-ups are copying, not creativity. But this presumes that fans rotely mimic the original. Hundreds of thousands of entries on fan-fiction websites dispel such an idea. They reveal instead painstaking efforts to develop one's own voice within existing, often almost overpowering, discursive frameworks. Fan communities help writers in this process of finding one's own voice within culture, critiquing and advising one another to better tell one's own stories, albeit within a framework of shared meaning.

Furthermore, the critic will argue that the existing rule promotes greater expressive diversity than would one that allowed for more working through culture. But this critique privileges diversity across culture rather than within it. The familiar idea is that diversity across distinct cultures allows individuals greater choice among ways of life. But as I have argued elsewhere, this vision often creates false choices. Rather than choosing to leave one's cultural communities, modern individuals prefer to remain within them, and to exercise choice and reason within those spheres. For example, many gays do not wish to leave the Boy Scouts of America but instead hope to be recognized within this association. Women typically choose not to leave patriarchal religious communities but rather to stay within and reform them. Thus the value of diversity within cultures begins to come into focus: such diversity allows for greater choice among a range of options within our normative communities.[34]

I offer a final critique of the traditional economic approach to fan and user-generated content. The traditional economic approach does not consider the distribution of the material benefits of this cultural production. Law is content to condemn YouTube videos, mash-ups, and fan fiction to a legal grey zone, in which authors of such material create in the shadow of the threat of lawsuits and dare not commercialize their work. The *Grey Album* was critically acclaimed, but DJ Dangermouse could not earn a single penny from the "pirate" work. While many fan-fiction writers enjoy participating in a noncommercial culture—indeed, they argue that a nonpropertied space allows for the development of more experimental creative products and communities—still others may seek, understandably, to profit from their creations. These distributive concerns are particularly poignant when we find that people from traditionally marginalized communities are producing cultural criticism that is also potentially lucrative. I shall return to these distributive questions in Chapter 3, "Fair Culture."

STORIES IN THE CUP: PARTICIPATION, MEANINGFUL WORK, AND LIVELIHOOD

Ethiopia is the birthplace of coffee. According to a local legend dating back to the ninth century, a shepherd boy named Kaldi observed that goats who ate wild coffee berries appeared to "dance" after consuming them. Kaldi, hungry and tired himself, tried the berries and found himself joining the dance.[35] Today, more than a thousand years later, 1.5 million Ethiopians earn their livelihood from coffee.

But the last decade has proven disastrous for many of these coffee farmers. In 2001 a global oversupply of coffee led to a sharp decline in prices, drastically affecting Ethiopian farmers' profits and well-being. Many were left with no money for basic necessities such as food and schools. The effect on Ethiopian coffee farmers from the fall in commodity prices was not, however, inevitable. Ethiopia produces some of the world's finest coffees, in particular Harar, Sidamo, and Yirgacheffe, which sell well above commodity coffee prices in Western specialty markets. Indeed, the top coffee buyer for coffee giant Starbucks declared Ethiopian coffee "the world's best coffee."[36] But the Ethiopian farmers failed to distinguish their specialty products from the pedestrian coffee purveyed around the world, and their specialty product sold at mere commodity prices.

In 2005, Getachew Mengistie, the director of Ethiopia's Intellectual Property Office, traveled to the United States, where he discovered a pound of his country's Sidamo coffee selling at a local Starbucks for a gourmet price of $26 a pound. He knew that his country's farmers only received $1.45 a pound for this specialty coffee, and sometimes even $0.75 at the commodity price. Ethiopia was capturing only 3 to 6 percent of the retail price, and Mengistie believed that the remaining value did not simply derive from roasting, distributing, and marketing the coffee. Indeed, estimates are that specialty coffee should return about 45 percent of the retail price to the owners of this coffee's high reputation.

Mengistie struck upon a bold plan to try to claim more of the coffee's value for his countrymen and -women. Ethiopia applied for trademarks in Harar, Sidamo, and Yirgacheffe coffees around the world. While most countries granted the trademarks, there was resistance in the United States from a formidable foe—Starbucks. The coffee retail giant argued that no other countries were using trademarks to control their coffees. Many countries used "geographic certification" marks instead, which ensure that the origin of a coffee is not misrepresented. With a geographic certification, for example, coffee not grown in Guatemala cannot be sold as "Guatemalan coffee." In Chapter 6, I discuss the growing use by developing nations of geographical indications such as these as a way to prevent their products from being copied and mass-produced elsewhere yet sold under the geographical name. I argue that these legal devices offer a good way of protecting "poor people's knowledge" because they are relatively cheap to acquire, they allow for multiple producers within a certain region, and they recognize, socially and materially, the cultural and scientific contributions of the community.

Ethiopia, however, insisted on trademarks. The legal difference is significant; the country did not simply seek to enjoin counterfeits but instead sought to control and develop a *brand*. Ethiopia sought to distinguish its high-end coffees from commodity products, which a geographic certification would do, but it also sought to build consumer desire for these coffees. Ethiopia proposed to license these trademarks to Starbucks and other coffee retailers only if they invested in building the brand among consumers. If Starbucks wanted to market this coffee under the Harar, Sidamo, or Yirgacheffe names, it would have to play by Ethiopia's rules. After a global consumer campaign led by Oxfam International, Starbucks relented, withdrawing its opposition to the trademarks and signing the license agreement.[37]

After centuries of making coffee, Ethiopia recognized that in today's global markets much of the retail value of the coffee lay in the coffee's *meaning*. Indeed, Starbucks trades as much on the social meaning of coffee as its taste. The latte-drinking Starbucks customer pays a premium for the story in the cup. Starbucks recognizes this, often enhancing the experience with photographs of indigenous coffee farmers around the world and text about their lives on its coffee packaging. Consider the evocative language of a Starbucks ad:

> Sometimes the coffee stirs you. A completed sentence ends
> with a small black dot, but that's how epiphanies begin. A cof-
> fee bean. A tiny, good thing from the earth. But the best ones
> have something special locked inside: *an exotic destination,* a
> spirited conversation, *a divine inspiration.* We search the world
> to find those beans and bring them to you.[38]

Starbucks even decorates some cafes with the bright colors and motifs found in some developing countries.[39]

Ethiopia sought to move from being the object of someone else's lucrative story to becoming its subject. Its trademark effort signals the country's desire to move from being the supplier of mere raw materi-als to a purveyor of social meaning with real economic value. Ethiopia's tactic suggests the next wave in "fair trade" practices. Rather than rely on a charitable act on the part of the Western enterprise or Western pub-lic, developing countries may claim their rights as intellectual property owners—thereby gaining control over their own reputation and destiny.

It is not commonplace for a developing country to apply for trade-marks in foreign lands. Ethiopia worked in conjunction with foreign not-for-profit groups such as Light Years IP and pro bono attorneys at the Washington-based law firm of Arnold & Porter. Ethiopia's campaign for its trademarks in the United States was championed by Oxfam International, a group better known for its activities combating hunger worldwide. But Oxfam saw trademarks for Ethiopian coffee as central to that very enter-prise. Such a move accords with Amartya Sen's insight that famine arises out of the lack of capacity to purchase the food one needs, not from the absence of food in the local marketplace.[40] To combat hunger, one needs to work on human capabilities to generate income.

A cultural approach to poor people's knowledge converges with the traditional economic approach to intellectual property on the following point: intellectual property rights related to poor people's knowledge can provide the incentives needed for the preservation, cultivation, and exchange of resources and knowledge. Yet the utility in the cultural approach goes beyond the creation of beneficial products. Anil Gupta, founder of the Honey Bee Network in India, which helps locate and sup-port innovation among India's rural poor, explains: "Once this knowledge becomes a basis for livelihood, conservation, lateral learning and social networking, a knowledge society starts emerging." Developing countries too seek to flourish as knowledge societies—communities in which all people have the capacity to participate in the cultivation and progression of knowledge. Intellectual property ownership makes up a significant proportion of the total value of world trade, but rich countries and businesses have captured most of this. Increasingly, some of the poorest countries and communities in the world are seeking a greater share of the global value of their products. As the Ethiopian example shows, this value lies not in the raw materials themselves, but in how they are marketed, especially to consumers in high-end markets. These consumers seek more than just a cup of coffee. Often they promote and support a set of global social relations based on recognition of others, shared meaning, and a conception of fairness.

The uproar about "biopiracy" in the field of patented inventions can be understood along similar lines. Attempts by Western corporations to patent the Indian staples turmeric, neem, and basmati rice, for example, drew sharp condemnation in the developing world. Another infamous case involves the hoodia cactus, a plant native to southern Africa. The San people of the Kalahari Desert of southern Africa eat this "miracle plant," which "tells your brain you are full," suppressing hunger and thirst during long desert crossings.[41] Upon learning of the San's use from a Dutch anthropologist, the South African Council for Scientific and Industrial Research patented the hoodia's appetite-suppressing element. The patent was eventually acquired by Pfizer, which sought to develop a diet drug to serve a market potentially worth billions. The central question in many of these cases is who should claim the value, and how much is their rightful claim, in these inventions. Even the European Patent Office (EPO) has acknowledged that yesterday's answers to these questions are inadequate. In *Scenarios for the Future,* a landmark work considering the pressures that will confront the patent office in the next quarter-century, the EPO writes that patent law must now respond to claims from below. "The key question that emerges," the report states, is *"[a]s new and powerful players emerge, who has power and authority?"*[42]

Despite calls to maintain our understanding of intellectual property simply as a utilitarian tool for stimulating creative production, intellectual property more and more demonstrates a claim on plural values, from participation to freedom, equality, mutual recognition, meaningful work, and development. The *intellectual-property-as-incentives* approach fails to account for the wide range of values at stake in global intellectual production today. Even the well-intentioned critics of maximalist intellectual property cannot address the giant-sized values implicit in current debates, from democracy to development, purely from within the traditional economic framework. The fundamental value of the intellectual-property-as-incentives approach is maximizing cultural production. This narrow theory presumes that maximizing cultural production in the aggregate will lead to the greatest good for the greatest number of people. We may assess this theory on its own terms—both from a narrow and from a broader utilitarian analysis. But this is not my project. My goal is to broaden the descriptive and prescriptive framework for understanding intellectual property. In so doing, I show that concerns about equality, social relations, and democracy animate contemporary intellectual property law and efforts to reform it.

But before proceeding, let me repeat: I do not reject the utilitarian account's central insights in toto; it remains a necessary tool in formulating intellectual property policy. Neither do I wish to exchange one metanarrative for another. Rather I argue that neither an economic nor a cultural lens alone provides a complete picture, and I urge intellectual property scholars to begin to integrate the two and come to recognize that the interrelationship between culture and economics goes well beyond incentives.

CHAPTER TWO

Bespoke Culture

A FOUR-YEAR-OLD GIRL jumps up from the couch and starts messing around behind the television. Her curious father asks, "What are you doing back there?" The little girl, who was born digital, replies: "I'm looking for the mouse."[1] Culture in the last century was marked by a mouse named Mickey—a canned product of a powerful media corporation held tightly under lock and key. Culture in this new century is symbolized by a very different mouse. The new mouse is *not a product, but a tool* for participating in the process of making culture oneself.

This chapter considers a principal raison d'être of intellectual property law: culture. The conceit is that intellectual property is a tool for incentivizing cultural production, from literature to art and science.[2] But thus far scholars of intellectual property have spent far too little time considering what culture is and how the object of law's desire, culture, is itself changing. The dominant law-and-economic theory of intellectual property law is premised on a thin theory of culture as commodities. But culture is not just a set of goods; it is a fundamental component of a good life. In this chapter, I turn to social and cultural theory to elaborate a richer theory of culture as critical processes of creative engagement and exchange that promote our humanity.

Intellectual property is one of the most important legal tools for regulating the production and circulation of culture today, from music, art, and film to scientific knowledge to expressive commercial speech in the form of trademarks. Yet law misunderstands the very nature of culture itself. What is perhaps most surprising is that social and cultural theory are largely absent from scholarly study of the field. In fact, culture studies, from anthropology to development economics to philosophy, have elaborated rich understandings of culture—its processes of production and circulation, its effects on social and economic life, and its role in human development.

In this chapter, I turn to these disciplines to contrast three views of culture that have dominated cultural studies (and influenced intellectual property law in turn): *culture as tradition, culture as commodity,* and *culture as participatory community.* From the late nineteenth century and for nearly a century thereafter, both anthropologists and the public at large understood culture as tradition, that is, as a set of learned customs and rituals transmitted from generation to generation. Culture as tradition presumed culture to be fixed, hierarchical, and unchanging over time. The rise of mass media during the last century fostered the corresponding emergence of culture as commodity. In Jürgen Habermas's account, the turn toward viewing culture as a commodity paradoxically had its roots in the Enlightenment. In *The Structural Transformation of the Public Sphere,* Habermas fascinatingly recounts how the Enlightenment coffee house culture of the late eighteenth century, in which people debated ideas, literature, and politics, evolved from a culture-producing society to a culture-consuming one. Mass media grew to serve a growing bourgeoisie that sought to mix learning and leisure. As Habermas reveals the irony, over time the consumption of books became the *end* of Enlightenment, rather than its means.

At the start of the twenty-first century, these two views of culture—as tradition and as commodity—are being challenged, by both social actors and scholars in the academy. On the ground, global social movements fueled by new technologies and political economies are challenging the conventional "take it or leave it" understanding of culture as either unassailable truth called "tradition," or as canned commodities poised to entertain. Whereas people of the last century understood culture as "off the rack"—a set of homogeneous goods and beliefs imposed on citizens by cultural authorities—increasingly people today understand culture as bespoke, tailored for the wearers themselves. On the Internet, young girls publish their own Harry Potter "fan fiction" that moves Hermione Granger from the periphery to the center of the adventure. In India, a fan renames Harry as Hari, taking the hero's adventures to the streets of Kolkata. Muslim youth fashion Islamic superheroes, challenging Marvel's and DC Comics' vision of who is a superhero. Players of the digital game *The Beatles: Rock Band* inhabit the world of John, Paul, Ringo, and George, collaborating and creating the world's most popular music "all together now."[3] And on YouTube, hundreds of millions of people have answered the challenge to "Broadcast Yourself," making an end-run around traditional commercial media by connecting directly with millions around the world on every topic under the sun. Welcome to the age of bespoke culture, aka DIY (do-it-yourself) or DIWO (do-it-with-others) culture.[4]

The enhanced ability—and willingness—of ordinary people to challenge cultural authorities, be they mullahs or Hollywood moguls, is notable in its own right. Some of the most popular videos on YouTube, for example, have been posted by ordinary Muslim men and women around the world, who use the medium to define and share their own answers to the oft-asked question after September 11, 2001: What is a Muslim? Homemade videos by and of ordinary Muslims around the world—in their college dormitories; as female police officers on the streets of Amman, Jordan; as moms debating mullahs in the United Kingdom—and even simple one-line "Tweets" such as those from the street protests of the "Arab Spring" of 2011 are a potent part of the content of culture today and are remaking Muslim identity in the twenty-first century. The result is that traditional cultural authority is eroding as more and more individuals in the modern world are questioning, debating, and collectively redefining their *cultural* communities just as they would their *political* communities. Web 2.0 is spurring and reflecting a much larger shift in the fabric of society: we are moving away from imposed cultural identities toward a conception of cultural identity based on autonomy, reason, and choice.

This is a big claim. Let me clarify that in making it, I do not deny the existence of participation and dissent within cultures for millennia. Indeed, we have long understood that *the very essence of culture is participation.* Culture is fundamentally collective, requiring the participation of many in making and sustaining shared meaning. Surely, this was true before the Internet: individuals and communities have always sought to participate in the cultural universes they love, by doing everything from singing, dancing, and telling stories together to playing with Star Wars action figures, dressing in elaborate DIY character costumes, and attending Star Trek conventions. As my own grandmother's story illustrates, culture has never really been a fixed tradition or static commodity simply handed down to people to imbibe; individuals have always had a hand in challenging cultural traditions and inventing new ones. Cultural theorists such as John Fiske have amply demonstrated how even before the Internet, individuals and disempowered communities reimagined the mass culture produced on television in active, not passive, ways to better reflect their own lives and desires.

But while this may have always been the case—that culture is always invented, not discovered—our *theories of culture,* combined with our *law* and *technological architectures* for producing and consuming culture, have not always reflected or promoted this vision. Indeed, as the culture-as-tradition and commodity views suggest, for most of the twentieth century, the dominant scholarly understanding in democratic liberal theory has been that "culture constrains."[5] A few select reformers challenge custom, but the masses obey it. As Anthony Appiah reminds us, it has long been the role of the artist to "disturb us and make us dissatisfied with our habitual life in culture."[6] But increasingly today, on blogs, YouTube, Flickr, Twitter, Weibo, and Facebook, we are all artists who, if not literally making our own news and art, are at least more ready to author our own lives and to not take the given culture lying down.

To be sure, culture does not represent a sphere of unlimited autonomy or choice. To the contrary, French theorist Pierre Bourdieu has famously described culture as a "habitus," referring to the constraints our social environment imposes on us. According to Bourdieu, cultural constraints may more or less determine our lives. But today, there is growing recognition that as cultures modernize and as more and more options are made available to people through technology, travel, and liberalization, "culture becomes less . . . habitus . . . and more an arena for conscious choice."[7]

Law's conception of culture matters. If law conceives culture as tradition, or as a fixed commodity to be handed down primarily to entertain the masses, it will instantiate traditional or commodity culture. In this chapter I argue instead that law ought to put its weight behind what I call a participatory culture. While the benefits of democracy in the *political* sphere are well known, scholars have spent far less time considering the benefits of participation and debate in the *cultural* sphere. I turn to social and cultural theory to elaborate the benefits of active and more widespread participation in the cultural sphere, which range from promoting learning and the critical thinking skills crucial in a democratic society, to incentivizing freedom and creativity, to challenging discriminatory cultural traditions and authorities, to promoting economic development and mutual understanding. Furthermore, I will show that the view of culture as participatory community is not only more in line with Enlightenment values than are the tradition and commodity views of culture, but also better takes into account the changes wrought by the Internet and shifting social expectations at the turn of the century. It is to the elaboration of this third view of culture as participatory community that I will soon turn. But first we must revisit the conventional understandings of culture, for these still have a powerful hold on our imaginations today, and are especially entrenched in intellectual property law.

CULTURE AS TRADITION

Scholars credit Edward B. Tylor with the first anthropological definition of culture, in 1871. Tylor called culture "that complex whole which taken includes knowledge, belief, art, morals, law, custom, and any other capabilities and habits acquired by man as a member of society."[8] Credited with being ahead of his time, Tylor's conception of culture found adherents among anthropologists well into the twentieth century. Bronislaw Malinowski in the early twentieth century defined culture as "inherited artifacts, goods, technical processes, ideas, habits, and values."[9] Ruth Benedict wrote of culture as "learned behavior" passed down from generation to generation.[10] Margaret Mead called culture "the whole complex of traditional behavior which has been developed by the human race and is successively learned by each generation."[11] Edward T. Hall wrote in 1966, "[N]o matter how hard a man tries it is impossible for him to divest himself of his own culture, for it has penetrated to the roots of his nervous system and determines how he perceives the world."[12] Émile Durkheim did not use the word "culture," but his description of "collective conscience" is similar in concept: "The totality of beliefs and sentiments common to average citizens of the society forms a determinate system which has its own life; one may call it the collective or common view."[13] These early theoretical views of culture are consonant with some popular conceptions of culture even today. The most recent *Merriam-Webster Dictionary* defines culture as "the integrated pattern of human knowledge, belief, and behavior that depends upon the capacity for learning and transmitting knowledge to succeeding generations."[14] In the culture-as-tradition view, culture is ancient, fixed, unitary, and transferable.

But by the late twentieth century the idea of culture as tradition began to morph considerably, at least in intellectual circles. Postmodern intellectuals began to question large, theoretical concepts such as "nation" and "culture," finding that the reified conception of culture as a "whole" made famous by Tylor "obscures a good deal more than it reveals."[15] Postmodernists observed that cultural groups were in fact more internally diverse—engaged in dialogue with other cultures, and subject to *change*—than the culture-as-tradition formulation allowed. Anthropologists like Renato Rosaldo observed that cultures are marked by fault lines such as class, race, gender, and sexuality. The postmodernist project was to highlight the suppressed or repressed voices that metanarratives sought to hide—that is, to de-reify and unmask culture.

But while postmodernism disintegrated culture, it did not destroy it. After postmodernism cracked open and fragmented the concepts of nation and culture, new movements in anthropology and "cultural studies" stepped in to pick up the pieces. Scholars in these disciplines attempted to navigate a conception of culture that is somewhere between the banks of culture as a static "thing" and culture as a "fiction." Today, whereas the dictionary may continue to define culture as refined traditions learned by individuals in discrete "cultures," the specialists who study culture, from anthropologists to social theorists, shun such a view.

As Clifford Geertz memorably characterized it in his influential *The Interpretation of Cultures,* "the concept of culture . . . is essentially a semiotic one. Believing, with Max Weber, that man is an animal suspended in webs of significance he himself has spun, I take culture to be those webs." Culture describes the meanings that individuals create in order to make a home in the world.[16] According to this view, culture is made, not found, and culture-making is an ongoing, dynamic process, not a finished product passed down through the ages. In the contemporary view, collective identity is "a hybrid, often discontinuous *inventive* process."[17] Cultural theorists today reject a notion of culture as natural or given and rotely learned, instead viewing culture as socially constructed webs of shared meaning.

CULTURE AS COMMODITY

Let us examine another powerful view of culture: culture as commodity. Return to Habermas's account *The Structural Transformation of the Public Sphere: An Inquiry into a Category of Bourgeois Society,* in which Habermas tells of the rise of the liberal bourgeois public sphere in late eighteenth- and early nineteenth-century Europe during the age of Enlightenment. There, for the first time in history, individuals rejected monarchy and feudal social relations in favor of republicanism. The Enlightenment motto, articulated by Kant as "Think for Oneself," extended beyond politics. From here on, the people would drive not only politics, but also art, philosophy, and literary meaning. "Public opinion" on this vast range of matters was formed in what Habermas calls the "public sphere," places and spaces where private individuals gathered as citizens to debate publicly the issues of the day. Salons, coffee houses, pamphlets, and journals became sites of critical-rational debate where public opinion could be freely formed, and reformed. Habermas's ideal public sphere has several key features: individuals are equals, debate takes place on rational terms, and persuasion involves mutual recognition, not coercion. Habermas adopts C. W. Mills's formulation for determining what constitutes "public opinion":

> In a public . . . (1) virtually as many people express opinions
> as receive them. (2) Public communications are so organized
> that there is a chance immediately and effectively to answer
> back any opinion expressed in public. Opinion formed by such
> discussion (3) readily finds an outlet in effective action, even
> against—if necessary—the prevailing system of authority.
> And (4) authoritative institutions do not penetrate the public,
> which is thus more or less autonomous in its operation.[18]

For Habermas, the promise of Enlightenment was not simply its commitment to public access to cultural knowledge in the form of literature, books, and essays, but also its commitment to truly democratic participation in cultural debates about the meaning of the works themselves. Simply stated: *intellectual works are the means, not the ends, of Enlightenment.* In a democratic public sphere, individuals should have more options than just "yes/no responses" to given works. In Habermas's view, without choice and the opportunity for individuals to engage with and debate given ideas, there would be no difference between republicanism and feudalism. For Habermas, the growth of an autonomous public sphere in newspapers, journals, reading clubs, Masonic lodges, and coffee houses in eighteenth-century Europe was crucial for maintaining the people's independence of thought. In an ideal public sphere, thought was not coerced by power—be it the king or media moguls. The essential characteristic of the public sphere is its "critical" nature, whereby the public no longer accepts the authority of the monarch and begins to rationally debate policy and morals among citizens themselves. Habermas holds that "ideal" discourse occurs where individuals recognize one another as equals, have equal capacity to engage in discourse, and can speak uncoerced by power. According to Habermas, to have truly public opinion, there should be the opportunity for "criticizable validity claims."[19]

But *The Structural Transformation* tells two tales. The second half of the book, Habermas's earliest work and now a foundational text in discussions of the public sphere, chronicles the decline of this Enlightenment culture of rational debate and its transformation into a culture of mass media and bourgeoisie commodity consumption in the twentieth century.[20] Habermas recounts an ironic transformation, whereby the Enlightenment ideal of access to knowledge led to the commercialization of cultural goods for the masses. Two simultaneous developments—the rise of mass media, and the introduction of the concept of leisure for a bourgeois middle class—transformed the participatory culture of the Enlightenment era, when citizens themselves debated and created meaning, into a culture of consumption. "[A]t one time the commercialization of cultural goods had been the precondition for rational-critical debate," but over time this access to cultural goods began, "surreptitiously," to become the end and not the means of debate. By the late nineteenth and early twentieth centuries, we were beginning to see "the replacement of a reading public that debated critically about matters of culture by the mass public of culture consumers."[21] Debate itself became a canned commodity for consumption and for enjoyment as entertainment and leisure, rather than a political activity of the people. Writes Habermas:

> Put bluntly: you had to pay for books, theater, concert, and museum, but not for the conversation about what you had read, heard, and seen and what you might completely absorb only through this conversation. Today the conversation itself is ad-

ministered. Professional dialogues at the podium, panel discussions, and round table shows—the rational debate of private
people becomes one of the production numbers of the stars in
radio and television, a salable package ready for the box office.[22]

The focus on cultural products for mass consumption went hand in
hand with the rise of the concept of leisure[23] and with democratization. In
Habermas's words, "Anyone who owned an encyclopedia was educated."[24]
Mass media acquired its power and cultural authority in the name of
making knowledge accessible to the public. Culture as commodity and
as entertainment stimulated mental relaxation rather than the engaged
and critical faculties required for the public use of reason.[25] Furthermore,
there was a heightened separation between cultural elites—intellectuals, artists, and big media conglomerates—and the general public. As
Habermas tells it, "the public is split apart into minorities of specialists
who put their reason to use nonpublicly and the great mass of consumers whose receptiveness is public but uncritical."[26] Intellectual property
rights such as copyright further protected and entrenched a creative elite.
In short: the public sphere became privatized. Meanwhile, the very core
of democratic society—a critical and innovative citizenry—was dulled.

Culture as commodities bears some resemblance to culture as tradition: again, cultural meanings are produced by a few and imposed on the
many. The irony of commercial "mass" culture is that while culture is
distributed to a mass public, it is produced only by a few. Furthermore,
the flow of culture from mass media to the public is largely unidirectional;
cultural products are presented as finished products and consumed "as
is." Habermas adopts C. W. Mills's distinction between "mass" opinion
and "public" opinion as defined earlier, noting that in a "mass"

> 1) far fewer people express opinions than receive them. . . .
> [as] individuals receive impressions from the mass media;
> (2) it is difficult or impossible for the individual to answer
> back immediately or with any effect; (3) authorities control
> possibilities for any action upon opinions; and (4) the mass
> is not autonomous.[27]

In a commodity culture, Habermas critiques, culture consumers are
"as little a 'public' as were those formations of pre-bourgeois society in

which the ancient opinions were formed, secure in their tradition, and circulated unpolemically with the effect of 'laws of opinion.'"[28] (Observing the similarities between commodity culture and traditional culture, the Brazilian musician and culture minister Gilberto Gil has decried advocates of "absolute [intellectual] property control" as "fundamentalists.")[29] Professional purveyors of culture and media solidify social control, and more and more the public comes to accept culture as a given. Commodity culture fails Habermas's ideal of a public sphere because although mass media reach a broad public, "they do not fulfill the requirements of a public process of rational-critical debate according to the liberal model. As institutionally authorized opinions, they are always privileged and achieve no mutual correspondence with the nonorganized mass of the 'public.'"[30] Habermas holds that mass opinion is the result of coercion, not consensus. Private interests and power drive debates and social change. In sum, the public sphere is "public" in name alone; once again, culture functions as imposed tradition.

John Philip Sousa was an influential early critic of commodity culture. Sousa famously lamented "the menace of mechanical music" when an improved phonograph was introduced in the early twentieth century. The American composer argued that mechanical delivery threatened to strip music of its human soul. "Canned music,"[31] he said, would lead to the death of amateur musicians and even impede the evolution of humans themselves to the point where "we will not have a vocal cord left."[32] While no such biological transformation came to pass, the changes in social culture Sousa feared are similar to those documented by Habermas. Sousa worried that the role of individual creators (now dubbed "amateurs") would diminish and be replaced by that of professional entertainers. "[I]t must be admitted that where families lack time or inclination to acquire musical technic [sic], and to hear public performances, the best of these machines supply a certain amount of satisfaction and pleasure," Sousa wrote, continuing:[33]

> Under such conditions the tide of amateurism cannot but recede, until there will be left only the mechanical device and the professional executant. Singing will no longer be a fine accomplishment; vocal exercises, so important a factor in the curriculum of physical culture, will be out of vogue! Then what of

the national throat? Will it not weaken? What of the national chest? Will it not shrink?[34]

Sousa laments the democratic society that loses its voice for lack of exercising it.

Sousa's critique, while powerful, is also overblown. Let me state at the outset that I acknowledge far more the benefits of commodified culture than Sousa did a century ago. As even the *New York Times* observed in an editorial response to Sousa in 1907, Sousa's tirade against "canned music" failed to acknowledge the significant ways that "the self-playing piano and the improved phonograph . . . are effective instruments in the spread of culture." The *Times* opined that "[a]ppreciation of the best music is largely growing through their influence," and "they are musically educating the multitude."[35] As Walter Benjamin later observed, mechanical reproduction or copies demystify the mystique of the original, allowing more democratic access to knowledge. Mass media also spurred the formation of national consciousness and identity, as Benedict Anderson has described, because the widespread distribution of common cultural referents helped cement communities of shared knowledge and experience.

There is another important context in which I do not reject wholesale the commodification of culture. In Chapter 1, I discussed the recent turn to intellectual property rights by poor peoples in the developing world, from the trademarking of Ethiopian specialty coffees to the San of southern Africa claiming patent-like rights in the medicinal properties of the hoodia cactus. In such contexts, commodification can have multiple benefits, from helping to preserve valuable art and knowledge, to giving recognition to the world's diverse authors and inventors, to offering a vehicle for sharing one's knowledge and culture with others, to providing a potentially lucrative means of economic development. As scholars like Arjun Appadurai and Rosemary Coombe have shown, cultural commodities have social and cultural lives and meanings.

My critique of the commodity view of culture is not Sousa's—that commodification itself is inherently profane and dehumanizing. Rather, my critique is of a twentieth-century mentality that began to view cultural commodities as the ends and not means of Enlightenment. As Habermas showed, the Enlightenment commitment to universalizing access to knowledge perversely led to a single-minded focus on the production of culture for the people, but not by them. Simply stated, and to take just one example, the production of books took precedence over a culture of book clubs and similar discussion groups. Driven by this logic, utilitarian intellectual property sought incentives for the production of more cultural goods, without care for who produced the goods and the terms under which they could be engaged.

Today, when scholars and practitioners of intellectual property law advocate for this law to promote "culture," it is largely this commodity view of culture. Law protects the incentives of cultural elites, from Apple to Disney, to produce cultural products for mass consumption. These cultural producers are praised for educating and entertaining the public; in turn, current law supports the expectation that the public should passively receive information products. Worse still, when confronted with revolutionary challenges to traditional and professional cultural authority at the dawn of the new millennium, we have witnessed new intellectual property laws that seek to actively maintain the commodity view of culture, giving creators even greater exclusive control over their cultural products. The recent Digital Millennium Copyright Act, for example, imposes criminal liabilities for circumventing technological encryptions on digital content and legally obligates Internet service providers such as Google to take down copyright-infringing material posted on sites like YouTube. The market failure rationale for fair use gives maximum value to incentives for professional creators and minimal value to public participation in making and sharing culture. In short, the utilitarian logic of intellectual property today, which is focused on incentives to produce goods, has led to a law that stands fundamentally at odds with the emergent participatory culture.

PARTICIPATORY CULTURE IN THE TWENTY-FIRST CENTURY

At the start of the twenty-first century, the century-old conceptions of culture as tradition and culture as commodity are being turned on their head. True to its motto "Broadcast Yourself," half of YouTube's nearly 100 million videos are "user-created."[36] A 2007 report by the Organisation for Economic Co-operation and Development (OECD) estimates that over one-third of all U.S. Internet users have posted content to the Internet and more than one-half of users under age thirty have produced and shared original content on the Web, from blogs to videos.[37] Web platforms deriving content from users are among the most popular and fastest growing in the world, with YouTube the fourth most popular website behind Yahoo, MSN, and Google.[38] In the music world, bands like Radiohead partner with iTunes and GarageBand to give fans the musical components to their songs—known as "stems"—to allow users to rip, mix, and burn their own tunes. Creators upload their remixes under Creative Commons licenses to share with others. The participatory culture of new media is converging with old media as well. Now even broadcast television shows invite audience participation, challenging fans to "create your own superhero," or to develop your own storyline to share with a show's creators and with other fans on a show's website. Some 20 million viewers call in to vote for their favorite talent on *American Idol*. As Jean Burgess and Joshua Green, authors of a new study on YouTube, write, "Consumption is no longer necessarily seen as the end point in an economic chain of production but as a dynamic site of innovation and growth in itself."[39]

Surely the Internet bears witness to the stupidity as well as the wisdom of crowds. An important new book edited by Saul Levmore and Martha Nussbaum, *The Offensive Internet,* highlights the prevalence of sexist and racist harassment in Internet communities, and excruciating instances of public shaming of young people who may be most vulnerable to peer pressure and abuse. But the solution to such abuses, as contributors to that book argue, is not to throw out the baby with the bathwater, but to ask what technological and legal architectures allow for these abuses to take place, and whether they can continue to be justified. The goal is to root out abusive activity that in fact stifles participation, while constructing law and technology that would allow for broader, productive engagement.

It bears repeating that participatory culture is fueled by more than technological change. Its roots are undeniably social and political. At its core is an Enlightenment claim that all men are intellectuals, capable of thinking for themselves and of making knowledge of the world. The movement known as "identity politics" in the 1990s grew out of this conceit. Disempowered groups argued that they lacked media power and the ability to control their own images and identities. Minorities and women pointed out that they were more often the objects of dominant culture, rather than allowed to be subjects capable of producing knowledge themselves. The social movement known as "identity politics" sought to enhance recognition of cultural others, namely those who had been written out of the dominant cultural discourse.

At the turn of the century this social movement converged with a technological one. The rise of the Internet and digital technology significantly enhanced the possibility of democratic influence over meaning-making. The Information Age of the late twentieth century has given way to the Participation Age of the twenty-first century. Several features of the high-technology architecture of the new millennium, from the digital medium to the Internet, offer the potential for a return to what Habermas calls the "unfinished project" of Enlightenment, that is, the promise of a time when cultural meaning comes from the people themselves. By disseminating more widely the levers of making cultural meaning, new technologies—what the legal scholar Michael Froomkin refers to as "hardware for democracy"[40]—assist us as we seek to think for ourselves, reflecting Kant's aspiration for humankind.

To be sure, obstacles to full participation remain, among them a continuing digital divide, lack of leisure time, and technical incapacity (the hardware is still difficult to use for many). Young white men still dominate the Internet. And traditional media retain strong control and influence in new domains, from YouTube to Twitter. But as I will emphasize, the rise of participatory culture is significant just in its *potential*. The relative ease of commenting on others' cultural expressions and making one's own content destabilizes traditional cultural authorities, making that authority more transparent and contingent. Moreover, the simple fact that individuals can more easily participate—even if they ultimately choose not to—can itself be empowering.

The technological features of participatory culture include:

- *Many-to-many interactivity*. While traditional media allowed for either one-to-one interactivity (a phone conversation between two people) or one-to-many non-interactivity (a broadcast radio or television program), the Internet allows many people at once to communicate with many others (described variously as "narrowcasting" or "multicasting"). Given that traditional media tend to privilege the message of those with access to the few channels of communication, the democratizing potential of this new communicative power has been well noted, even by the U.S. Supreme

Court: "Through the use of chat rooms, any person with a phone line can become a town crier with a voice that resonates farther than it could from any soapbox. Through the use of Web pages, mail exploders, and newsgroups, the same individual can become a pamphleteer. . . . '[T]he content on the Internet is as diverse as human thought.'"[41]

- *Amenability to manipulation and revision.* Information stored in digital form is far easier to manipulate than information in analog form. Cutting and pasting once involved scissors and glue. The digital medium facilitates the rearranging of text, art, music, and video, and permits the addition of new elements along the way.

- *End-to-end architecture.* The architecture of the Internet shifts the development of culture away from popular media with top-down control to a system known as "end-to-end architecture." The current infrastructure of the Internet offers a system in which intelligence is located not in the middle but at the ends—that is, in the computers of the users themselves. This open architecture facilitates democratic resistance to dominant cultural discourses. As I argue in Chapters 4 and 6, the digital technologies empower minorities, girls, women, and the poor who have not been reflected in traditional media to represent themselves and foster mutual understanding.[42]

- *Digital hardware.* Digital video cameras now abound, creating amateur auteurs. Sony's latest high-definition video camera, whose $2,000 price tag makes it an expensive luxury for most home users, brings even high-quality video imaging within the reach of some middle-class households. The computer itself, of course, is the most powerful piece of digital hardware. Its increasing penetration in American households has extended access to the digital revolution, though a digital divide still persists.

- *Authoring software.* Consider Apple's iMovie, or the music software GarageBand, which lets you, depending on your preferences, feel and sound like a rock star or conduct a full orchestra. Both iMovie and GarageBand come free with the purchase of an Apple computer. The Web itself comes with authoring software. Tim Berners-Lee, the Web's inventor, insisted that Web software include not just a browser, which would enable one to access content on others' computers, but also an editor, which would enable the user to add her own content.[43] "Mod" software, such as Machinima, enables users to not merely watch a movie or play a videogame, but also to turn the games into film and to "modify" or "re-skin" existing characters to look like themselves. Increasingly, software will allow our children to insert themselves into their favorite make-believe worlds. Dollhouses now face virtual competition.

- *Peer-to-peer networks.* Technologies of creation require technologies of communication. Peer-to-peer networks give us each a bullhorn, mercifully without forcing anyone else to listen to what we have to say. Peer-to-peer services capitalize on the fact that at any moment most computers exhaust only a small percentage of their computational power and their network access. Bandwidth access can be expensive, but peer-to-peer services reduce the need for the author to purchase large amounts of it by making the file available for download from a variety of distribution points across the Internet. Even very large files—typically ones including video—can be disseminated rapidly using software such as BitTorrent. The more popular a file, the more readily it becomes available via peer-to-peer services. By sharing computing resources across the Web, each of us becomes more powerful than we would be standing alone.

- *Blogs.* Companies such as Google and Moveable Type offer free software to create Web-based diaries that enable any individual or group to comment on the issues of the day—or on the issues of their own lives. They also host such blogs for free. By 2008, worldwide blogs numbered over 150 million; nearly 350 million people worldwide were reading blogs.[44]

- *Wikis.* Even the task of writing a major encyclopedia of the world is no longer in the hands of a small group of editors at a major publishing house. Wikipedia takes advantage of the distribution of human knowledge by permitting individuals worldwide to contribute bits and pieces to a large encyclopedia. It is written and edited "collaboratively by volunteers, allowing most articles to be changed by anyone with access to the website."[45]

- *Podcasting and vidcasting.* The radio station now faces competition from home-brewed talk and music available on the Internet. The wide distribution of mobile digital music players enables users to download readily their favorite audiocast and listen to it at their convenience. Rather than rely on editors at radio stations to determine audio programming, podcasting permits anyone to supply material, subjecting herself only to the mercy of the audience. Fast on the heels of podcasting has been vidcasting, in which individuals—equipped with digital camcorders, editing software, and a home computer—offer television clips, music videos, political commentary, and amateur video blogging on popular sites such as YouTube, without requiring the intermediation of large studio houses.

- *Social networking sites.* Individuals have found a powerful means of expressing themselves to a community of their own choosing through social networking sites such as MySpace, Facebook, Orkut, and Twitter. In these sites, individuals can initiate the topics—they can set the agenda. Some might protest that much of the conversation responds to items in the mass media, from television to movies to news.[46] But it is in this communal conversation that individuals can question, debate, and criticize what is happening around them. Social networking sites also provide for a forum for political association. Members of Facebook can create or join a "group" with a specific goal or purpose and then initiate or comment on discussion topics. Due to social networking sites, countries such as Egypt have seen increased grassroots movements by women toward political participation. Facebook's "event" feature, for instance, allows individuals to publicize events, including ones that they are initiating. Because of such features, authoritarian governments across the world have come to see Facebook as a threat. When Ahmed Maher Ibrahim used Facebook to organize a protest against the Egyptian president, the police beat him—and demanded his Facebook password.[47] And while most social-networking sites consist of communities of "friends," they are not necessarily parochial. Questions like "do you like my new haircut" and commands to "see how much the baby grew today" are "the ephemera that keep . . . people related to each other."[48]

CULTURE AND LIBERAL DEMOCRATIC THEORY

My account thus far has been largely descriptive. The question remains: Why does participatory culture matter? Should we support the rise of participatory culture or seek a return to the logics of cultural production and consumption that governed the last century? To answer these questions, we need to turn to theory. Today there is increasing recognition that participatory culture is centrally linked to freedom, equality, democracy, and development. It is to the elaboration of these connections that I now turn.

I suggest that John Rawls is much less relevant in this context than is Habermas, or Aristotle as elaborated by Nussbaum. Rawls, who is credited with elaborating the most important theory of justice in the twentieth century, focuses on the requirements for structuring a society that betters the least well-off. But Rawls's concern is *political institutions, not culture,* and he expressly limits his theory to the political sphere, specifying that judges, legislators, and citizens should engage in rational debate in the public sphere over political matters.[49] Rawls's theory of public reason does not apply to normative communities or commitments—what he calls the "background culture."[50] Rawls intentionally "leaves untouched all kinds of doctrines, religious, metaphysical, and moral, with their long traditions of development and interpretation."[51]

My own interest is culture rather than political institutions. For although Rawls takes as a given the "background culture," this is precisely the arena of privately created and contested meanings that liberal and postmodern theories must more critically explore today. In fact, democracy, participation, freedom, and equality are just as important in the cultural sphere as they are in the political.

In contrast to Rawls, Habermas takes a much broader view of the "public sphere." Where Rawls takes the background culture as a given, and focuses on the creation of public discourse apart from it, Habermas views the background culture itself—what he calls the "lifeworld"—as his real subject of interest. In his magnum opus *The Theory of Communicative Action,* Habermas describes the lifeworld as the background culture in which we live and act, including everything from traditions and communities to language, beliefs, and institutions. While the lifeworld is usually taken for granted as self-evident or natural, the challenge of a robust public sphere, says Habermas, is to debate everything openly and free from coercion, including and especially the lifeworld itself. The public sphere becomes corrupted, or in Habermas's terms "rationalized," when power controls the lifeworld, making certain ways of being appear natural and uncontestable.

Habermas's lifeworld is not something an individual can exit. The lifeworld forms us and provides the language and symbols through which we speak and act. And yet the lifeworld can and must be transformed—thus, Habermas's conception here stands in contrast to the view of culture as tradition that I described earlier. In Habermas's view, a robust public sphere frees culture from being fixed and determined and reveals the lifeworld as something that individuals create, challenge, and can change of their own free will. While Rawls leaves the "background culture" untouched, Habermas urges that those very normative commitments and truths that appear sacrosanct are the ones we should be willing to question and critically engage with reasoned arguments. Habermas envisions a culture that "puts itself on trial."[52]

Surely, Habermas highlights the instrumental role that culture plays in liberal democratic society. Habermas credits the eighteenth-century salons and coffee houses of the Enlightenment with creating the spaces in which citizens could develop their critical faculties and form "public opinion" by debating the political issues of the day. Significantly, here culture was not only an end of Enlightenment but also its means. The public use of reason was exercised through the medium of literature and literary debates. For Habermas, a robust and autonomous public sphere is constitutive of republican democracy. But in Habermas's view, the benefits of ideal communicative action go further, from facilitating self-development and equal recognition of participants in an inclusive public sphere, to engendering social solidarity and mutual understanding among participants.

Michel Foucault, most often understood as a postmodern critic of liberal theory, at the end of his life penned an important exchange with Habermas about cultural critique. In that later work, Foucault also advocates critical engagement with the cultures in which we live. The Enlightenment is to be understood not as a specific age or epoch, Foucault writes, but as a critical "attitude" toward the present.[53] Revisiting Kant's essay "What Is Enlightenment?" Foucault concludes that Enlightenment is "the attitude of modernity," which he describes as a commitment to engage in "a permanent critique of our historical era."[54] For Foucault, Enlightenment is at once "a task and an obligation."[55] The modern individual can simultaneously revel in the present yet assert the liberty to transgress it and *transfigure the world*. We must recognize "the limits that are imposed on us" and then engage in "an experiment with the possibility of going beyond them," Foucault writes. The modern individual "simultaneously respects [her] reality and violates it."[56] For all their differences, in this final exchange between them, Habermas and Foucault both rejected the passive acceptance of culture as tradition in favor of cultural critique.

My praise of participatory culture builds on the insights of these philosophers. Habermas and Foucault expanded the focus beyond political process, noting how culture constitutes self and society while also providing the very building blocks for reconstructing the social edifice. To repeat: we can never leave the lifeworld. But as modern beings we must be empowered to question and transform it. Indeed, it is precisely because culture is so influential in shaping our world and our selves that individual rights to debate it and participate in its making are imperative. As Jack Balkin has persuasively argued, we need "democratic culture" because people must have a say in critiquing and remaking the cultural forces that shape their lives, just as democratic citizens have a say in shaping the politics that govern us.[57] Democratic culture may be even more important than democratic politics. Balkin explains, "[L]aw and governance are only parts of this world. Culture is an even larger part, and in some ways it has an even more capacious role in structuring our lives."[58]

THE BENEFITS OF PARTICIPATORY CULTURE

Participatory culture is instrumentally and intrinsically related to promoting freedom, engendering equality, and fostering human and economic development. I consider here in some more detail particular benefits of participatory culture in these regards.

Freedom and Equality

Freedom to participate in cultural life stands at the very core of *liberty*. As Salman Rushdie has stated, "Those who do not have power over the story that dominates their lives, power to retell it, rethink it, deconstruct it, joke about it, and change it as times change, truly are powerless, because they cannot think new thoughts."[59]

Additionally, there is a liberty interest in engaging cultural works not just intellectually but also physically, with one's whole body. Consider the human imperative for physical interaction with cultural works by singing, dancing, dressing up, or acting out favorite lines from a film. Martha Nussbaum describes how physically performing in dance or theater can itself be liberating, particularly for women. She recalls the Indian intellectual Rabindranath Tagore's emphasis on empowering women through the arts, particularly dance and drama. "Women were his particular concern, since he saw that women were typically brought up to be ashamed of their bodies and unable to move freely, particularly in the presence of men," Nussbaum writes. "A lifelong advocate of women's freedom and equality, he saw that simply telling girls to move more freely would be unlikely to overcome years of repression, but giving them precisely choreographed moves to perform, leaping from here to there, would be a more successful incentive to freedom."[60]

Today, we can witness precisely these types of liberating moves that simultaneously recode popular culture on YouTube. Beyoncé's hit song "Single Ladies (Put a Ring on It)" has inspired hundreds of individuals to post themselves dancing to the song on YouTube. Although each video entails fans mimicking the pop star's moves in the original video, the *individuality* of each dancer is unmistakable. Particularly interesting are the numerous videos of "Single Ladies" by gay men, a phenomenon noted on the popular television show *Glee,* which focuses on the tribulations of high school. Recognizing that young gay men struggle to come out to their families and peers during high school, one episode featured a gay football player videotaping himself and two female friends doing their own rendition of "Single Ladies"—until his father walks in and abruptly stops the recording. The young man provocatively lip-syncs Beyoncé's words, "Acting up . . . I could care less what you think." He continues, "I need no permission, did I mention, don't pay him any attention."[61] In the hands (and feet) of these men, the song "Single Ladies" is reworked as a comment both on the possibility of gay marriage and on the performance of femininity. These videos persist on YouTube, generating literally millions of views, because Beyoncé invited fans to create their own versions of her hit song. Unlike some artists, Beyoncé seems to embrace participatory culture. She even aired some of the videos during her world tour.

In this example, we can also see how cultural liberty has important implications for *equality.* The liberty to contest hegemonic discourses has particularly profound possibilities for women and other minorities who have not traditionally had power over the stories that dominate our lives.

We have an intuitive understanding for the value of political dissent in a democratic republic. First Amendment theory views dissent as crucial to autonomy and choice, and as a means for discovering truth. But what about cultural dissent—that is, the right and ability to disagree with cultural traditions or norms? Is not cultural autocracy just as constrictive of freedom and equality, especially as experienced by women, gays, and others who have suffered under oppressive cultural traditions? Theorists from Bourdieu to Foucault have described the profound ways in which culture governs human capability—in Nussbaum's words, what people "are actually able to do and be."[62] Women may have equal rights on paper, for example, but cultural norms about women's roles profoundly influence women's aspirations and opportunities. Misrepresentations and the lack of representation of gays and lesbians in mainstream media contribute to their leading closeted lives, at times unable to reveal their identities publically or express themselves. Participatory culture is a means of challenging oppressive cultural constraints that negatively affect both individual liberty and social status. As Stuart Hall writes, "Popular culture is one of the sites where this struggle for and against a culture of the powerful is engaged. . . . It is partly where hegemony arises, and where it is secured. . . . That is why 'popular culture' matters."[63]

Intellectual property laws are often implicated in contests over cultural meaning, and particularly in challenges to dominant cultural discourses, because many of the most popular cultural images, which generate far-reaching understandings of gender, race, sexuality, and dominance, are protected by copyrights and trademarks. The YouTube videos using Beyoncé's song may violate her copyright, leaving the participants at the mercy of her generosity. In 2005, DC Comics demanded that a New York gallery cease and desist from showing artist Mark Chamberlain's homoerotic watercolor depictions of Batman and Robin kissing and embracing. Mattel has ruthlessly gone after individuals and artists who put Barbie in a compromising and unflattering light. While many artists have emerged victorious in legal battles over their right to rework such popular icons, their victories have cost millions of dollars in legal fees and have entailed years of protracted battles. Worse still, many artists and amateur creators simply "cease and desist" because they do not have the funds to legally discern whether theirs is a "fair use" of intellectual property.

Michel de Certeau describes such acts as resistance to cultural hegemony. Individuals engage in everyday resistance to dominant culture by a process called "bricolage," which entails making do and tinkering with the cultural images around us to create subversive meanings. Bricolage involves "artisan-like inventiveness" by ordinary people; often, the texts to which people respond are owned by others.[64] "Everyday life invents itself by poaching in countless ways on the property of others,"[65] writes de Certeau. According to de Certeau, individuals do not receive culture as fixed products, but rather "inhabit" cultural texts "like a rented apartment." The individual "transforms another person's property into a space borrowed for a moment by a transient." Just as "renters make comparable changes in an apartment they furnish with their acts and memories," de Certeau writes, so "do speakers, in the language into which they insert both the messages of their native tongue and, through their accent, through their own 'turns of phrase,' etc., their own history."[66] For de Certeau, the question is not what cultural products are handed down to the people but what they make of them. His analysis is both descriptive and prescriptive. Culture is the web of meanings in which we make a home; it is where we live and the discursive space we "inhabit." At the same time, we are actively spinning our own meanings, contesting hegemony through everyday acts of resistance.

Autonomy and Self-Development

In our examples of Indian women acting and dancing and gay men lip-syncing on YouTube, we can begin to see more clearly how cultural participation is a vehicle of self-development. Simply put: individuals develop themselves *through* culture. In one of the most important pieces of American writing on the significance of art in human life, *Art as Experience,* John Dewey writes that individuality "is realized only in *interaction* with surrounding conditions."[67] Dewey is critical of both the "classical" approach to art, which views art as outside of culture, and the "romantic" view that searches for that which is fresh and spontaneous.[68] Notably, Dewey describes the creation of the self and of a work of art in nearly identical terms. Both are the creation of what Dewey calls "intercourse" between the self and society. "[T]he self is both formed and brought to consciousness through interaction with the environment," and it is the result of such intercourse that we call a "work of art."[69] Self-cultivation, like art, is work—something actively made, not discovered. Both arise only from sustained interaction with one's cultural surroundings.

A "School of Political Participation"

John Stuart Mill described local government as a "school of political participation and skill."[70] Similarly, today we are recognizing the ways in which cultural participation serves as an arena for developing engaged and active political citizens among the young and old. The election of President Barack Obama in 2008 was spurred by an enormous surge in cultural creativity shared on the Internet, from Will.i.am's "Yes We Can" video to Shephard Fairey's now iconic street art ripped and mixed from a digital photo. More profoundly, the surge in cultural participation by *ordinary* Americans, especially youth, illustrated how democratic cultural participation can bring about broad cultural change.

The relationship between cultural participation and political democracy goes further still. We often hear that the goal of intellectual property is to foster innovation. Yet innovation ought not simply mean the production of more technical goods. *The essence of innovation is critical thinking.* Participation rather than passive reception in the production of culture and science enables a democratic citizenry ready to question convention and to seek novel answers to problems, old and new.

Children, too, develop themselves as future democratic citizens by actively sharing, debating, critiquing, and re-creating copyrighted and trademarked literary works. The central characters in Harry Potter are themselves role models for democratic citizenship: they question authority, confront evil, and defend the rights of the weak. (In contrast, the benighted "Muggle" family that raises Harry, his aunt and uncle the Dursleys, lives by the motto "Don't Ask Questions."[71]) The rise of participatory groups around the Potter series enables readers to go even further, acting out these values themselves in the real world around them. I have already mentioned Heather Lawver's *The Daily Prophet,* the fan-created virtual newspaper for the fictional wizarding world of Harry Potter. This online newspaper was written and edited by hundreds of children from around the world. The stories they penned do not simply mimic the original Potter stories but take them further, making the case for the rights of Muggles and house elves, and illustrating by example that children should make themselves aware of current events and the news of the day.

We need to ask: Is children's time best spent in front of a computer? Should children not be outdoors, running and playing? In other words, critical thinking may be developed by new and enhanced forms of on-line cultural participation, but what is lost? Will we replace parks with computer labs, or relationships with our neighbors and classmates with virtual friendships and online communities? I reply that multiple forms of engagement—local and global, real world and virtual—are important for developing ourselves as individuals and as citizens. Cultural engagement with mass media, in particular, is an important tool for developing critical faculties—participatory culture online can teach children to criti-cally assess and reconstruct information rather than passively receive it.

Furthermore, cultural texts can serve as vehicles for questioning or critiquing something in the real world. The Harry Potter Alliance is an-other real-world extension of the fictional Potter universe that illustrates this phenomenon. Through the Alliance children are coming together to form an army of young citizens dedicated to upholding the Potter books' values of being kind, having the courage to question authority and cultural norms, and fighting for justice in the real world. The Alliance website describes itself as "dedicated to using the examples of Harry Pot-ter and Albus Dumbledore to spread love and fight the Dark Arts in the real world," imploring, "Please join us in creating the real Dumbledore's Army."[72] Protesting the banning of books (including the Potter books), one member asks "everyone to stand up against the Dolores Umbridges of the world," making reference to the narrow-minded teacher in the Potter lore. Young members of the Alliance are challenged to "think of a banned book that you've read that means a lot to you . . . [and then] leave a short blog post explaining what that book is and what it means to you."[73] The Alliance post concludes: "Let's prove Hermione right by continuing to read books that deal with big ideas and hard issues, despite those who would try to keep them off our shelves and out of our heads."[74]

Henry Jenkins describes a partnering between the Harry Potter Alli-ance and a citizen watchdog group critical of Walmart.[75] Young members of the Alliance made campy videos casting themselves in the familiar roles of Harry, Ron, and Hermione, but here they are battling the Lord Waldemart, who nefariously underpays employees and runs smaller businesses into the ground. We can witness similar play that engenders democratic engagement in the multiplayer online gaming worlds, where children in middle school run for elected office and edit the newspapers of their online communities.

The increased transparency of knowledge production gives youth a healthy skepticism of truth claims, and helps them filter fact from fiction—critical skills necessary in a democracy. Furthermore, Jenkins argues that simply having the capacity to participate and effect change empowers youth, regardless of whether they actually participate or not. "Even if many of them have chosen not to participate," concludes Jenkins, "they understand their place in the media ecology differently because they know how easy it is to contribute content."[76]

This important point—that simply having the capacity to have a say in political affairs empowers individuals to make their voices heard—applies equally well to children and adults. Today even if individuals are not blogging, they may still be more likely to produce some political content—even if that simply means posting comments on citizen blogs and traditional media sources, which increasingly invite and air emailed questions and "Tweets." At this juncture, actual participation by the masses may be less significant than the widespread knowledge of the potential to contribute, which may be empowering enough and threatening to traditional cultural and political authority.

Participatory culture affects democratic citizenship in a number of other ways as well. Participation greatly enhances the sheer *amount* of information available to citizens as they critically assess their governments and societies. I am far from the first to observe that Wikipedia harnesses the wisdom of crowds. This people's encyclopedia collects the knowledge of many diverse peoples rather than simply the knowledge of a few homogenous cultural elites. Today there is more knowledge in circulation than ever before, and even better, it is free and readily available at one's fingertips on mobile devices as well as desktop computers. The immediate accessibility of information, with the enhanced ability to search for more information (revolutionized through Google Books), and then finally the ability to modify the information itself, democratizes access to knowledge in terms of both consumption and production.

To be sure, enlightened public debates about issues from climate change to health care reform mandate deeper knowledge and study than

cursory online encyclopedia entries allow. And there are real concerns
that Wikipedia spreads inaccuracies and is dominated by white males.
But these critiques apply equally to traditional media.

Perhaps more fundamentally, *participatory culture demystifies knowledge itself.* Wikipedia's transparency—illuminating who added or modified
what information—reveals knowledge production as the result of human
agency exercised here and now, not something static, given, or natural.
Publicly airing dissent and the plurality of opinion also delegitimizes
authorities, whose claims to represent the will of the people may be revealed as false. Ultimately, the challenge to traditional authorities may
be profound; as Hannah Arendt notes, a "loss of authority" precedes all
revolutions.[77]

There is an ethical component to fostering critical thinking within
cultural spheres. As Amartya Sen has written, "To see identity as merely a
matter of discovery can not only be a conceptual confusion. It can also lead
to a dereliction of duty by thinking human beings."[78] Passive acceptance
of cultural authority or tradition feeds autocracy and inequality. Cultural
critique, in contrast, is in Foucault's words "a task and an obligation" of
democratic citizens.[79]

Learning Through Play
The very first copyright law, the Statute of Anne enacted in England in
1710, was described as "An Act for the Encouragement of Learning." Born
during the Enlightenment, copyright has always been a critical tool for
facilitating learning. Today, we largely focus on the learning that accrues
from accessing copyrighted works created by others. Yet in the fields of
education and human development, nearly a century of clinical studies
and theory have elaborated how children learn not by imbibing knowledge from the top down, but by actively working through the cultural
discourses that surround them through "pretend play."[80] Role-playing is
not just a descriptive term for how children learn; studies document that
it is a normatively beneficial way of learning, and one that schools have
increasingly adopted and encouraged. Elaborating on the world around us,
children mime to learn social roles and yet also take creative liberties that
test established expectations. Culture for children is a sphere not only of
entertainment and enjoyment but also of experimentation and innovation.

When my daughter was six, rather than restrict her schoolyard play to house, fairies, or princess games (the dominant culture sold to young American girls), she took on the roles of knights and star warriors. My son at four pretended he was a boy version of Mei, an inquisitive four-year-old girl in the film *My Neighbor Totoro*. Even such simple pretend play that challenges gender stereotypes, studies show, has benefits, from disrupting dominant discourses about gender roles (a girl can be a knight) to engendering sympathy for the other (a boy sees the world through the eyes of a four-year-old girl). Indeed, a worldwide phenomenon for adults celebrating these same principles, called cosplay (short for "costume role play"), has spread from Japan to other parts of the globe. In cosplay, individuals develop and wear elaborate costumes mimicking their favorite anime or manga characters. Within the game gender-switching called "crossplay" is common as a vehicle for gaining greater understanding of the other and of challenging traditional gender roles.

Recent studies show other benefits of role-playing include helping children to negotiate conflict and develop language and collaborative skills.[81] Perhaps most importantly in our diverse and increasingly interconnected world, physically and emotionally inhabiting the role of the other helps children learn empathy, as they contemplate what it may be like to walk in another's shoes.[82]

To be sure, child's play at recess or at home does not threaten copyright holders. The children's work is not "fixed" or recorded—thus it does not even constitute a "copy" under law. But the new online worlds of fan fiction, interactive gaming, and videotaping for widespread distribution on platforms such as MySpace and YouTube threaten copyright owners unlike in the past, as the quality of children's creations—and the reach of their work—are significantly enhanced through technology. Consider, for example, what happens when yesterday's most interactive toy—Legos—combines with digital technology and the Internet. For seventy years, the Danish company Lego, which literally means "play well" in Danish, has been making interlocking plastic bricks and components for creative young minds to build whatever they imagine. In 2007, then-fourteen-year-old Coleman Hickey filmed a short video starring his Lego figurines performing "Tonight I'm Gonna Rock You Tonight" from the album to *Spinal Tap* (the film, a spoof documentary of a rock band, is a cult classic from the early 1980s). Hickey posted the video on YouTube and received an overwhelming response, with over 80,000 hits. But his success did not end there. The band Spinal Tap itself began showing the video to audiences during its recent concert tour—that is, until the Lego company objected, claiming copyright ownership in the Lego images in the clip. Spinal Tap reluctantly agreed to stop showing the video.

For its part, the Lego company, which has seen a significant resurgence in popularity,[83] claimed it objected to the video because its depiction of the rock stars was inappropriate for most Lego users, who mostly range in age from six to twelve.[84] Yet Lego has allowed numerous other questionable fan-made videos posted on YouTube. One stop-action video, "Lego Weapon Store," opens with the main character entering a (Lego) weapon store stating, "I'd like to buy a weapon to kill my neighbor." The store features numerous tiny weapons that Lego actually sells to kids, from pickaxes to chainsaws, small pistols, and dynamite.[85] "Lego Weapons Store" has been viewed by over two million people. And in a parody video of the "Girls Gone Wild" video series, called "Legos Gone Wild," the narrator invites hundreds of thousands of viewers on YouTube to watch as "the hottest chicks in town 'Lego' their inhibitions"—the video features female Lego characters exposing themselves.[86] On YouTube, Legos even have sex.

Thus far, Lego has not objected to these videos, regarding them as noncommercial use.[87] To the extent that individuals are not making money using Lego's copyrighted characters, the company has continued to uphold the value of interactivity on which it has been built. Indeed, corporate copyright objecting to interactivity may soon be a thing of the past. Lego itself unrolled an online interactive version called Lego Universe in 2010.

There is a final point about learning by doing or playing with copyrighted works. Individuals learn and master skills by copying and putting themselves in the shoes of masters, from musical greats to literary giants and star scientists. A new interactive video game, *The Beatles: Rock Band,* hailed by the *New York Times* as potentially "the most important video game yet made,"[88] is premised on this insight. The game allows users to "come together" with John, Paul, George, and Ringo, jamming and creating songs. Learning is a key goal of the game. As Paul McCartney acknowledges, even great musicians hone their skills through imitation.[89] Just as McCartney emulated "Buddy Holly, Little Richard, Jerry Lee Lewis, Elvis," so too will tomorrow's musicians learn by miming The Beatles and other rock bands.[90]

Greater Sociability and Sharing

Cultural activity cements social solidarity and community in much the same way that social scientist Robert Putnam argues that civic engagement in activities like bowling does. Dancing, singing, story-sharing, and acting are often group activities, as are fan-related activities such as cosplay and fan fiction. To repeat: shared meaning is what makes culture tick.

Mutual Understanding

For Habermas, there is a moral component to discourse, because public deliberation requires "mutual recognition" of others as equal participants to the dialogue.[91] Communication requires recognizing and understanding the other. As Antje Gimmler writes, much of the interactive and participatory culture of Web 2.0 is built on an implicit understanding of Habermas's discourse ethics. YouTube, he observes, is primarily about "sharing" and "social connections, not high quality commercial content."[92] The jury is still out on whether YouTube will fulfill Habermas's rigorous standards for an ideal public sphere in which dialogue involves "genuine negotiation of complexity and difference."[93] Burgess and Green optimistically opine that YouTube "is an enabler of encounters with cultural differences and the development of political 'listening' across belief systems and identities."[94] Tweets and blog posts by Iranian protesters during that country's mass protests in the summer of 2009 offer an example. The moving images posted on YouTube of the death of the youthful Iranian woman Neda Agha-Solten, who was tragically murdered by authorities as she peacefully protested for democracy and human rights in her country, awakened the world to the courageous quest of millions of Iranians. The rapid and spontaneous accumulation of financial support for victims of the Haiti earthquake, elicited in part by the dissemination of pictures and video of the aftermath, may be another recent variation on the theme of digitally facilitated empathic feeling. Long ago, Dewey observed that "the art characteristic of a civilization is the means for entering sympathetically into the deepest elements in the experience of remote and foreign civilizations."[95] Today, ordinary citizens are artist-ambassadors and their videos and Tweets are documentaries.

I have already described the important role that art plays in cultivating children's creativity, collaborative skills, and empathy for others. In adulthood, these same skills and emotions continue to be engendered through participation in the arts. David Winnicott has argued that art is the sphere in which childhood play is extended into adulthood. Martha Nussbaum describes the arts as a crucial sphere for recognizing the humanity in others because the arts afford a rare opportunity to feel emotion and contemplate the other as human. In his classic treatment on the role of art in social life, *Art as Experience,* John Dewey concluded that "art is the most effective mode of communication that exists."[96]

Nostalgia and Remembering

Milan Kundera writes: "Remembering our past, carrying it around with us always, may be the necessary requirement for maintaining, as they say, the wholeness of the self."[97] Just as culture can connect disparate peoples from across the globe, it also facilitates connections across generations and connections between past and present. A simple song, film, or story can immediately evoke nostalgia, triggering memories and perhaps even a reconsideration of one's youth. Burgess and Green observe that YouTube has become an "accidental archive" of cultural memories. People "spend hours at a time watching old music videos, half-forgotten TV commercials, or clips from Sesame Street—recapturing memories from their childhood or young adulthood."[98] These cultural artifacts are historical and yet also elicit personal, emotional responses among listeners and viewers. And again, intellectual property often becomes implicated as individuals seek to tell and broadcast their own personal histories told through the brands, characters, music, and films owned by corporations. Copyrighted songs often form the soundtrack to individual video-biographies. Cultural works can become the basis of memories in other ways as well. The first generation of youths to read and fall in love with Harry Potter has grown up. Now in college, they maintain their connection to the stories of their youth by forming real-life "Quidditch" teams, with tournaments to boot. "I associate 'Harry Potter' with my childhood," says one senior at Northwestern.[99] For these young adults, the games are a way to feel secure and to stay connected with their past.

Economic Development

President Obama's mother, the late Ann Dunham Soetoro, spent much of her life living and working with poor communities in Indonesia. An anthropologist by training, Ms. Soetoro observed that far from evincing wholly different mores and a way of life, the villagers and craftspeople with whom she lived and worked had ambitions and lifestyles similar to those in the United States. Their heartfelt desire was to participate actively in culture and commerce. Inventiveness in rural Indonesia was "in plentiful supply," she observed—indeed, crafts and trade were their tradition—and these innovators were also "keenly interested in profits."[100] The anthropologist in Ms. Soetoro sought to show that studying a different culture can ultimately help illuminate the common human aspirations that bind us all. Her work reveals a common desire for recognition as a creator of the world, and for fair remuneration in global markets. In the next chapter, I elaborate on the connections between culture and development created by democratic participation in making culture.

CRITIQUES OF PARTICIPATORY CULTURE

Some scholars have objected to the idea that intellectual property law should support individuals' participation in the development of their culture. Their arguments generally fall into the following categories.

Law Should Promote Originality, Not Mimesis

There is a powerful critique of participatory culture: if we do not allow people to play in other people's worlds, perhaps they will create their own worlds. And should we not be especially concerned when individuals, and perhaps especially children, are mimicking the dominant culture, which often exhibits sexism, racism, and class hierarchies? Lego has itself come under scrutiny for its recent adoption of play sets with commercial themes featuring, for example, Star Wars, Indiana Jones, and yes—Harry Potter. As one observer worries, "When you have a less structured, less themed set, kids have the ability to start from scratch. When you have kids playing out Indiana Jones, they're playing out Hollywood's imagination, not their own."[101] More to the point: Do we want children to emulate the popular culture with which they are bombarded? Superman and Batman are hyper-masculine, praised for their might and not prone to expressing their feelings. Female characters are no better; from Tinkerbell to Snow White they set up unattainable and misguided standards of perfection for girls, from physical appearance to their accommodating qualities. Does the emulation of popular culture in pretend play simply encourage the next generation to mimic and replay the unfortunate traditions of the past?

These are important concerns, but my approach neither rejects originality nor condones inequality. Instead, I argue that a closer look at participatory cultural communities, such as the elaborate cosplay and fan-fiction communities among adults, reveals that participants subvert given texts in radical ways. In Chapter 5, I describe some of the ways that fan fiction often contests the hierarchical norms of the original—centering the girl, for example, or making gay relationships more explicit. As mentioned earlier, in cosplay gender switching is not unusual, with women playing male roles and vice versa (a feature dubbed "crossplay"). This is also true in the context of children's play. Studies show that children learn *creativity* and *divergent thinking* through pretend play that emulates their existing worlds, as children extend the original stories in new directions.[102] Furthermore, we have seen that even strict mimesis can have positive effects; the struggle to re-create the work teaches the individual the skills she needs to perhaps create her own original work in the future. But play, too, especially for children, must be properly supervised and directed. The essence of the participatory culture I advocate is critical engagement in contrast to passive reception.

Participatory Culture Breeds Factionalism and Narcissism

Habermas himself has observed that the "Internet has certainly reactivated the grassroots of an egalitarian public of writers and readers."[103] But he has worried publicly about the loss of shared meaning that may result when the mass media culture of the last century is fractured into millions of individualized channels and blogs. Is "bespoke culture" culture at all? More recently the legal scholar Cass Sunstein has argued that a benefit of mass media is that it served as a common reference point for a broad swath of people. Mass media may have been imposing, but its dominance led to the creation of cohesive nation-states with common memories and shared values. Sunstein fears that the proliferation of chat rooms and social networks dedicated to narrow interests of relatively homogeneous groups—from Star Trek fans to Sarah Palin foes—will lead to cultural fragmentation. Sunstein worries that dissent may decrease on the Internet, as individuals tune away from the "Daily Us" to the "Daily Me"— social networks that reinforce our views rather than challenge them.[104]

A related critique is that a world of iP (culture as a community that individuals make together) and MySpace is narcissistic. Posters on You-Tube are self-aggrandizing and seek glory, not mutual understanding. Again, the idea is that individualism is trumping community.

But as I have shown, what is most significant about cultural production today is that new creators are not leaving the community of others, but rather, they increasingly seek to participate in the collaborative project of *making our culture together*. Minorities and gays are inserting themselves into a popular culture that would otherwise either ignore or debase them—as with the gay Batman and Robin, or an empowered girl figure in a story where the original hero is a boy. In Chapter 4, I consider one of the most important cultural rewritings of our day—the African American author Alice Randall's revision of Margaret Mitchell's classic *Gone with the Wind* in the unauthorized parody *The Wind Done Gone,* which is told from the perspective of a black slave girl during the Civil War period. Rewriting iconic cultural works with themselves front and center is a radical tool for historically disadvantaged minorities, who have thus far been denied this subjectivity. As Anupam Chander points out, for many minorities, Sunstein's idealized "Daily Us" is the "Daily Them."[105] Claims by girls and minorities to retell popular stories from their perspectives are not a rejection of shared culture, but a call for the "Daily Us" to better reflect who we really are.

Participatory Culture Threatens Professional Creators
In the face of the challenge of participatory culture, some scholars argue that law must be first and foremost a tool for incentivizing the work of *professional* creators. Behind Andrew Keen's lament in *The Cult of the Amateur* is the fear that while "intoxicated by the ideal of democratization" we will kill "professional mainstream media."[106] The legal scholar Rob Merges has similarly expressed concern "that an over-emphasis on the conditions of participation may significantly worsen the conditions for original creativity." He concludes that "IP policy has as one of its central functions to attend to the care and feeding of creators of original works."[107]

Keen and Merges are coming from different places. Keen is not a fan of participatory culture, which he decries as inferior and shameless.[108] But current copyright law is not, in fact, focused on promoting only "quality" content or professional creators, as Keen would suggest. The inference of the law's relatively low bar on "originality" and the lack of any rigorous registration process, for example, suggest the opposite—that nearly anyone can be a legally recognized creator. Even if we concede that quality matters, copyright law implicates more than the production of more and better things. Copyright law plays a central role in facilitating learning (not only *from* books but through active and critical engagement *with* them), democratic citizenship, freedom, equality, and mutual understanding.

In contrast to Keen, Merges has much more sympathy for participatory culture—indeed, he would likely concede many of the benefits I have described here. But he feels that "IP policy has a special obligation to promote and encourage professional creatives," without whose efforts, Merges argues, "our collective culture would suffer enormously."[109] I am sympathetic to the claims of professional creators—indeed, in subsequent chapters, I argue that many people who have not traditionally been considered authors ought to be recognized and rewarded for their cultural contributions. I agree that intellectual property law ought to contend with issues of livelihood, fairness, and incentives to participate in creating our culture. But I do not believe that incentives to participate in cultural production should be our only concern. I have shown in Chapter 1 how an increasingly exclusive focus on incentives and market failure has made fair-use analysis narrow. Furthermore, as I have just argued, it is simply not the case that current copyright doctrine is structured to favor professionals over amateurs, as the low bar on originality and the ease of obtaining a copyright suggest.

There is another important point. Merges seems to presume that the "creative professionals" are more deserving of protection than others because their creations are "original" while those of remixers are derivative. But characterizations of romantic authorship are often overblown; such distinctions often overlook the extent to which all creativity is derivative. I examine these issues in more detail in Chapter 6, where I focus on cultural sharing—and stealing—between Hollywood and Bollywood.

We Do Not Need Law to Promote Participatory Culture
Some suggest that while participatory culture is important, we may not need law to promote it. These observers are optimistic that markets will facilitate such participation, offering enhanced tools for users to make

culture themselves if this is indeed what the public demands. Moreover, they argue that even where copyright owners have rights to exclude the public from using their works, high enforcement costs will mean that many users will be able to make use of others' copyrights without either permission or payment. Scholars thus seek to justify the current distribution of entitlements favoring professional creators using a range of arguments, from incentives to Lockean labor theory.

But we could argue that law should put its weight on the side of those who would dissent from cultural authorities, or those who seek greater autonomy to play and share in cultural communities, in order to actively balance competing claims and interests. Cultural authorities already have the force of tradition and market power supporting them; legal authority to suppress dilution and change may be overkill. Just as the First Amendment recognizes the importance of political dissent, intellectual property law should acknowledge the importance of cultural dissent.

Notably, recognizing the value of freedom and participation *within* culture need not require wholesale rewriting of the law. The statutory fair-use provision of U.S. Copyright Law, for example, expressly privileges "comment" and not just parody or critique. But as I argued in the last chapter, the statute has been narrowly interpreted in recent decades to promote a singular economic vision of fair use as market failure. In fact, fair-use law, with its required balancing of numerous factors and express concerns for transformative uses of copyrighted material, can accommodate uses that critically engage copyrighted works and put the original works to new educational purposes and expressive uses. Broader social and cultural theories that recognize the central role of working through culture in promoting freedom, equality, democracy, and self-development would help ground the law surrounding intellectual property and promote human freedom in ways that narrow economic theory alone does not.

This is not to rule out doctrinal reform—but specific doctrinal reform is not my project here. Instead, I urge that what we need is a *new normative vision of culture and how it matters* to be incorporated into intellectual property law. A law that presumes culture to be static products or imposed tradition reinforces the power of a few cultural authorities and thwarts the ability of ordinary citizens to challenge existing cultural discourses and make cultural meaning themselves. These outcomes, in turn, have profound effects on freedom, equality, social relations, politics, and economic development.

If the raison d'être of intellectual property law is the promotion of culture, we need to know what vision of culture we are promoting. The theories of culture from anthropology to philosophy I have elaborated here usefully complement our current economic analysis of intellectual property. The goal of economic analysis is well intentioned: maximizing the social welfare. I have sought to show, however, that we need input from different fields as to just what constitutes social welfare, and how conceptions of welfare change over time, in light of new technologies and social relations. "Economics as a discipline cannot determine what goods or activities provide value to individuals," Omri Ben-Shahar has written in response to my call for the elaboration of social and cultural theories of intellectual property to stand beside the economic account. "It welcomes any insight from other disciplines, regarding sources of value, including insights from cultural perspectives." Cultural and social theories provide insight into the value of cultural *production, not just consumption,* and of working through culture, not simply against it or outside of it. Law ought to recognize these benefits and consider them when determining the metes and bounds of intellectual property.

CHAPTER THREE

Fair Culture

AS A YOUNG CHILD IN THE South African hinterlands, Solomon Linda spent his nights protecting cattle from lions in the jungle. Later, when he was living in a squalid Johannesburg hostel reserved for black migrant workers, he recalled this time and composed a song called "Mbube," which means "lion" in Zulu. "Mbube" was sung a cappella, but Linda borrowed the syncopation of contemporaneous American music and added his own haunting falsetto overlay. It was 1939. The song became Africa's first pop hit.[1]

"Mbube" would cross the Atlantic and be reborn first as "Wimoweh" and later, "The Lion Sleeps Tonight." It would go on to be recorded more than 170 times, generating millions of dollars, and was eventually incorporated into Disney's immensely profitable movie *The Lion King*. The "most famous melody ever to emerge from Africa"[2] added to the wealth of many, especially in the United States, but not its composer, who, as I mentioned in the Introduction, died destitute from a curable kidney disease in 1962 at age fifty-three, with less than $25 to his name. Linda's children had heard their father's song playing over the radio, but remained unaware of their intellectual property claims until a South African writer chronicled the injustice in 2000. In February 2006, the publishing house, which claimed the song on the basis of an apartheid-era assignment from Linda that paid him less than one dollar,[3] settled with Linda's family. The settlement would come too late for his daughter Adelaide, who died of AIDS in 2001, lacking the resources to purchase antiretroviral treatment. Two of Linda's other children had died as babies, one of malnutrition.

The international circuit traveled by "Mbube" links north and south, past and present, copyrights and patents, songs and medicines, intellectual property and development. This story of international injustice illustrates a number of points. First, it demonstrates *the intercultural dimensions of creativity.* Linda's creation offers an exemplar of Paul Gilroy's "Black Atlantic" thesis, evidencing the interchange of cultures across the African diaspora. Second, it shows that *cultural exchanges can take place in the presence of sharp differences in power and knowledge.* Taking the warning of Linda's story to heart, African lawyers today urge local creators to protect themselves from a similar fate by learning their rights. Third, Linda's tale tragically illustrates the *interrelationships among intellectual property rights and other freedoms.* Linda's failure to be recognized—and remunerated—for his contribution to our shared culture in turn prevented him and his family from having the resources to access life-saving medicines, first for himself, and then for his daughter. Intellectual property law both incentivized the creation, and in due course, exacted a high price for their retroviral drugs, a price his family could not afford even to save a life.

In this chapter, I will try to articulate a vision of intellectual property that comprehends the complexities and import of cultural production in a global context and, in so doing, helps to promote more just global social relations. Intellectual property does not merely incentivize and reward creators; it structures cultural and social relations. Intellectual property not only governs the production of life-saving medicines or work-saving machines, but also disciplines their distribution. The relationship between intellectual property and development goes well beyond GDP. Economic, social, and cultural rights are interconnected and mutually reinforcing: as in the case of Solomon Linda, intellectual property rights affect one's social standing, health, and overall well-being.

Intellectual property utilitarianism neglects these deeper connections between culture and economics. Law's focus on the economics of cultural activity is narrow, recognizing law's role in stimulating the optimal level of creative production (however elusive this goal may be), and the market's in rationing distribution. As I have argued, the goal is creating the greatest number of cultural artifacts to be trickled down to the greatest number of people. The utilitarian approach to intellectual property does not ask: Who makes the goods? Who profits, and at whose expense? The approach ignores the moral failure to distribute essential knowledge goods, from textbooks to medicines, widely, so long as there is no market failure afoot. But in this chapter my critique goes further. I argue that the current narrow economic approach to intellectual property has failed to comprehend the broad effects that this law has on structuring cultural and social relations, and how differences in power and knowledge, in turn, affect one's ability to acquire intellectual property. Intellectual property recognizes some authors and inventors, and misrecognizes others. In turn, law apportions the material spoils of creativity unequally. Cultural standing ultimately affects social standing and individual well-being, as some people come to lack the resources to furnish themselves with the basic accoutrements to live a healthy and fulfilling life.

Furthermore, the economic approach, with its reliance on the market to distribute cultural and social benefit, has failed to recognize asymmetries in the world, including the unequal capacity to participate on fair terms in global markets. The Solomon Linda story illustrates how intellectual property laws exacerbate these incapacities rather than relieve them. This must no longer be the case. Today, the World Intellectual Property Organization (WIPO) has pledged to reorient intellectual property law from its exclusive focus on incentives to the broader promotion of development. I believe that meeting this ambitious goal will require a theory of culture and development that goes beyond those that have been offered by contemporary intellectual property scholars.

WHY FREE CULTURE IS NOT ENOUGH

A principal critique of the intellectual-property-as-incentives story is that broad and durable property rights might jeopardize further creation. Lawrence Lessig and James Boyle have demonstrated the risk that maximalist intellectual property laws pose to innovation.[4] Their concern resonates with the economists' concern for efficiency. The fear is that property rights that are too many and too broad will stifle innovation. A maximalist intellectual property law proves to be poor innovation policy.[5] Before we can stand on the shoulders of giants, we will need to beg their permission. The libertarian might respond by arguing that one should not borrow—that one should be clever enough to make one's point without relying on others' production. But scholars such as Suzanne Scotchmer have shown that innovation is often incremental, with new discoveries building on older ones.[6] Requiring downstream innovators to purchase licenses from upstream ones might at times run aground on the difficulty of assembling (and paying for) all the necessary licenses.[7] A vibrant public domain, however, becomes a fount of creativity, and thus preservation of such a domain is vital to innovation.

Lessig's insight goes beyond innovation policy to consider the requirements of a free society. In his book *Free Culture,* he worries about the development of a culture where we will need permission to speak if that speech involves borrowing someone else's words. A free culture is not merely efficient; it is essential to a democratic society. Lessig affirms the value of freedom to participate "in culture and its growth."[8]

But there are several reasons why Lessig's passionate plea to protect a free culture is yet incomplete. First, the dynamics of culture itself remain unexplored in Lessig's account; the cultural vision embedded within the call for a free culture remains obscure. But without a cultural account we cannot fully understand the relationships among intellectual property, culture, and freedom. This book seeks to set forth a fuller vision of culture itself and some of these rich relationships.

Second, Lessig's account fails to acknowledge people's unequal capacity to exercise the freedoms that law provides. Freedom in theory is not freedom in fact. Contemporary public domain scholars hold as their paradigm figure the "commoner" who easily appropriates popular art and innovations for his or her own purposes. But this conception fails to acknowledge disparities in the ability of individuals to exercise their freedoms. In truth, the public domain movement leaves the common person to the mercy of an unregulated marketplace where she must struggle to realize her rights. Public domain advocates seem to accept that because a resource is open to all by force of law, that resource will indeed be exploited by all.[9] In practice, however, differing circumstances—including knowledge, wealth, power, and ability—render some better able than others to exploit a common resource.[10]

Third, Lessig's vision of freedom sometimes leads him to give short shrift to other values. In 2004, the Creative Commons, which Lessig and Boyle helped found, introduced a Developing Nation's License, which would allow authors to commit their work for free use in the developing world, but retain their full rights in the developed world.[11] Lessig praised the license as allowing creators to participate, firsthand, "in reforming global information policy." But the license was quickly retired for failing to "meet the minimum standards of the Open Access Movement" because it "does not free work in any way" in the West.[12] In short, Lessig's libertarian vision of "free culture" would give up on those authors who hoped to use copyright to promote more egalitarian values and development.

Fourth, the vision of freedom embedded in Lessig's free culture is ultimately expressed through the marketplace. This leaves cultural and other knowledge production to the mercies of the market. Governments must consider directly whether knowledge production requires more direct support, through alternative mechanisms such as prizes and subsidies. The U.S. Congress recognized that certain diseases may affect too few people to incentivize drug companies to invest the enormous resources required to produce treatment. The Orphan Drug Act of 1983 offers tax breaks to drug companies that produce treatments for such diseases (though it is unclear whether the tax benefit is greater than the resources required to produce the drugs). The realization that states may need to step in to support some cultural activity applies to minority cultures as well. Markets may not be the best mechanism for stimulating poetry in the vernaculars of less economically powerful communities. The support of the arts often has many knock-on economic and cultural benefits, and is often regarded by governments as key to a successful economic development policy.

Fifth, Lessig's theory of free culture tends to romanticize freedom in the past. Lessig begins from the premise that a "free culture has been our past."[13] But the story of Solomon Linda begs the question: even when copyright terms were shorter, were people equally free? Who could participate, and who was left out? A more critical historical account would recognize that we have traditions of both freedom and oppression, and that not all of our traditions are worth preserving—indeed, our public domain tradition is rife with examples of exploitation of the knowledge and creativity of traditionally disadvantaged groups and the poor (I explore some examples in Chapter 6). Furthermore, Lessig's privileging of free culture in the past does not acknowledge the important ways in which our conceptions of culture *have changed*. As I showed in Chapter 2, for more than a century the prevailing view of culture has been one of static tradition and imposed authority—a far cry from free culture.

Finally, public domain advocates do not sufficiently acknowledge the extent to which the romantic rhetoric of the public domain obscures unjust appropriation. Pioneering public domain scholars such as Boyle point out that the rise of the "romantic author" helped to mask the importance of the public domain for innovation. The romantic author presumed that artists create out of thin air, rather than borrow from a rich and diverse public domain.[14] In truth, however, most innovation is derivative, building on earlier works and discoveries. Even the world's most famous copyright owner, Disney, thrived by mining the works of past creators, from Rudyard Kipling to Victor Hugo to Robert Louis Stevenson, as I discuss further in Chapter 6. But the romance of the public domain is guilty of its own subterfuges. Unlike the works of Kipling that Disney appropriated, Solomon Linda's song suffered the common fate of being *falsely* and conveniently cast as belonging to the public domain. Linda's composition was performed *and recorded* by the Original Evening Birds. But recording artists across the Atlantic treated the song as African "folklore" and therefore as part of the public domain and free for the taking. Pete Seeger, one of the fathers of American folk music and world music, heard the African hit. He turned "Mbube" into "Wimoweh" in the 1950s and registered the copyright in the new composition under his alias Paul Campbell.[15] (Seeger has recently decried this apparently common practice on Tin Pan Alley, and I will return to his confessional at the end of this chapter.[16]) A decade later, by the time "Wimoweh" was being rewritten as "The Lion Sleeps Tonight" by the American music legend George Weiss, Weiss "leapt to the obvious conclusion: 'Wimoweh' was based on an old African folk song that didn't belong to anyone. As such, it was fair game."[17] The South African journalist Rian Malan notes that the liner notes to the song by Weiss, who later rose to become president of the Songwriter's Guild of America, described "Mbube" as "a familiar Zulu song about a lion hunt."[18] Lest one think that I am testing the actions of earlier generations with the copyright ethics of our generation, I should point out that Seeger's father, Charles Seeger, published an article titled "Who Owns Folklore?" in 1962. "American and European copyright law has been designed to encourage the acquisition and retention of property under rules favoring the more enterprising citizens," he wrote. But, he concluded, the folk song is "entirely a product of plagiarism" and the act of claiming copyright in it "unethical."[19]

Solomon Linda's story serves as warning that intellectual property should not be the law of the jungle. As Linda's tale shows, simply leaving a resource in the public domain is not enough to satisfy societal ideals. Our laws must serve to facilitate the free flow of culture but on fair terms. This will require, first, recognizing inequalities in people's capacity to participate in cultural production, and second, ensuring fairness in cultural exchanges, which may otherwise exploit innovators with unequal wealth, knowledge, or social status.

The skeptic will object. Solomon Linda's tragic story is one of the past, and a distant past at that. Apartheid is no longer; no limits to freedom of contracting exist for Africans even in South Africa. Moreover, does not Linda's story prove the importance of economic compensation as essential to intellectual property? Thus, does it not underline the economic rationale for intellectual property offered by contemporary law and economics accounts of the subject? Indeed, does it not link that account with a view of justice?

Solomon Linda's tale is the grossly magnified version of commonplace inequities.[20] Today, creativity around the world flourishes, but few have the knowledge to commercialize on fair terms and sustain a livelihood. Even the Beatles sued their publisher for unpaid royalties. Furthermore, Linda's story shows that respecting a creator's rights can sustain livelihoods, even if exclusive rights prove unnecessary to incentivize the original creation. At the same time, unequal marketplace treatment can discourage people from sharing their knowledge, leaving creators to adopt the strategy that intellectual property lawyers call trade secret. This defeats a central purpose of culture—sharing, participating, and making meaning together.

TOWARD A FAIR CULTURE

The critique of free culture must be supplemented with a more complex vision of the relationship between culture and freedom. My vision builds upon Lessig's free culture, but seeks a role for law in promoting equal capacity to meaningfully participate in making our culture. Others have spoken of the importance of *fair culture*. A report by the Finnish Ministry of Education, Science, and Culture defines "fair culture" as "the realization of cultural rights and the inclusion of everyone in cultural signification, irrespective of their age, gender, ability, or ethnic, religious or cultural background."[21] I adopt that definition here, and elaborate on the normative vision that underlies fair culture.

Like free culture, a central value animating fair culture is still freedom. But where Lessig found his inspiration for free culture in the writings of technological guru Richard Stallman, who decried permissions to access software code from a largely libertarian position, I find my inspiration in Amartya Sen's concept of "development as freedom," an idea that relies on Sen's and Nussbaum's focus on expanding human capabilities. Both Stallman and Sen take freedom as their touchstone value. "Greater freedom enhances the ability of people to help themselves and also to influence the world," Sen explains.[22] Sen's conception thus sees freedom not only as an end but also as a means of development. Sen praises "agency-oriented" programs for development, whereby the poor improve themselves not by being the passive beneficiaries of "cunning benefit programs," but rather by freely exercising their capacity to work and participate in markets. Hence freedom is both a right and a tool for advancing further freedom. Moreover, Sen's approach recognizes that differences in individuals' social, cultural, and economic standing affect their capacity for exercising freedom. Like free culture, fair culture values freedom but, going further, seeks to spread the capacity for citizens to meaningfully exercise their freedom.

In earlier chapters I have argued that participatory culture is normatively valuable in its own right. As Amartya Sen has shown, development requires far more than meeting basic needs and enhancing GDP. Sen's vision of development as freedom requires improving each person's capacity to make choices and meaningfully participate in political, economic, and cultural life. The capacity to participate in *cultural* life has particularly important implications for human flourishing. First, the cultural spheres of life are those we typically associate with the communities or experiences that give one's life *meaning*. Participating in a religious or cultural community; listening to or making music with others; posting a video to YouTube of your child dancing or creating a "video response" to someone else's post; reading, watching, and then rewriting *Harry Potter*—promoting freedom to partake in these activities may be thought of as central to *what development is for,* that is, the opportunity to innovate, share ideas, and enjoy life with others. Singing, reading, writing, innovating, and sharing: these cultural activities are crucial to human flourishing. Indeed, the right to freely "participate in the cultural life of the community,"[23] to enjoy the arts and to share in scientific advancement and its benefits," is recognized in article 27 of the Universal Declaration of Human Rights and countless other human rights instruments.[24]

At the same time, freedom to create and share with others in work and play has important implications for other freedoms. In this chapter, I elaborate how enhancing participation in culture can also serve as a means of development. A central insight of Sen's theory of development as freedom is the recognition of "the mutually reinforcing connection between freedoms of different kinds."[25] Let me consider two important connections here. First, cultural participation helps secure *livelihood*. As Solomon Linda's story illustrates, all people—rich and poor, from North or South, white or black—may serve as the source of culture that can be shared globally. Additionally, Linda's story illustrates that tremendous wealth may be generated from cultural knowledge production; experts value Linda's single song in the millions of dollars. This wealth may, in turn, be used to promote basic needs, such as health and safety. In short, at the turn of the millennium, the Participation Age and the goal of poverty eradication have dovetailed. The concept of fair culture yokes together meaning and livelihood. Indeed, as knowledge in the new millennium leads to social and economic power, the role of culture in development promises to be profound.[26]

Ironically, the law-and-economics analysis often gives short shrift to the actual economic consequences of intellectual property. Of course, property rights facilitate marketplace transactions that generate wealth. But the vision pays little heed to questions about who has access to life-saving medicines, who earns money from her creativity or industry, and whether the legal system promotes innovation in cosmetics or vaccines for tropical diseases. As Linda's story shows, the answers to these questions are interrelated.

There is another important connection between participatory culture and social and economic well-being. Social power derives from controlling knowledge, or discourse. Who is speaking matters. We may reconsider one of the most important recent decisions in U.S. copyright law with this in mind. For much of a century, the most popular account of life on a slave plantation has been *Gone with the Wind*. That was until one Alice

Randall disturbed Margaret Mitchell's idyll by retelling the story from the perspective of a slave protagonist on the O'Hara plantation, and thereby laying bare the racism and objectification of the original.[27] A U.S. appellate court held Randall's *The Wind Done Gone* to be a parody, and therefore a "fair use" of the original. Most accounts of this case champion the decision as enhancing free speech in the form of criticism, and promoting the production of more intellectual works (viewing copyright as the "engine of free speech"). But they have missed the novel's act of cultural revolution. *The Wind Done Gone* represents a shift in the distribution of power in cultural production and meaning-making. We must see intellectual property law as regulation of meaning and, in turn, of the social relations that flow from how we envision our world. Indeed, there are even claims, likely exaggerated, that the depiction of black presidents in Hollywood media paved the way for President Obama (a particularly surprising claim given Hollywood's resistance to calls for greater diversity in its casting).[28]

These claims reflect the rise of the late twentieth-century social movement that Charles Taylor calls "the politics of recognition." Taylor eloquently described the emergence of a new paradigm for understanding equality, where minority groups decried not material deprivation but psychological injury deriving from demeaning and misleading cultural images expressed in mainstream media and markets. "Nonrecognition or misrecognition" of one's identity, Taylor wrote, "can inflict harm, can be a form of oppression, imprisoning someone in a false, distorted, and reduced mode of being."[29] Power derives from the ability to shape and influence culture; inversely, those who do not have the power to create and contest culture "truly are powerless."[30]

Some critique identity politics for its temptation to place representation above other concerns, such as the distribution of social and economic power.[31] The challenge, as Iris Marion Young described it, is when "misrecognition" becomes a "problem independent of other forms of inequality or oppression."[32] I embrace an understanding of identity politics that recognizes the "interpenetration" of culture and economics. Cultural representation—in the form of who is represented, how, and under what terms—affects economic and social power, and vice versa. To be sure, analyses of "cultural differences" are often overblown and essentializing; for this reason, some scholars are wary of cultural analysis altogether. But the mere fact that many have taken an overly simplistic or erroneous view of identity and culture does not mean that we ought to turn our heads from the important ways in which a cultural analysis matters. As I have argued earlier, we ought not to discard cultural analysis but rather we should employ it more critically, retaining a commitment to recognizing the heterogeneity, dynamism, and interconnectedness of cultures. We must avoid the trap of viewing "culture" as separate from other factors related to inequality. As Arjun Appadurai writes, "The challenge today . . . is how to bring the politics of dignity and the politics of poverty into a single framework."[33]

This is beginning to happen. Nancy Fraser has led the charge that identity politics, with its focus on representation and dignity, abandoned the traditional goal of social movements: redressing material inequality.[34] But the more recent linking of identity politics to *intellectual property,* which I describe in this book, brings social movements back, full circle, to issues of distribution. In India, local artisans apply for "geographical indications" in Darjeeling tea and Mysore silk, which would grant an exclusive right to peddle goods under these names. In Australia, aboriginal communities assert copyright in their artwork. And, as described earlier, Ethiopians have trademarked the names of their specialty coffees, often praised as the best coffees in the world, in the hopes of retaining more control over the global social meaning of the coffees and the hearty profits they command in global markets. Diasporas, the Internet, and international travel have brought the danger of distant foreign exploitation to the attention of local artisans. Increasingly today, diverse authors and inventors seek recognition and to benefit materially from their cultural production, especially where recognition and material benefit were denied in the past.

These claims suggest, as a UNESCO Convention on the Protection and Promotion of the Diversity of Cultural Expressions makes plain, the complementary nature of the cultural and economic aspects of development. The UNESCO Convention urges that the cultural contributions of the poor be encouraged, recognized, and materially rewarded. These new claims for intellectual property understand rights not just in the familiar terms of incentives-for-creation, but also as tools for both recognition and remuneration. Tracking a shift in human-rights thinking away from first-generation rights (civil and political rights) toward second-generation rights (culture, development, and distributive justice), new claims for intellectual property rights by the historically disadvantaged tether social justice movements to the attainment of greater cultural, social, and economic power. Intellectual property is increasingly understood as a legal vehicle for facilitating (or thwarting) the recognition of diverse contributors to cultural and scientific discourse. Call it the property turn in identity politics. Wielders of this law increasingly deploy the law to create and benefit from the processes of meaning-making.

Current intellectual property law addresses economic incentives but focuses little on livelihood. Current law's raison d'être is to promote culture but it pays no heed to the value of participating in communities or the importance of shared meaning. Law is concerned with producing more goods but is indifferent to the kinds of goods being produced, or more aptly, to which goods fail to get produced in the absence of market incentive. This need not be the case. Intellectual property law can be understood through a broader cultural and economic lens focused on livelihoods, social relations, and well-being. Solomon Linda here becomes a metonym for those human beings involved in the transnational processes of collaboration, cultural production, and wealth creation. Cultural theory takes as a starting point that human beings are creative, continually seeking to make and remake our world, contributing to commerce and culture, science and spirituality. Individuals demand and deserve both recognition and remuneration for their intellectual production. As a United Nations report puts it, "At its best, the Knowledge Society involves all members of a community in knowledge creation and utilization. The Knowledge Society is not only about technological innovations, but also about human beings, their personal growth, and their individual creativity, experience and participation."[35]

To repeat: the vision of culture here is not one of enclaves fenced off from one another seeking "protection" or making claims for "survival." Recall that "fair culture" is committed to free culture in the sense of facilitating open cultural exchanges. Fair culture promotes the view that individuals can claim the world's heritage as one's own. "Whatever we understand and enjoy in human products instantly becomes ours, wherever they might have their origin," Rabindranath Tagore famously asserted. "I am proud of my humanity when I can acknowledge the poets and artists of other countries as my own. Let me feel with unalloyed gladness that all the great glories of man are mine." Indeed, the impact of "Mbube" has been truly global. The song has appeared at Navajo powwows, President John F. Kennedy's last birthday party, and the Apollo space launch.[36] It has been rendered by generations of artists, from Glen Campbell to R.E.M. to Phish. Solomon Linda's tune, journalist Rian Malan writes, "has penetrated so deep into the human consciousness over so many generations, that one can truly say, here is a song the whole world knows."[37] Furthermore, in order to create new cultural or scientific works, individuals need access to globally produced knowledge, which serve as building blocks for this future innovation. Solomon Linda himself relied on American jazz for his innovation.

At the same time, a cultural approach would acknowledge that global asymmetries of capability threaten cultural production and sharing, and raise important ethical questions about global culture flows. Not everyone can realize his or her creative aspirations if, for example, the home country lacks a research and development infrastructure, funding for innovations, adequate health care, access to information, or a lack of access to capital, especially venture capital. Moreover, dominant culture industries have economies of scale that enable easier production and dissemination of cultural products around the world. Thus some cultures are more capable than others of being heard and having influence.

WHAT IS A "FAIR CULTURE"?

A "fair culture" should seek to promote free cultural exchange on fair terms. A central concern of a cultural approach to intellectual property should be how to facilitate cultural production that involves inter- and intra-cultural borrowing in a socially just manner. The UNESCO Convention on the Protection and Promotion of the Diversity of Cultural Expressions, mentioned earlier, recognizes the twin goals of promoting sharing of cultural expressions, on the one hand, and providing fair recognition and remuneration, on the other. The convention celebrates "interculturality"—that is, the exchange of ideas among cultures—and eschews a conception of cultures as hermetically sealed off from one another. Yet the convention also recognizes that rapid globalization and new technologies simultaneously "afford unprecedented conditions for enhanced interaction between cultures" and "represent a challenge for cultural diversity, namely in view of risks of imbalances between rich and poor countries." The convention links culture to development goals and would foster respectful and equitable interactions between and within cultures.

A richer cultural vision of *how people create* (within and across communities), *why people create* (to share experiences and make meaning with others), and *which obstacles threaten cultural sharing* (especially unequal human capacity and global asymmetries of power) should include the following tenets:

Fairness as the capability to participate in cultural production. A narrow focus on spurring innovation through intellectual property rights fails to differentiate between capacities to innovate or, perhaps more importantly, capacities to commercialize innovation. Such capacities may be limited because of small home markets or the absence of government funding for research and development.[38] Furthermore, the expansion of intellectual property rights globally has not been coupled with a reinvigorated commitment to global development. Foreign aid budgets have largely stagnated or declined—and so are hardly likely to compensate for the huge net royalty payments for intellectual property now flowing from the South to the North as a result of the Trade-Related Aspects of Intellectual Property Rights (TRIPS) Agreement, which I consider in more detail in Chapters 5 and 7.[39] Recognizing the fact of global inequalities (both within and across communities) requires focusing on improving the capacity to participate in knowledge production. Some examples of affirmative assistance to boost local innovative capacity include World Bank lending programs that build capacity in science and technology, government assistance to secure export markets for local producers, and the enactment of local laws in developing countries that require developed world partners to involve and train local scientists in joint projects conducted in the developing country. Microloans to poor entrepreneurs who do not otherwise qualify for bank loans are yet another important tool for addressing the capital deficit that impedes innovation in the developing world. Finally, local innovators need to be educated about prospects for commercializing their innovations on fair terms.[40]

Crucial to this goal is improved access to information tools, from innovative programs such as "One Laptop per Child," which produces and disseminates laptops endowed with software designed to spur "collaborative, joyful, self-empowered learning," to technology transfer under TRIPS, to the development of Web 2.0 software that empowers users to make culture themselves. Additionally, being attentive to the most basic human capabilities, for example, health, is vital: intellectual property laws should thus recognize the moral claims to promote access to essential medicines. The Doha Declaration on TRIPS and Public Health promotes such capacity by ensuring countries' flexibility to provide essential medicines to their people. Similarly, a proposal for an international treaty on copyright exceptions and limitations would enhance the poor's access to educational materials. All of these efforts, inside and outside formal intellectual property law, seek to promote free culture *in fact,* not just as abstract theory, by improving the human capacity to create.

Fairness as recognition. Even where people do create, law can fail to recognize their creativity as authorship or invention. Recognizing poor people's claims to their creative knowledge need not require the creation of new intellectual property rights, but likely will entail critically examining our preconceptions of what is "public domain." Often, the poor's contributions meet the requisite requirements of novelty demanded by intellectual property law—as they did in Linda's case—but the poor lack knowledge of their rights, as well as the skills and capital necessary for commercializing their contributions. In Chapter 5, I show that our distinctions between "traditional" and "modern" knowledge are often overdrawn. What is often cast as traditional, created by anonymous collectives, passed down over generations, and remarkably, static over millennia, is in fact often vibrant, novel, and created by recognizable and identifiable living individuals. In India the Honey Bee Network, founded by innovation professor Anil Gupta, sets out to show just this: that Indians are economically poor but knowledge rich. Twice yearly, Gupta and nearly a hundred students and colleagues set out on a "Shodh Yatra," a trek by foot of sometimes hundreds of miles to remote villages in order to access the knowledge of India's poor. The network has helped to locate inventors of a natural nonstick coating for pots and pans, a foot-powered washing-machine, and, my personal favorite, an "amphibious bicycle" created by one Mr. Saidullah so he could cheaply, and quickly, cross the river to meet his love.[41]

Gupta's Shodh Yatras illustrate well that the rallying call for "Access to Knowledge" should not mean simply redistributing the knowledge of the West to the rest. We must search out, recognize, and if need be translate the knowledge of diverse creators around the world. At the same time, asymmetries in cultural and economic power threaten ethical sharing of the knowledge of the poor. For its part, the Honey Bee Network seeks to model sharing that is open and yet also fair—like a honey bee, which connects flower to flower through pollination without diminishing the beauty of any one. The network gives prizes to inventors, shares their inventions across communities, helps find partners who would commercialize ideas, and, on occasion, helps inventors to seek intellectual property rights in the inventions.

Issues of fairness through recognition and reward of diverse authors apply at home and abroad. Recall that under current copyright law, those who use copyrighted material without the authorization of the copyright owner, and outside the protections of fair use, are not eligible for copyright protection in their creations, however transformative they may be. Thus fans who create by using copyrighted work without authorization can never be "authors," unless the court finds fair use. This approach to improvements in copyright law is distinct from the approach in patent law, where the improver may receive a patent for the improvement, but must still seek a license from the original patent owner. The result is that copyright owners may freely appropriate from fans that create under the threat of injunction and have no rights in their contributions. A recent case pitted a fan with encyclopedic knowledge of the Harry Potter universe against the series' author, J. K. Rowling herself. Steve Vander Ark had produced and edited on the Internet the *Harry Potter Lexicon,* an A–Z compendium of the spells and bestiary of Potter's world. Vander Ark's *Lexicon* was so complete that Rowling and Warner Bros., producers of the Harry Potter films, admitted to using the site as a guide during the production of the films. Just as Vander Ark free rode on Rowling's creations, Rowling and Warner Bros. also free rode on his.

Fairness as livelihood. Enhanced capacity for participatory culture is not only a good in itself, but also, as I have argued here, a key to economic development. In a Knowledge Age, wealth increasingly derives from the capacity to produce knowledge for the world. From Ethiopian coffee farmers to indigenous Australian artists to Indian scientists perfecting methods of farming basmati rice, intellectual property rights, from trademark to copyright to patent, can be used as tools for generating wealth for the poor.

Fairness as recognizing vulnerability to exploitation. The very essence of culture is sharing knowledge and meaning with others. But differences in power and past mistreatment affect people's willingness to share culture. That is, fear of exploitation may discourage people to share and distribute their knowledge, be it music, literature, or local knowledge of the medicinal properties of plants. Anthropologists now report resistance to their ethnographic studies, with potential local informants refusing to participate in what they perceive to be objectification and global exploitation of their knowledge. Indeed, histories of colonial exploitation may go further to explain cultural insularity than do assertions of essential cultural differences. Promoting fairness among global creators makes for good innovation policy, fosters free speech, and promotes better cultural relations. Modern intellectual property law ought to be attentive to crafting rules that promote ethical extraction of knowledge. Recent proposals in the World Trade Organization to amend the TRIPS agreement to require patent applicants to disclose the origin of genetic materials and traditional knowledge are premised on this very insight.

We have come to believe that property rights in intellectual creations are there simply because they incentivize creative activity. But there is an older understanding that flows out of notions of unfair competition and more visceral feelings of justice. It is now commonplace that in fact people create without exclusive property rights—as evidenced by open-source software, fan fiction, mash-ups, and Solomon Linda's story. But behavioral economists have identified a natural sense of justice that may lead people to "irrational" decisions if they feel that they are being treated unfairly.[42] Even the premise of the "intellectual property as incentives" thesis can be understood as responding to the "vulnerability" of the creator in the absence of intellectual property rights, given the often high costs of production and the typically low costs of copying.[43]

Focusing on fairness rather than incentives to create also helps reveal intellectual property's role in releasing information to the public. Left to themselves, scientists may not share but rather hoard their knowledge, fearing exploitation. Patents address this possibility by protecting innovators through property rights. The first copyright statute in England, the Statute of Anne, did the same: recall that this "Act for the Promotion of Learning" established limited copyrights for authors in order to wrest knowledge from the monopoly control of a few publishers. Intellectual property law from the beginning was crafted to promote fairness and access to knowledge.[44] This insight ought to empower us to recognize and accept broader visions beyond the narrow incentives vision alone. Indeed, we may usefully reconsider numerous intellectual property doctrines through this lens.

Fairness as support for non-market-based cultural production. I have emphasized the links between participatory culture, global markets, and livelihood. As I will further argue in Chapter 5, markets provide incentives for cultural preservation through transformation. For example, obtaining geographical indications encourages communities to invent new applications for old traditions, thus keeping the community alive through dynamism, not stasis. But should markets determine which cultural products and activities are supported? I have argued no in the case of essential goods, such as drugs to treat tropical diseases (an issue to which I return in more detail in Chapter 7). And we have already recognized that states commonly support the arts through subsidies, because they appreciate the importance of cultivating robust artistic activity. But more detailed questions about which cultural activities should be subsidized and how far state support should go are more difficult. The aforementioned Orphan Drug Act in the United States, for example, may offer subsidies to corporations in excess of their costs to make the drugs. Subsidies to prop up some withering artistic or literary traditions, or translation efforts to preserve local languages, are perhaps even more difficult to assess. What, precisely, does democratizing the capability to participate in making culture require? For example, how far if at all ought the state go to support the niche literary community of Bengali feminist poets?[45] Subsidies for poetry in the vernacular?

Cultural diversity is a good in itself but markets, especially large multinational corporate actors within them, often promote mass culture. Preserving diverse cultural traditions, languages, and works may offer people near and far, and over generations, new ways of thinking by exposing them to more ideas. State subsidies can serve as a critical mechanism for promoting participation, diversity, and cultural vitality, and indeed states routinely engage in supporting local cultural industries, often as part of a development policy. At the same time, we should be wary of state preservation of tradition for its own sake. As I have argued elsewhere, we ought to critically probe whether certain traditions are harmful, for example to women or children, and are therefore not worthy of preservation. Indeed, the theory of participatory culture developed in Chapter 2 is premised on full participation by all members of a culture in order to critically engage traditions and bring about cultural change.

But the case of Bengali poetry does not raise such concerns. Furthermore, we should not confine such support to grant mechanisms. Awards and recognition systems can also generate cultural creativity outside of markets. Support from appreciative communities on the Internet can spur one to keep on producing as well. Indeed, despite the common perception of homogenization resulting from globalization, niche cultures may fare better in markets today than in the past. The Internet and other technological improvements in distributing knowledge make Bengali feminist poetry potentially a more lucrative activity today, as the diaspora of Bengalis and all other interested parties become easier to connect and access. This is the phenomenon known as the "long tail," where larger numbers of people are able to purchase (or support implicitly through advertising) "non-hit" items.

This example reinforces a broader point. I do not reject the incentive analysis in full, but rather propose that plural values and goals animate intellectual property law. Property rights in information clearly can incentivize innovation that would otherwise draw insufficient investment. But they can also promote freedom, cultural dynamism, human capabilities, and more fair cultural and social relations.

A further clarification: I do not mean to treat intellectual property as an end in itself. Rather, the end is participation in meaning-making and in having the capacity to earn a livelihood to achieve the life one scripts for herself. Intellectual property remains a tool, not a right. But it may now be seen as a tool for incentivizing participation in processes of intercultural sharing on fair terms, not just the creation of more products by a select few.

CRITICISMS AND RESPONSES

Skeptics will object. Intellectual property law is a human construction designed to solve a fundamental problem of information economics: without intellectual property protections, the ready duplicability of information undermines incentives to create information. Armed with this economic insight and fortified by a constitutional mandate to "promote the Progress of Science and useful Arts," some intellectual property scholars—we have labeled them "Intellectual Property Originalists"—would keep intellectual property's focus solely on incentivizing the production of information.[46] They would thus resist any call to expand the values of intellectual property to the broad array of values I have offered, from freedom to fairness. But let me answer some specific critiques here.

Whose values? How do we identify the myriad values to be considered? And whose values? The values I champion in these pages, from democracy to development, to freedom and equality, reflect long-standing commitments to Enlightenment, international human rights, and in many cases constitutional mandates. Furthermore, social theories from Nussbaum's capabilities approach to Sen's view of development as freedom resonate as normative guides for a revised intellectual property. Within these larger frameworks, details will be elaborated through political processes. Brazil and Thailand, for example, have stronger constitutional commitments to public health than do some other nations, as I elaborate in Chapter 7. We may also allow for some reconsideration of intellectual property to be determined dynamically through the politics of the age, just as the social movements of the past influenced real property law.

Adding to the law would make it too complex. Introducing additional values to intellectual property analysis will necessarily complicate that analysis. But if this move adds complexity, it is just the complexity necessary to get things right. Narrowing the calculus to ease the calculation will likely lead to the wrong answer. Economy should not come at the expense of achieving a just outcome. Moreover, a single-minded focus is not true of most other areas of the law. Property rights in land serve myriad values, and are justified and cabined accordingly.

Changes would threaten the public domain. Many intellectual property scholars have mounted a heroic effort to staunch the enclosure of the public domain of information, and they worry that broadening our understanding of intellectual property will buttress maximalist intellectual property claims.[47] But a single-minded focus on incentivizing creation could also lead to maximalist intellectual property claims, because the only limits on intellectual property would occur when (1) additional intellectual property rights are unnecessary to spur creation, and (2) situations where expanding intellectual property rights for some will interfere with others' ability to create. A broad range of human values, in contrast, should help restrain maximalist intellectual property demands. Human rights are a principal source for delimiting intellectual property, not simply expanding it. For example, the arguments for access to medicines (and the compulsory license schemes they often entail) typically rely not on claims of authorship or incentive, but rather on the desire to expand human capabilities. Similarly, recent efforts to reconstruct the fair-use doctrine as principally an effort to head off a market failure caused by excessive transaction costs might jeopardize the doctrine itself. As the transaction costs of finding the copyright owner and negotiating a license decrease in the digital age, the rationale for fair use can vanish, transforming fair use into fared use. A broad understanding of intellectual property values might justify fair use in the face of potential obsolescence of the doctrine due to technological change. In short, rather than shrinking the public domain, my argument may expand it. Recognizing the diversity of values underlying intellectual property should lead us to share certain rights in intellectual products, rather than reserve them more closely. Recall that new theories of property, from personhood to social relations, enhanced our ability to explain and justify legal limits on property, even while they served to bolster some property claimants.

Intellectual property law should have a limited purpose. The originalist objects, claiming that intellectual property was not intended to promote such ends. But intellectual property laws have always sought to promote development and principles of Enlightenment. Intellectual property has long harbored multiple values, such as the First Amendment values implicit in fair use.[48] This plural tradition notwithstanding, the fact that a legal regime might be created for one purpose should not mean that the implications of that regime for all other purposes should be ignored. The state raises an army because of the need to assure its security against foreign invasions. Yet the state might deploy the army domestically in case of natural disasters. And it might need to create limits on how the army might operate (such as prohibitions on torture and sexual harassment)—limits stemming not necessarily from self-defense but from other human values. Similarly, the fact that intellectual property law might be established for instrumental reasons does not mean that other purposes should not be considered when we set its metes and bounds.

Why focus on distribution? Why not mete out any distributive justice explicitly through the tax system? Those who disfavor a social justice agenda for intellectual property are not necessarily antagonistic to social justice itself. They would often simply prefer what they find to be a superior forum for considering such issues: tax.[49] But it seems unrealistic to expect the effects of intellectual property law I have discussed here to be sorted out through a redistributive tax regime. First, as in the case of Solomon Linda, such a regime would have to be global, redressing unjust appropriation across borders. Second, a tax regime that offered credits to the poor would keep them wards of the state, rather than recognizing their contributions and fairly remunerating them. It is a very different thing to give people a handout rather than acknowledge their contributions to cultural life. Such a regime would also negatively affect people's incentives to create and share their knowledge with the world in global markets. As I have pointed out, vulnerability to exploitation can serve as a strong disincentive to the poor, diminishing their desire to contribute to world science and culture. The potential for closing oneself off to the world, and hoarding knowledge, would deprive all of humanity of that knowledge. Finally, why compound disadvantage through an intellectual property system indifferent to equality in the usually vain hope that it might be sorted out later through a tax system?

Rights intended to aid the poor are more likely to be wielded ultimately by those already in power. This suggests that it is analytically difficult to distinguish Disney from the dissident, or Monsanto from a mountain tribe. In fact, courts can make such distinctions when they are justified by other normative reasons. Furthermore, this is the risk of any legal reform effort—even the public domain movement itself. The campaign to preserve the public domain, which has been taken up in everyone's name, in fact may benefit the powerful, who are in a better position to quickly appropriate for themselves ideas and goods in the public domain. An intellectual property regime that expressly acknowledges and confronts its social and cultural effects will be best suited to resolve these issues.

Now in his nineties, Pete Seeger is spearheading what he calls the Committee for Public Domain Reform. In a letter to the United Nations, he decries the standard practice in the music industry of copyrighting songs supposedly in the public domain. Many of these works are not public domain at all, Seeger argues. He quotes Joseph Shabalala of the South African vocal group Ladysmith Black Mambazo, who notes that when the word "traditional" is used, "it means the money stays in New York."

Seeger proposes that a share of subsequent copyright royalties "go to the place and people where the song originated."[50]

On the ground, international actors are developing new understandings of intellectual property as a tool for promoting not just free culture, but also fair culture. No human domain should be immune from the claims of social justice. Intellectual property, like property law, structures social relations and has profound social effects. If the twenty-first century will be the Age of Knowledge and Participation, surely we must acknowledge and grapple with the reality that intellectual property law will help define the possibilities and human capabilities of this age. Intellectual property regulates the production and distribution of culture. Considerations of social justice cannot be peripheral to such a central human enterprise.

Newsweek's Pakistan edition ran a cover in April 2011 featuring the Muslim superhero and superheroine characters from Dr. Naif Al-Mutawa's comic book series *The 99*. (Courtesy of The 99)

In 1999, Mattel sued Utah-based artist Tom Forsythe for his series of photographs entitled *Food Chain Barbie*. (Courtesy of Tom Forsythe)

Photo of Solomon Linda (farthest left) and The Original Evening Birds in 1941.

The energy drink Guaraná Power, conceived and produced by a farmers' collective in Maués, Brazil. The farmers sought to compete with the global company Ambev's popular guarana berry–based drink, Antarctica, in order to retain more of the profits for cultivating the berries. The logo "Guaraná Power" is stamped across the more familiar Antarctica label. (Courtesy of Superflex)

In collaboration with the Danish artists' group Superflex, a farmers' collective in Maués, Brazil, brainstormed ideas for developing commercial products derived from their crops. Here one member suggests "Mauescafé" coffee. (Courtesy of Superflex)

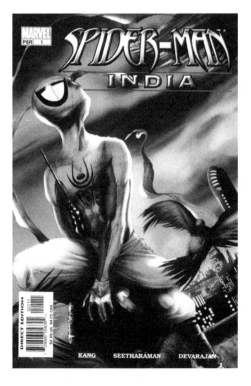

The cover of the first issue of *Spider-Man India*. (Spider-Man ™ and © Marvel Entertainment, LLC. All Rights Reserved and used with permission.)

Mark Chamberlain's watercolor of Batman and Robin kissing. (Courtesy of Kathleen Cullen Fine Arts)

Comparisons between Tezuka's *Kimba the White Lion* and Disney's *The Lion King*. (Courtesy of MUSHI PRODUCTION Co., Ltd.)

CHAPTER FOUR

Everyone's a Superhero

"Gee, golly, gosh, gloriosky," thought Mary Sue as she stepped on the bridge of the *Enterprise.* "Here I am, the youngest Lieutenant in the fleet—only fifteen-and-a-half years old." Captain Kirk came up to her.

"Oh, Lieutenant, I love you madly. Will you come to bed with me?"

"Captain! I am not that kind of girl!"

"You're right, and I respect you for it. Here, take over the ship for a minute while I go for some coffee for us."

Mr. Spock came onto the bridge. "What are you doing in the command seat, Lieutenant?"

"The Captain told me to."

"Flawlessly logical. I admire your mind."[1]

GOING WHERE ONLY MEN had gone before, Lieutenant Mary Sue took the helm of the USS *Enterprise,* performing to acclaim and earning the Vulcan Order of Gallantry. This was, of course, fantasy, but doubly so. By 1974, no woman had commanded the *Enterprise* bridge, according to the *official* Star Trek fantasy. Indeed, it would take another two decades before a woman would command the principal starship in a later Star Trek series. Trekkie Paula Smith, however, was impatient. So she inserted the young

Lieutenant Mary Sue into the Star Trek universe, not as a communications officer, nurse, voice of the onboard computer, or passing Kirk love interest, but as commander. In so doing, Smith began the modern incarnation of an old and often celebrated phenomenon—retelling a canonical story to better represent oneself.[2]

The name of Smith's character, Mary Sue, has come to stand for all such characters in the universe of fan fiction. Fan fiction spans all genres of popular culture, from anime to literature. In every fan literature, there is the Mary Sue: "She fences with Methos and Duncan MacLeod; she saves the *Enterprise,* the *Voyager,* or the fabric of time and space; she fights with Jim Ellison in defense of Cascade; she battles evil in Sunnydale alongside Buffy Sommers."[3] She stands as the only female member of the fellowship of the ring. According to Wikipedia, a "Mary Sue" is an idealized "fictional character . . . lacking noteworthy flaws."[4] Often she appears in the form of a new character beamed into the story or a marginal character brought out from the shadows.

"Mary Sue" is often a pejorative expression, used to deride fan fiction perceived as narcissistic.[5] But we may also consider Mary Sue to be a figure of subaltern critique and, indeed, empowerment. Cultural studies scholars define empowerment "as a function and possibility of participation in popular culture."[6] We may see empowerment also in terms offered by the civil rights movements—as increasing social, economic, and political power. As exemplified by Lieutenant Mary Sue, this figure serves to contest popular media stereotypes of certain groups such as women, gays, and racial minorities. Where the popular media might show such groups as lacking agency or exhibiting other negative characteristics, Mary Sues are powerful, beautiful, and intrepid. Indeed, the gendered appellation for this form—Mary Sue—reflects its popularity among female authors, who often work against the gender stereotypes of the canon work. Through a survey of social science research that reveals how media affect our racialized and gendered view of occupations, the connections between cultural and economic power become apparent.

The emergence of the World Wide Web has amplified this relationship. In the past, Mary Sue authors might have stashed what they penned in a drawer, distributed photocopies, or, at most, published their work in an underground magazine. The Web offers writers a relatively inexpensive and simple mass distribution vehicle. Posting a story to a fan-fiction website is literally free, at least for those with access to the Internet. Lacking the global distribution channels of print media, Mary Sue authors now find an alternative in the Web, which brings their work to the world. In fact, the increasing power and affordability of digital tools may make it possible to go beyond rewriting stories in words to permit video and audio creations, often through mash-ups of existing copyrighted material. Such spin-offs can usher in a whole new universe of imagined possibilities—if the law will allow us to go there.

This chapter has two goals, one practical and the other theoretical. The first goal is to clarify the law so that writers of Mary Sues will not be chilled by possible legal threats to such speech. Such authors should not readily "cease and desist," as copyright owners demand. Rather than illegal art, Mary Sues may well constitute fair use. Second, Mary Sues usefully probe the theory of fair use itself. Mary Sue can be seen as a metonym for fair uses that rewrite the popular narrative. Implicitly, I defend fair use against efforts to narrowly interpret it as merely a defense against a market failure caused by high transaction costs, an explanation that would lead ultimately to its evisceration as technologies reduce such costs. Under that view, the cultural and speech consequences of transformative uses of copyrighted works lay hostage to the ability of the transformers to pay. I also defend against the foremost cultural critique of fair use—that reinterpretation (or "recoding") of the text destabilizes cultural foundations.[7]

Mary Sues challenge a patriarchal, heterosexist, and racially stereotyped cultural landscape. These popular stereotypes have subtle yet important consequences for our social, political, and economic relations, as social science research reveals. The phenomenon of rewriting the story to revalue one's place in it is not simply an exercise in narcissism. Mary Sues offer important epistemological interventions in the reigning discourse, confronting the traditional production of knowledge by reworking the canon to valorize women and marginalized communities. They exemplify the tactic that Arjun Appadurai describes as *commodity resistance*—a strategy of popular struggle through the resignification of common goods.[8] One of the most important recent copyright cases, which I touched on earlier, revolves around a Mary Sue: Alice Randall's take on *Gone with the Wind* called *The Wind Done Gone*. In the latter, a slave protagonist illuminates the oppression of the age and African-American characters are imbued with complexity and agency.[9]

Mary Sues that challenge the orthodox representations in the original work should constitute fair use under U.S. copyright law in many cases. The skeptic will ask the Mary Sue author: Why not write your own original story rather than inserting yourself into a story written by someone else? Alternatively, why not license the original? Such arguments go far beyond Mary Sues: they represent the fundamental challenges to any fair-use claim. I respond to these challenges, relying on theories of cultural critique and change. Specifically, I argue that semiotic democracy[10] requires the ability to resignify the artifacts of popular culture to contest their authoritative meaning. I also show that concerns regarding any resulting cultural destabilization misunderstand the nature of culture itself.

MARRY, SUE!

When *Star Trek* debuted on television in 1966, it was groundbreaking. Its creator, Gene Roddenberry, "envisaged a multi-racial and mixed-gender crew, based on his assumption that racial prejudice and sexism would not exist in the twenty-third century."[11] Lieutenant Uhura was the first African-American woman to be featured in a major television series.[12] Officer Sulu offered a rare Asian-American face outside a martial arts milieu.[13]

But despite these laudable aspirations, equality was not yet truly complete in Federation space. Uhura, for example, was relegated to the communications station. Women generally played secondary roles, often serving as episode-long love interests for the white male members of the crew. Uhura broke ground again when she participated in network television's likely first interracial kiss—with Captain Kirk, of course.[14] (Same-sex romantic relationships, however, apparently did not survive into our future.)

Women, gays, and racial minorities have certainly made major strides over the past four decades of television. In 1993, for example, an African-American actor commanded the station in the Star Trek series *Deep Space Nine*.[15] And in 1995, more than two decades after Lieutenant Mary Sue, Captain Kathryn Janeway commanded the deck of the starship in *Star Trek: Voyager,* the only Star Trek series to have a lead female captain.[16] Yet there remains a long way to go, as demonstrated by American television, a principal source of information about our world. A recent Children Now report shows that male characters remain dominant, consistently outnumbering female characters by nearly two to one between 1999 and

2004.[17] Primetime television portrays "a world in which women are significantly younger than their male counterparts and where older women
are hard to find."[18] Perhaps especially telling is the occupational differen-
tiation of men and women: "Male characters outnumbered female characters as attorneys (71% were male), executives/CEOs (80%), physicians
(80%), law enforcement officers (82%), paramedics/firefighters (84%),
elected/appointed officials (92%) and criminals (93%)."[19]

The racial divide on primetime television remains alarming. While
40 percent of Americans ages nineteen and under are children of color,[20]
nearly three-quarters of all primetime characters during the 2003–2004
television season were white.[21] The racial diversity that does exist is found
mostly during the evening ten o'clock hour, when American children are
least likely to be watching: "The 8 o'clock hour remained the least racially
diverse hour in prime time with one in five shows (20%) featuring mixed
opening credits casts."[22] Latino characters are often cast in "low-status
occupations."[23] Even when they were represented, Asian-American characters "were far less likely than characters from other racial groups to
appear in primary roles."[24] An earlier study by Children Now concluded
that youth watching primetime television would most likely see a "world
overwhelmingly populated by able bodied, single, heterosexual, white,
male adults under 40."[25] When minority groups are depicted in the media, they are generally stereotyped, with Asian women, for example, cast
as "China dolls" or "dragon ladies" and Asian men denied any positive
sexuality.[26] Latinos are commonly depicted as "criminals, buffoons, Latin
lovers, or law enforcers."[27]

Movies may not be much better. In a study of black female characters
in the top movies of 1996, 89 percent were shown using profanities, 56
percent were shown being physically violent, and 55 percent were shown
being physically restrained. By contrast, 17 percent of white female characters were depicted using profanities, 11 percent were shown being physically violent, and 6 percent were shown being restrained.[28]

Popular books evince similar disparities. A study on children's books
published in the early 1980s showed that adult male characters appeared
almost three times more frequently than females.[29] Even more importantly, central characters were almost two-and-a-half times more likely
to be boys than girls. Consider Winnie the Pooh. The lovable bear is
Disney's most valuable character, generating revenues of a billion dollars

annually.[30] But despite his apparently wide appeal, the bear's universe is quite narrow. Of the nearly dozen characters in the Hundred Acre Wood, only one is female—Kanga, Roo's mother, who often dons an apron.[31] Winnie the Pooh and his friends, of course, were created in a different era, written to cheer a young boy, but today these characters appeal to both boys and girls.[32]

While Winnie the Pooh is the British literary creation popular among younger children, older children are currently entranced by the magic of Harry Potter. But although the stories are penned by a woman, J. K. Rowling, the lead role is played by a boy, and the principal parts are mostly male.[33] Moreover, the vast majority of Hogwarts teachers and pupils—especially the principal characters—are white.[34]

Even magazines written specifically for girls fail to guarantee an empowering experience. Reviewing *Seventeen* magazine, sociologist Kelley Massoni observes that "men dominate its pages, as both subjects and job holders." It is not only what is depicted that is important; it is also what is omitted. Magazines for teenage girls, according to Massoni, "overtly suggest, through content and pictures, how women should look, dress, and act; they more subtly suggest, *through exclusion of pictures and content,* what women should not do, be, or think." Massoni concludes: "In the occupational world of *Seventeen,* Prince Charming still exists as the ultimate goal."[35] The implicit instruction in the pages of teen-girl magazines: "Marry, Sue!"

Such images are not confined to U.S. borders.[36] Hollywood and other American media multinationals have globalized American television shows, the Hundred Acre Wood, and Harry Potter. Disney and Time Warner offer their fare on the many television channels they own around the world. The fictional worlds envisioned therein now charm the real world's youth. Hollywood's global cultural hegemony translates Hollywood's prejudices to the world.

Psychological and sociological research reveals that cultural representations may have social and economic consequences.[37] Racial and gender stereotypes depicted in popular media may impact children's perceptions of career paths. Children "as young as five years of age learn to gender stereotype occupations based on the gender of a television role model."[38]

Early media research established a correlation (though not necessarily a causation) between large amounts of television watching and stereotyped views of gender occupations and traits. In one study published in 1980, children in the first, third, fifth, and seventh grades were asked to associate a given trait, such as shyness or confidence, with a man or a woman. Children who were heavy television watchers showed a marked increase with age in male stereotyped responses, while children who watched relatively little television demonstrated a decrease in such answers with age.[39] In another study published in 1974, children between the ages of three and six were asked about their career aspirations. The result showed that 76 percent of children who were classified as "heavy viewers" chose professions stereotypical for their gender, compared with 50 percent of "moderate viewers" who chose stereotypical professions.[40] The occasional counter-stereotypical media portrayal may not suffice to overturn engrained prejudices. In a study published in 1979, five- and six-year-olds were shown four films shorter than two minutes each and questioned afterward about what they had seen. Each film presented two actors who portrayed doctors and nurses in various gender combinations. Of the films with a female doctor and a male nurse, 53 percent of the children stated that they had seen a movie about a male doctor and a female nurse. In contrast, 100 percent of the children correctly identified the actors' genders in the film with a male doctor and a female nurse.[41]

A recent study also demonstrates stereotypical correlations with respect to race. Researcher Rebecca Bigler and her colleagues invented new, fictional occupations and presented various combinations of white and black persons in those occupations to children. Poorer African-American children were less likely to aspire to jobs that had been depicted with white workers exclusively. The study authors point out the potential for a vicious cycle: African-American children, especially those from disadvantaged backgrounds, may preferentially seek out low-status jobs in which minorities are well represented, thus perpetuating the skewed models for new generations of poor African-American children.[42]

The effects of media portrayals reach beyond children. One study asked college students to complete questionnaires about their racial and gender attitudes after they viewed stereotypical or counter-stereotypical racial and gender portrayals in a newsletter. Those who first viewed stereotypical portrayals were more likely to favor policy judgments against blacks or women when asked who bears responsibility for Magic Johnson contracting HIV and the police beating of Rodney King, and whether to accept the credibility of Anita Hill and Patricia Bowman in their respective claims.[43]

Minorities internalize the stories they read, see, and hear every day. A U.S. Civil Rights Commission study found that minority stereotypes in the media reinforced the negative beliefs that minorities have about themselves,[44] echoing one author's argument that "the television roles in which Blacks are cast communicate to Black children the negative value society places on them."[45] The importance of televised role models is not lost, even on the National Aeronautics and Space Administration. It hired Nichelle Nichols, who had played Lieutenant Uhura on *Star Trek,* to help recruit women and African-American astronauts.[46]

Self-Insertion as Self-Empowerment

Lieutenant Mary Sue and those Mary Sues that have followed in her wake appear against this backdrop. Yet within fan subcultures, Mary Sues are typically derided because of their perfection. Indeed, websites offer budding writers tutorials on how to avoid the pitfall of writing a Mary Sue.[47] "Flaming" and negative reviews are deployed to discipline fan-fiction writers who stray from acceptable additions to the particular fictional universe.[48] Where texts have long been subject to socially regulated readings,[49] the fan-fiction community—formed today principally through cyberspace—extends this discipline even to acceptable reworkings of the text.

The Mary Sue needs reclaiming not only from the *official guardians of the official story,* but also from the *unofficial guardians* of the *unofficial story.* The fact that Mary Sues are marked by relentlessly superlative qualities becomes more understandable when viewed against a popular culture that marginalizes certain groups. Flattering self-insertion offers a partial antidote to a media that neglects or marginalizes certain groups. Victims of prejudice often internalize its claims; indeed, oppressive societies have often relied on this psychological trick to maintain hierarchies.[50] A process of consciousness-raising and self-empowerment requires that one recognize one's own potential, even if others do not. Denied the principal role in the official canon, Mary Sue is no passive peripheral character: "She *does,* not just simply *exists.* She slays, she runs a starship, she types, she wields a sword."[51] Mary Sues help the writer claim agency against a popular culture that repeatedly denies it.

Some commentators worry that the "Mary Sue often reinforces the impossible idea that women must strive for effortless perfection." But would not the intrepid Captain Kirk or the invincible Superman suggest the same goal for men? Based on the social science literature canvassed earlier, I suggest instead that relentlessly positive portrayals of people who look like you may lead to (1) others thinking that people who look like you are capable and desirable; and (2) a belief in your own capability and self-worth. Rewriting popular culture is a step toward breaking the cycle of dominance, as the following three examples demonstrate.

Same-Sex Romance: Kirk/Spock
Even though *Star Trek* envisioned a purportedly egalitarian future, the reality it posited was far from the ideal. Just as Paula Smith had introduced Lieutenant Mary Sue to make up for the absence of female leaders, early fan-fiction writers often imagined same-sex romantic relationships among the ship's crew. Referenced often as "K/S" for "Kirk/Spock," such same-sex pairings in fan fiction came to be known as "slash."[52] Slash thus functions as a kind of Mary Sue, reflecting a desire to introduce homosexuality where it has been omitted.

This may be true even when the author is a heterosexual woman. Consider the following accounts of why women write male same-sex pairings:

- Given the priority given to the hero in the original, the female reader may identify with the hero, not the heroine, and then use the hero to "'feel' the adventure with" another character;
- Rewriting masculinity places emotional responsibility on men;
- The male slash is erotic to the female writer; and
- It rearranges the expected sexuality.[53]

That is, the ripping, mixing, and slashing of traditional sexual roles may allow the writers to reimagine their own places in the sexual order.

Heroes and Heroines: The Adventures of Hermione Granger
Some *Harry Potter* fan fiction gives center stage to Hermione Granger. Given that the *Harry Potter* books already depict Hermione with extraordinary, positive characteristics, it may have seemed unnecessary to rewrite her story. But the stories offer two twists on the official tale. First, they make it *her* story, not someone else's story in which she plays a part.

Second, the stories often find her a romantic partner, especially Ginny Weasley, Draco Malfoy, or Harry Potter. As one critic points out, the last pairing is especially satisfying for some: "As the Potter series' brilliant bookworm, Hermione is a role model for smart girls (and boys) who find themselves overshadowed by their flashier peers. There's a certain appeal to thinking that a young academic could couple with the hero of the wizarding world."[54]

Cultural Adaptation: Harry Potter in Kolkata
"Harry gets onto his Nimbus 2000 broom and zooms across to Calcutta at the invitation of a young boy called Junto," reads the text of an Indian tale, *Harry Potter Kolkataye* (Harry Potter in Kolkata).[55] Written in Bengali, the book brings Harry Potter to Kolkata where he "meets famous fictional characters from Bengali literature." Uttam Ghosh, the author, describes the story as a "poor man's Potter," costing just thirty rupees—less than one U.S. dollar.[56] But does this poor man's Potter simply further insinuate a foreign character into the imagination of Bengali youth? To some extent, yes, but we must not overlook the power of global mass media, which makes Potter difficult to avoid for the middle-class Kolkata youth likely to buy the book. *Harry Potter in Kolkata* is yet another variant of the Mary Sue. It introduces a young Indian boy into the Harry Potter legend and within a new environment—Kolkata—rather than Harry's familiar England. By situating Harry in Kolkata, it makes it easier to imagine the local street corner as a place of magic.

SUING MARY
Potter in Kolkata was rapidly taken off the market. Indian lawyers for Rowling and Warner Bros. issued a cease-and-desist letter to the "pirate" work's Indian publisher, which quickly complied.[57] J. K. Rowling has generally tolerated literally hundreds of thousands of other fan-fiction stories based on her characters, including stories that focus on Hermione—but these have been largely noncommercial and web- rather than print-based. The owners of the Star Trek franchise contemplated legal action against Star Trek slash, but did not bring suit because of strategic considerations.

What are the respective legal rights of the owner of the official work and the author of the Mary Sue? I argue that U.S. copyright law permits Mary Sues that challenge the orthodox depictions in the original.

The Fair Mary

U.S. law permits the copyright owner to claim not only his or her own stories, but also the characters in those stories.[58] It also grants to the copyright holder the exclusive right to make derivative works.[59] The unauthorized author of a derivative work such as fan fiction cannot claim a copyright in that work. This practice places the fan-fiction writer at the mercy of the copyright owner, unless the fan fiction constitutes fair use. Thus, a fan-fiction writer can pen stories employing copyrighted characters only if (1) the copyright owner explicitly permits such fan fiction, (2) the copyright owner chooses not to pursue legal action against the fan-fiction writer, or (3) the fan fiction constitutes fair use of the copyrighted work.

This third avenue allows fan-fiction writers the freedom to create using existing creative worlds without needing the permission, either explicit or tacit, of the copyright owner. If a use is judged "fair," then the copyright owner cannot bar it. Whether a use is fair depends on a number of factors, including the character of the work (is the use either commercial or transformative?), the nature of the underlying original work, the amount copied, and whether the use injures the copyright owner's market for the original work.[60] Courts enjoy wide discretion when weighing these factors, referring in their deliberations to the statute as well as to a long lineage of interpretive case laws.

Campbell v. Acuff-Rose Music, Inc.

The leading case defining the contours of fair use as it applies to critical commentary concerns a rap group's reworking of an earlier song, "Oh, Pretty Woman." In *Campbell v. Acuff-Rose Music, Inc.,* the copyright owner of Roy Orbison's song sued the rap group 2 Live Crew for copyright infringement for its song "Pretty Woman." The Supreme Court reversed the Sixth Circuit's decision that the use was presumptively unfair because of the song's commercial nature, holding that 2 Live Crew's parody of the original might constitute fair use. Justice Souter, writing for the Court, characterized 2 Live Crew's version as a parody of the original: "[W]e think it fair to say that 2 Live Crew's song reasonably could be perceived as commenting on the original or criticizing it, to some degree. 2 Live Crew juxtaposes the romantic musings of a man whose fantasy comes true, with degrading taunts, a bawdy demand for sex, and a sigh of relief from paternal responsibility. The later words can be taken as a comment on the naiveté of the original of an earlier day, as a rejection of its sentiment that ignores the ugliness of street life and the debasement that it signifies."[61]

The Court observed that parodies like 2 Live Crew's "Pretty Woman" transform the original, providing "social benefit, by shedding light on an earlier work, and, in the process, creating a new one."[62] Even the commercial nature of 2 Live Crew's work did not defeat the group's fair-use defense, though the Court remanded the case for fact-finding, in order to determine whether the 2 Live Crew rap parody harmed the copyright owner's market for a *non*-parodic rap version of the song.[63]

Similarly, many Mary Sues comment on or criticize the original, while creating something new. They highlight the absence of society's marginal voices in the original works, the stereotyped actions or inactions of certain characters, and the orthodoxy of social relationships in the original. Lieutenant Mary Sue beamed on board, finally bringing a leading woman character to the bridge, saving the day while parrying Captain Kirk's advances. The depiction of Lieutenant Mary Sue served to challenge the original in a uniquely powerful way. It demonstrated the glaring lacuna in the original, despite its pretensions of egalitarianism (exemplified in the first Star Trek movie's risible use of "Mr." to reference both male and female crew members). Such Mary Sues comment on the disappointments of the original, particularly its racial, gender, and sexual hierarchy.

The Wind Done Gone

Mary Sues help us rewrite not just the future, but also the past. For nearly a century, the most popular account of life on a slave plantation has been Margaret Mitchell's literary classic *Gone with the Wind (GWTW)*, a book second only to the Bible in worldwide sales.[64] That account presented an idyll disturbed only by the actions of the North:

> In the world of *GWTW*, the white characters comprise a noble aristocracy whose idyllic existence is upset only by the intrusion of Yankee soldiers, and, eventually, by the liberation of the black slaves. . . . Mitchell describes how both blacks and whites were purportedly better off in the days of slavery: "The more I see of emancipation the more criminal I think it is. It's just

ruined the darkies," says Scarlett O'Hara. . . . Free blacks are
described as "creatures of small intelligence . . . [l]ike monkeys
or small children turned loose among treasured objects whose
value is beyond their comprehension, they ran wild."[65]

In *The Wind Done Gone (TWDG)*, Alice Randall, an African-American
novelist, retold the tale from the perspective of a slave, Cynara, on the
O'Hara plantation. Mitchell's heirs sued for copyright infringement. The
trial court held that Randall had infringed Mitchell's work. On appeal,
the Eleventh Circuit reversed, holding that *TWDG* likely constituted a parodic fair use.[66] The two novels' depictions of race and sex relations could
hardly be more different, as characterized by the Eleventh Circuit: "It is
clear within the first fifty pages of Cynara's fictional diary that Randall's
work flips *GWTW's* traditional race roles, portrays powerful whites as
stupid or feckless, and generally sets out to demystify *GWTW* and strip
the romanticism from Mitchell's specific account of this period of our
history. . . . In *GWTW*, Scarlett O'Hara often expresses disgust with and
condescension towards blacks; in *TWDG*, Other, Scarlett's counterpart,
is herself of mixed descent. In *GWTW*, Ashley Wilkes is the initial object
of Scarlett's affection; in *TWDG*, he is homosexual."[67]

The Sue-ification of the African Americans in the story is unmistakable. As the Eleventh Circuit noted, "[i]n *TWDG*, nearly every black
character is given some redeeming quality—whether depth, wit, cunning, beauty, strength, or courage—that their *GWTW* analogues lacked."[68]
Given the racist caricatures in the original, Randall's redemption of the
African Americans is not only understandable but overdue.

Whether Mitchell's heirs must tolerate *The Wind Done Gone* did not
turn on whether either they or *even the public* liked the retelling. Courts
have insisted that "public majority opinion" is irrelevant to the question
of whether a work is a parody;[69] making the inquiry an issue of law helps
insulate uses that society disfavors. Of course, relying on judges to make
the parody determination inserts judges' own prejudices into the decision-
making. Yet on occasion, judges have endorsed as fair use those parodies
they have found objectionable. For example, the Second Circuit upheld
an actor's right to poke fun of the pregnant female body, even though it
found the act "unchivalrous."[70]

While parodies often constitute fair use, satires often do not (though they may). Satires employ the original work "as a vehicle for commenting on some individual or institution and not on the work itself." As the Supreme Court explained in the *Campbell* case: "Parody needs to mimic an original to make its point, and so has some claim to use the creation of its victim's (or collective victims') imagination, whereas satire can stand on its own two feet and so requires justification for the very act of borrowing."[71] That decidedly does not mean that parodies cannot comment simultaneously on the underlying work *and* on society at large. Indeed, this is the norm for parodies that courts have found fair. Justice Souter recognized that a particular work might exhibit both satire and parody: "[N]o workable presumption for parody could take account of the fact that parody often shades into satire when society is lampooned through its creative artifacts, or that a work may contain both parodic and nonparodic elements."[72] This will be especially true of source works that are cultural icons—because of their popularity, critiquing these icons carries a larger message. When the canon works stand for an era, a mood, a history, the Mary Sue becomes a subversive intervention.

Mary Sues can be commercial and still be fair.[73] Indeed, the history of fair use is replete with commercial uses, including all of the cases cited earlier.[74] In *Campbell,* the Supreme Court declared that "the more transformative the new work, the less will be the significance of other factors, like commercialism, that may weigh against a finding of fair use."[75] While amateur fan fiction is typically authored without remuneration in mind,[76] not all Mary Sues have a noncommercial motive. The possibility of remuneration is important, because it spurs creation by allowing writers a livelihood in such work, while potentially giving them the financial means to reach a larger audience. Alice Randall, for example, found a commercial publisher for her story, and will have the right to challenge Mitchell's film version with her own.

Even when a work is found to be a parody, courts will analyze the effect of the parody on the market both for the original work and for potential derivatives in the work. But when a new work transforms the original in some substantial way, the market harm resulting from the copying can be difficult to ascertain. The *Campbell* court noted that "as to parody pure and simple, it is more likely that the new work will not affect the market for the original . . . by acting as a substitute for it."[77]

Mary Sue works—which by their very nature are subaltern critiques of the dominant stories—are not likely to supplant the market for the originals. Rather, they are likely to serve a different market of specialized consumers who identify more closely with Mary Sue versions than with dominant versions. If part of the market for the original disappears because the Mary Sue exposes the original's prejudices, this is not a harm that copyright law protects against. The Copyright Act is properly concerned with illegitimate free riding, not the speech effects of the use.[78] Take, for example, scholarly criticism that borrows quotes or images from the subject of the critique. That criticism might ridicule or deride the original and thus harm the market for that work, yet that market harm should not be cognizable in the fair-use inquiry. While scholarly criticism can be effective, critiques written in the language of the original may prove equally persuasive.

Not all Mary Sues that challenge stereotypes constitute fair use under existing law. Fair use is a contextualized, fact-specific determination requiring courts to carefully consider the factors enumerated in the statute. In deciding whether a use is fair or unfair, a court must "work its way through the relevant factors, and . . . judge[] case by case, in light of the ends of copyright law."[79] While parodies by their nature require some amount of borrowing in order to evoke the original,[80] the question of how much is too much can only be determined by considering the particular context. For example, a Mary Sue masquerading as the canon work would likely go too far. Indeed, fan-fiction authors have developed conventions to avoid such false advertising.[81] In the case of *Warner Bros. Entertainment, Inc. and J. K. Rowling v. RDR Books,* a federal district court judge ruled in 2008 that a fan-published encyclopedia of all things Harry Potter did not constitute fair use because the fan, Steve Vander Ark, copied too much from Rowling's original works, thus prompting Vander Ark to put more of the encyclopedia into his own words before he could sell it.

COMMON CRITIQUES OF THE "MARY SUE"

Like any claim to use another's original work, the author of a Mary Sue will face three fundamental objections. Let us consider some responses here.

Why Not Write an Entirely Original Story?

In *Campbell v. Acuff-Rose,* the Supreme Court indicated its distaste for
someone who borrows someone else's copyrighted work merely "to avoid
the drudgery in working up something fresh."[82] Indeed, a skeptic might
ask: Why not simply write your own world? In a letter to her fans, this is
precisely the advice of the writer Anne Rice: "I do not allow fan fiction.
The characters are copyrighted . . . . I advise my readers to *write your own
original stories* with your own characters."[83]

Both the preference for parody over satire and the penchant for entirely original stories have typically turned on economic analysis and the
underlying notion of substitutability. The critical legal inquiry is: Is there
a viable substitute for the copyrighted work? That is, can the later writer
employ a public domain work or invent a wholly original work as an alternative vehicle for his or her critique? Paul Goldstein expresses confidence
that, for satire at least, such alternatives will be readily available: "There
will rarely be a shortage of works, including public domain works, that
with some ingenuity can be made to serve as equally effective vehicles for
the intended satire."[84] If a viable substitute exists, it is no longer necessary
to use the copyrighted work. The focus on substitutability explains why
courts generally favor parody over satire. For satire, as Goldstein reminds
us, a substitute generally exists. But if the point is to comment on a particular work, and to seek to resignify it for oneself, there is no substitute
for the use of the original work.

Furthermore, there is only one Superman. In such cases, social commentary gathers its unique power *because* of its use of cultural icons.
The abstract statement may not hold the same cultural currency as the
one directed at, and employing, Superman. Thus, it is not the absence of
creative genius on the part of the later author that requires the use of an
earlier work. Rather, while the canon work's inventiveness or brilliance
may have contributed to its current cultural status, it is the very popularity of the canon work that is the focus of the Mary Sue. Of course, by
piggybacking on the canon work, the Mary Sue cannot guarantee itself
a share in the original's popularity. But for the author and a particular
set of readers, the Mary Sue helps reimagine the world by reworking the
most powerful elements of popular culture.

This dynamic is particularly important where the popular culture is
widely discriminatory and noninclusive. As Henry Louis Gates, Jr., testi-

fied in a declaration before the Court in the *Wind Done Gone* case, *"Gone with the Wind*—especially in its book form—is widely regarded in the black community as one of the most racist depictions of slavery and black slaves in American literature."[85] In her declaration in the same case, Toni Morrison asked simply, "Who controls how history is imagined? Who gets to say what slavery was like for the slaves?"[86] Randall's retelling of the master narrative is a hoary tactic: as Gates testified, "African Americans have used parody since slavery to 'fight back' against their masters."[87] As Keith Aoki has described, parody offers a "cultural space for 'talking back' at, or *through,* the pervasive and dense media languages which constitute much of our social environment."[88] Rosemary Coombe powerfully asks: "What meaning does dialogue have when we are bombarded with messages to which we cannot respond, signs and images whose significations cannot be challenged, and connotations we cannot contest?"[89] Theorists, both traditional and postmodern, affirm the discursive nature of creativity: all creators borrow from earlier masters.[90] But contemporary cultural theorists recognize as an important discursive tactic the reworking of a *discriminatory* narrative to retell history and empower oneself.[91] Building on Michel de Certeau, Henry Jenkins describes fan fiction as "textual poaching," in which fans "reconstruct meanings according to more immediate interests."[92] Rewriting the popular narrative becomes not only an attempt to change popular understandings, but also an act of self-empowerment. In Gates's words, "[S]ignifying can also be employed to reverse or undermine pretense or even one's opinion about one's own status."[93]

But would not women and minorities who find themselves misrepresented in culture be better off creating wholly new stories, rather than redeploying the icons already offered by cultural authorities? This is a common criticism of Star Trek slash fiction, which paradoxically *is often penned by women but at the same time often excludes women* in its glorification of the male bodies of Kirk and Spock. Though I have already posited some possible explanations for this phenomenon, here I consider it as an example of a discursive practice known in cultural theory as "bricolage"—the act of creating by "making do" with the hodgepodge of cultural elements that already exist.[94] One study, for example, found that women writers of Star Trek slash fiction focused on the lead males in the show because (1) the women characters in the story are not interesting, and (2) the writers were just "working with what's out there" already.[95]

Going further, I have posited a theory of cultural belonging and participation that goes beyond describing how individuals create within culture.[96] I argue that, more and more, individuals seek a right to develop their autonomous selves within the normative communities that matter most to them. Mary Sue fan fiction affirms Jane Austen's observation that "[o]ne does not love a place the less for having suffered in it."[97] Writers responding to discriminatory texts they nonetheless love may simply seek to reclaim the works as their own, and in more affirming ways.

There are, of course, brilliant, entirely original texts that reflect an egalitarian worldview. Yet for whatever reason, few such texts have attained the popular cultural status of a small set of iconic works. Popularity may arise through a grassroots, word-of-mouth groundswell, which the Internet has made increasingly possible. More often than not, however, popularity is carefully cultivated, often requiring a large capital investment that is out of reach for many marginalized communities.[98] Even when popular alternatives emerge, they can be co-opted by the dominant players simply through acquisition. Take the alternative teenage girl magazine *Sassy*, purchased by *Teen* magazine, "which first integrated it as a column and later phased it out completely." *Teen* itself was later acquired and integrated into *Seventeen* magazine.[99]

Yet another obstacle to "wholly" invented alternatives is the possible use of intellectual property law by dominant players against newcomers. For example, Marvel and DC Comics both claim a joint trademark in the use of the phrase "Super Heroes" in comic books. Faced with a threat of suit, the creator of the comic book "Super Hero Happy Hour" changed his comic's name to "Hero Happy Hour."[100] While there are reasons to doubt the validity of the "Super Heroes" mark (for example, the term "super hero" is generic; the mark owners have failed to meet their obligation to police unauthorized uses of the mark),[101] Marvel and DC can employ their questionable trademark against those parties lacking the resources to test their claims in court.

Why Not License the Original?

Why not require that the Mary Sue be licensed from the copyright owner? Copyright law assumes that copyright owners will be reluctant to license criticism of their work. The Supreme Court so stated in *Campbell v. Acuff-Rose:* "Yet the unlikelihood that creators of imaginative works will license critical reviews or lampoons of their own productions removes such uses from the very notion of a potential licensing market."[102] The Court accordingly concluded that, if there is no derivative market for criticism, criticism of the original work cannot interfere with the potential market for the copyrighted work. This supports the conclusion that critique of the work itself will likely constitute fair use. But some might argue that this is too pessimistic. If there is a market for a work, then the copyright owner should seek to maximize his or her profit by exploiting it—even if it means tolerating criticism. (An alternative view is that rather than calling for fair use for criticism, any reluctance to license criticism should simply imply a compulsory license, requiring a royalty payment in lieu of a royalty-free use.) For instance, DC Comics, the owner of Batman, Superman, and other popular characters, has authorized "Elseworld" alternative universes, in which the heroes are villains, and the villains, heroes.[103]

Two recent moves by corporate America further suggest that "Official Mary Sues" are not entirely unlikely. Marvel Enterprises, Inc., licensed an Indian version of Spider-Man, with the superhero donning a traditional Indian loincloth and sparring with the Green Goblin recast as a Rakshasa, a demon from Hindu cosmology.[104] As the Indian publisher announces, Spider-Man India interweaves the local customs, culture, and mystery of modern India, with an eye to making Spider-Man's mythology more relevant to this particular audience. Readers of this series will see not the familiar Peter Parker of Queens under the classic Spider-Man mask, but rather a new hero—a young, Indian boy named Pavitr Prabhakar. As Spider-Man, Pavitr leaps around rickshaws and scooters in Indian streets, while swinging from monuments such as the Gateway of India and the Taj Mahal.[105]

In late 2005, Disney revised its most lucrative story, *Winnie the Pooh,* by replacing the central human figure, Christopher Robin, with a "redhaired six-year-old tomboy" girl.[106] The reaction to Disney's announcement was mixed. Nicholas Tucker, author of *The Rough Guide to Children's Books,* declared the new character "a huge error," explaining that the original stories are "built around a boy who arrives and puts things right, like little boys do."[107] Yet another scholar of children's literature doubts whether the absence of female characters in *Winnie the Pooh* has a deleterious effect: Kathleen Horning, who instructs children's book librarians at the University of Wisconsin–Madison, reports that, "growing up, I had no problem relating to Christopher Robin. He almost had a non-specific gender."[108] Do these two events—involving what are likely to be the single most popular superhero in the world and the single most popular children's cartoon character—suggest that underground versions of popular culture are unnecessary? Indeed, recently even the producers of *Sesame Street*, acknowledging their failure to produce "a single female character with anything close to the name recognition of Big Bird or Cookie Monster or Ernie and Bert" (not to mention Elmo), introduced a new girl character, "Abby Cadabby" (although her iconic status remains to be seen). This introduction comes in this progressive television show's thirty-seventh season.[109]

Despite these examples, the possibility of an official Mary Sue for *Winnie the Pooh* is unlikely for at least three reasons. First, Disney's move comes after almost eighty years of the male-dominated Hundred Acre Wood; Spider-Man's new ethnicity comes after more than forty years of a white-only superhero. It seems unreasonable to expect the world's women and minorities to wait patiently for each such move. Second, the official Mary Sue may still leave much to be desired in the characterization of the newly represented group. Third, even where it expands the representation, it still leaves large omissions: the tomboy girl replacing Christopher Robin was white. And finally, the masters of popular characters are unlikely to license the most disfavored uses. When the Mitchell estate sought out an author for a sequel to *Gone with the Wind*, it required a pledge that the author "will under no circumstances write anything about miscegenation or homosexuality."[110] Similarly, while DC Comics produced an alternative strip featuring an evil Batman, it issued a cease-and-desist letter to an artist depicting Batman and Robin as lovers.[111] An evil Batman, it seems, is more palatable than a gay one.

Won't "Recoding" Popular Icons Destabilize Culture?

If popular icons are recoded, will a society's culture suffer? The legal scholar Justin Hughes worries that a permissive attitude toward transforming social meanings will undermine cultural stability; according to another scholar, "Hughes worries that a generally passive audience will suffer as cultural minorities disturb their icons."[112] I disagree for four reasons.

First, human beings have the capacity to hold multiple, even contradictory, meanings simultaneously. Despite the multiplicity of meanings that any given word can hold, communication stumbles on. It may at times require disambiguation, but that does not seem an unreasonable price for a richer discourse.

Second, the canonical text itself might have multiple interpretations, both official and unofficial. Authors of literary criticism do not seek to uncover the one authentic meaning of a text, but rather understand that it can accommodate multiple interpretations. Homosexual readings of Batman have been offered since at least the 1950s, yet Batman's womanizing remains a popular motif. Official owners have themselves promoted "forked" meanings—consider Frank Miller's "grittier" Batman, which was offered by DC Comics to revive the classic character.[113]

Third, the meaning of a text evolves over time, and cannot be firmly fixed to some romantic original intention. Our contemporary understanding of culture rejects the static, thing-like terms of early cultural anthropology. Today's anthropologists understand culture as "traveling," engaging "in both internal and external dialogue" along the way.[114]

Fourth, demeaning representations in popular culture need to be challenged. A semiotic democracy in which the power of meaning-making has been democratized cannot declare certain icons sacred, especially those icons that valorize only the already dominant segments of society. While many in society may not wish to despoil their romance with Scarlett and Rhett Butler, the pair's position in the fiction as lords of a slave plantation cannot be whitewashed.

> Everyone's a superhero, everyone's a Captain Kirk.
> —Nena, "99 Red Balloons"

Reworking the proprietary icons of our age can lead to both political resistance and economic empowerment. Media stereotypes play an important role in educating us about the capacities of others. Even more alarming, they are a central way in which we learn about our own capacities. Given a popular media that marginalizes various segments of society, the act of reworking popular stories to assert one's own value is empowering: it opens the path to new livelihoods and roles. Self-insertion changes popular meanings, laying the foundation for economic change. Copying can be an act of both homage and subversion.

CHAPTER FIVE

Can Intellectual Property Help the Poor?

IN LATE DECEMBER 2004, I traveled to India to witness the social rup-
tures that India's entry into the modern intellectual property world would
likely trigger. The deadline for developing nations to be fully compliant
with the Agreement on Trade-Related Aspects of Intellectual Property
(TRIPS), the preeminent global intellectual property law of the Information Age, was January 1, 2005. From that date on, India would have
Western-style intellectual property rights for everything from medicines
to seeds. For more than a decade, the developing world had resisted this
moment. Since they had been pressured into signing TRIPS during the
Uruguay Round of WTO negotiations, countries such as Brazil and India
had argued that strong intellectual property rights helped the West but
would devastate the rest.

Sadly, my visit to India that December coincided with an all too literal
tsunami that shook the subcontinent. The tsunami focused the world's
attention on the rural poor in the countries at the perimeter of the Indian
Ocean. I will seek to keep my focus on these people in this chapter.

Much to my surprise, India rang in the New Year without much ill
note of TRIPS. In the intellectual property storm, the dust had settled, for
now. TRIPS was finally in India, seemingly to stay, and the intellectual
property scholars and practitioners there with whom I spoke had little
interest in prolonging the battles of the last decade. "TRIPS has entered,

and India took a U-turn because it felt it could not [continue fighting against TRIPS]," V. C. Vivekanandan, an intellectual property professor at NALSAR, a leading national law school in Hyderabad, told me. "It has been grudgingly accepted."[1]

But in that characteristically Indian way of absorbing every contradiction and all the diversity of life, this was not simply an expression of passive acceptance of destiny. After a decade of resisting the Western imposition of intellectual property, now many in India—from the intellectual property professors and lawyers in the cities, to the farmers and artisans in the villages—were beginning to ask: how can intellectual property rights work for us? TRIPS protected the knowledge and economic interests of the developed world, the rich corporations of the West. But can intellectual property be a tool for protecting poor people's knowledge as well? Some seem to think so. Take the case of an award-winning farmer in Kerala who developed a high-yield method for planting rubber trees. An intellectual property professor from Kerala related the farmer's story: "Later when somebody tried to plant [rubber trees] in the same way, [the farmer] said, 'No, I will get a patent in this.'" The professor noted, "Five years back this concept [of patenting] was totally lacking. This farmer had only studied up to [the] sixth or seventh [grade]. But he has some idea about this particular law where you can stop somebody else from using the method."[2]

Certainly, the shift to appropriating intellectual property in India is neither complete nor uncontested. When the Kerala farmer took his claims to the Rubber Board, there was fierce debate among the farmers. "One young farmer stood up and said, 'I [wouldn't] want any monetary benefit from this. I [would] just want this to be propagated freely. Uncle, I [wouldn't] want a patent. For me the honor of the award [would be] enough.'"[3] But if the daily headlines are any indication, the country's approach is shifting from this traditional view. The front pages chronicle a rising tide of applications filed with a national registry established pursuant to the Geographical Indications of Goods (Registration and Protection) Act of 1999 (also known as the GI Act).[4] Required by TRIPS[5] originally as a means to protect French makers of wines and champagnes, the law gives trademark-like protection to distinctive goods or services whose quality and reputation derive from the geographical area in which they are produced. In a country such as India, which has a vast cultural heritage and a store of traditional knowledge dating back to the Vedas, the GI Act is seen as a potentially important source of recognition and income for India's rural poor—the very same poor who otherwise have been displaced and forced further into poverty by globalization. One hope is that Geographical Indications (GI) protection will allow local artisans to stay in their communities and fend for themselves, without having to renounce their traditional work for life in the overcrowded cities. When I visited India in 2005, farmers and artisans from across the country were getting in line to register their wares, from Darjeeling tea to Alfonso mangoes, Kolhapuri chappals, Mysore silk and sandalwood, and the uniquely woven sarees from the village of Pochampally, in the shadow of high-tech Hyderabad.[6]

Turn the clock back ten years. When intellectual property found its way into the sanctions regime of the international trade order, there were no marchers in the streets to mark the occasion. The White House had issued a white paper declaring the need to strengthen intellectual property law in the face of the digital revolution. Congress was just about to undertake enormous giveaways to intellectual property holders—granting famous brands rights even in the absence of consumer confusion, extending copyright terms by another two decades, and securing technological copyright protection schemes against hacking. Courts signaled their willingness to accept patents on business methods. In the new economy of the information age, patents, trademarks, copyrights, and even domain names[7] were being distributed with abandon. Conventional wisdom was that the digital world to come would require bigger and stronger intellectual property rights.

Amid this euphoria, some scholars recognized a dark side of intellectual property. In this narrative of progress, James Boyle, for example, saw us sowing the seeds of our own destruction. Just as the first enclosure of the commons and industrialization had threatened our natural environment, this new "land grab" in cyberspace and on our cultural commons, Boyle observed, threatened to ruin our cultural landscape and deplete our cultural heritage. Boyle's critical insight was that expanding intellectual property rights were fed by the conceit of romantic authorship: the idea that individuals (and even corporations) create out of thin air rather than borrow from a rich public domain of freely circulating sources and inspirations. "The author vision blinds us to the importance of the commons—to the importance of the raw material from which information products are constructed," he wrote in his 1996 book *Sha-mans, Software, and Spleens: Law and the Construction of the Information Society*.[8] The process of creation, Boyle noted, requires the conservation of cultural raw materials; if these are themselves owned, the process of creation may be stunted.

Boyle's vision of a political movement to protect and preserve the public domain, complete with private institutions dedicated to the project modeled after Greenpeace, spurred the establishment of the Creative Commons. The metaphor Boyle offered, "cultural environmentalism," helped lay the foundation for the recognition and protection of traditional knowledge and natural resources found in the developing world. Taking a cue implicitly from the environmental justice movement, which demonstrated the disparate effects of environmental harms on disadvantaged minorities, the cultural-environmental movement illustrated how third-world peoples are disproportionately disadvantaged by intellectual property law, which historically has not recognized their cultural contributions.

Indigenous people and those in the third world benefited from the attention to our cultural commons. It provided a moral and economic basis to reward their cultivation of the world's biodiversity and ancient cultural knowledge about that biodiversity, both of which were required inputs for innovation. By "reifying the negative"[9] and focusing needed attention on the "other side" of intellectual property,[10] Boyle invented the public domain.

But now, in the developing world, scholars, lawyers, and activists are turning the light on what they call "poor people's knowledge."[11] For them, *this* is "the other half of intellectual property"—the knowledge that is not protected by TRIPS, but perhaps should be.[12] In this chapter, I consider how "cultural environmentalism" both bolsters and obstructs the project of protecting poor people's knowledge and promoting development through intellectual property. I argue that although the metaphor spurred the invention of traditional knowledge as a political and legal category, the same metaphor may also inadvertently obscure the *inventiveness* of traditional knowledge. Reifying the public domain may have the unintended effect of congealing traditional knowledge as "the opposite of property,"[13] presenting poor people's knowledge as the raw material of innovation—ancient, static, and natural—rather than as intellectual property—modern, dynamic, scientific, and culturally inventive. According to this view, traditional knowledge holders may receive remuneration for conserving biodiversity and contributing the raw materials of innovation, but they are not recognized as intellectual property holders in their own right. What's more, a binary view of "intellectual property versus the public domain" rejects new claims for intellectual property in traditional knowledge on the premise that these rights would shrink the public domain.[14]

In truth, the line between what law considers "raw material" versus "intellectual property" is less stable and more fraught with bias than the binary approach would acknowledge. While politically effective, reifying the negative may have the perverse effect of reinventing these categories as real and stable, obscuring the degree to which they are constructed and insecure.

If anyone understands this, it is Boyle himself. The author of "Foucault in Cyberspace,"[15] Boyle articulated in *Shamans, Software, and Spleens* one of his fundamental concerns: the contested concept of authorship. Why was the shaman's lore unprotected "traditional knowledge" but W. R. Grace's appropriation of that knowledge "innovation"? Why was the patient Mr. Moore's spleen "raw material" but the UCLA researchers' cell line derived from the spleen "intellectual property"? These were more than the sharp questions of a law professor challenging first-year property students. Boyle offered up the "romantic author" not to justify these categories but to deconstruct them. Boyle persuasively argued for the need to critically probe authorship and its premise of a "transformative originality more often assumed than proved."[16]

How is it, then, that the cultural environmentalism metaphor may now be inadvertently helping to reconstruct some of the very same false binaries that Boyle set out to tear down more than a decade ago? The answer, I believe, turns on the historical contingency of the work, its intellectual history. In *Shamans, Software, and Spleens*, Boyle was concerned about the morality of legally recognizing some members of society as authors and not others. He bemoaned the distributive effects of such intellectual property laws as "colossally unfair"[17] and boldly called for "a critical social theory of the information society"[18] that would consider these difficulties. But by and large, Boyle's own work did not stray far from intellectual property's economic tradition. While Boyle acknowledged the broad social, cultural, moral, and distributive effects of intellectual property, his primary prescriptions stuck to a law-and-economic analysis of intellectual property. Failure to protect a public domain was, above all, *inefficient*. Destroying the raw materials necessary for creation would stunt creation itself. This approach was admittedly strategic; Boyle openly stated that economic appeals "will sometimes convince when more frankly moral appeals do not."[19] Boyle acknowledged that his approach was not radical, but rather that it evinced "a conservative strand," advocating "a return to the rational roots of intellectual property."[20]

Boyle displayed a rare combination: postmodern acuity and political savvy. His analogy to the environmental movement was a brilliant move. But given the discursive restraints of the time, Boyle was not able to fulfill his ambition completely. He openly acknowledged "the dangers of embracing too closely a language that can express only some of the things that you care about."[21] Boyle was fully aware of the contingency of his economic argument, recognizing that "our concerns with education and the distribution of wealth, with free speech and universal access to information, can never be fully expressed in the language of neo-classical price theory."[22]

Today, the space for discussing intellectual property's distributive and social effects is expanding. Notably, a vast coalition of hundreds of intellectual property practitioners, scholars, and activists from around the world are calling for intellectual property to be approached in the context of broader societal interests and development-related concerns, and not just from the narrow lens of economic incentives for innovation.[23] As ever, we are enriched by tradition, but not beholden to it. We are still in need of "a critical social theory of the information society" for which Boyle's work offers a foundation. But since then, the discursive space for crafting that theory has expanded beyond the narrow confines of understanding intellectual property rights as incentives alone.

By foregrounding the important role of "raw materials" in the process of innovation, cultural environmentalism helped provide a theoretical and political basis for recognition and recompense for the purveyors of those raw materials—often indigenous peoples who have cultivated the earth's biodiversity and who hold "traditional knowledge" about that biodiversity. The invention of the public domain helped to foster "the invention of traditional knowledge" as a political and legal category worthy of rights. But while theorizing the public domain provided intellectual heft to new claims for traditional knowledge protection, it has also proved a stumbling block. Today, the 1992 Convention on Biological Diversity (CBD) and more recently the 2011 Nagoya Protocol to the CBD promote an international legal regime that would reward traditional knowledge holders for their role in preserving biodiversity and ancient knowledge—that is, for their role in preserving the public domain.

But these international legal documents do not expressly recognize the *inventiveness* of traditional knowledge, nor the attendant intellectual property rights claimed by the world's poor as authors and inventors of new knowledge. In truth, traditional knowledge is much more dynamic and innovative—indeed *evolving*—than the "environmentalism" metaphor, with its connotations of *conservation*, acknowledges. A legal regime that recognizes poor people as agents—that is, as the subjects of intellectual property, and not just as the objects of intellectual property, offering up raw materials for others to transform—is premised on a broader view of the relationship between intellectual property and development itself. Here yet another side of intellectual property is revealed: its social and cultural face, not just its economic aspects. World actors are beginning to recognize that intellectual property is about more than incentives for innovation. Just like real property rights, intellectual property rights can promote freedom and security, potentially enabling knowledge societies in which the rich and poor alike may cultivate and materially benefit from their ideas.

VIEWING THE POOR AS WARDENS OF "TRADITIONAL" KNOWLEDGE

The invention of the public domain helped lay a foundation for "the invention of traditional knowledge" as a political and legal category worthy of rights. Boyle's metaphor for a politics of the public domain, "cultural environmentalism," helped focus the world's attention on the value of ecological and cultural biodiversity for the process of scientific and cultural innovation, and on the need to preserve those resources. Although Boyle offered cultural environmentalism as a metaphor, at points cultural environmentalism coincides with environmentalism itself. Recall the shamans of Madagascar. In this poverty-stricken nation, medicine men had developed therapeutic uses for the indigenously grown rosy periwinkle. Enter Eli Lilly & Company, which transformed this plant and the shaman's lore into a drug to treat Hodgkin's disease. At the time, the drug was valued at some $100 million annually.[24] As Boyle pointed out, even a fraction of the company's profits would have been a significant boost to the economy of this poor country.[25] But through the vagaries of Western intellectual property law, the people of Madagascar received none of the profits derived from this new drug. Western intellectual property, as Boyle explained, was premised on an authorial regime that "values the raw materials for the production of intellectual property at zero," yet judges Eli Lilly's contribution, refining the shaman's traditional knowledge, in the hundreds of millions of dollars.[26]

For Boyle, the rosy periwinkle symbolized more than just a moral problem, or a problem of postmodern authorship. The rosy periwinkle, Boyle wrote, "exemplifies *the utilitarian failures* of the current regime."[27] Absent any reward for their preservation of biodiversity and traditional knowledge, the people of Madagascar had "chopped down most of their forests to feed [their] people"[28]—an irony Boyle decried. In this context, the cultural environment was not merely metaphor. Boyle was concerned about the literal environment, the earth's forests and all of its abundant biodiversity, from which medicinal and other cultural knowledge could be derived. *Cultural* environmentalism called our attention to the *traditional knowledge* of the shaman and other people, often poor, who cultivated disease-resistant wheat and rice and held the secrets of which plants could cure our ills. Going further, cultural environmentalism highlighted the need to preserve diverse cultures, the repositories of such knowledge. "Who knows what other unique and potentially valuable plants disappear with the forest, what generations of pharmacological experience disappear as the indigenous culture is destroyed?" Boyle pointedly asked.[29]

The trope of the romantic author obscured the contributions of biodiversity and traditional knowledge to innovation. "Who needs a public domain if you can create out of nothing?" Boyle asked.[30] By exposing how companies such as Eli Lilly did not, in fact, create out of thin air, but rather often benefited from the rich biodiversity and knowledge found in the global South, Boyle made the strongest case for preserving the public domain: *the public domain saves lives.*

Boyle's theory of the public domain provided intellectual grounding to arguments for recognizing the value of the cultural contributions of indigenous and third-world peoples to innovation. Both the CBD and

the recent Nagoya Protocol to the CBD promote an international legal
regime that would reward indigenous peoples for supplying the raw materials of innovation and preserving the public domain. Employing the
combined language of environmentalism and economics, the CBD refers to local peoples as "resource managers" and their trade as "species
management,"[31] and grants countries sovereign rights of ownership over
genetic resources found within their borders. These rights serve as both
ex post reward for biodiversity conservation and ex ante incentive for
continued conservation. The CBD would grant both sovereignty in biological resources and the right to share in the benefits of patented products
that arise from the appropriation of a country's biodiversity or traditional
knowledge. Similarly, a draft Treaty on Access to Knowledge seeks to
"protect, preserve and enhance the public domain, which is essential for
creativity and sustained innovation,"[32] by similarly requiring patent holders to seek prior informed consent for use of biological materials from the
country of origin and to "equitably share the benefits derived from use
of that biological material."[33] The dual recommendation of both resource
sovereignty and equitable benefit sharing seeks to recognize indigenous
peoples as the wardens of the world's "raw materials" and to reward them
materially for their role in preserving the public domain.

   Whereas this theory of the public domain has served to undergird
claims for traditional knowledge protection, so too has it proved a stumbling block. In the last decade, we have seen indigenous peoples and the
poor, not unlike the Kerala rubber-tree farmer, turning their attention
to appropriating intellectual property to their own ends.[34] Today claims
by indigenous people and the poor go beyond equitable benefit sharing;
increasingly, the poor seek to own copyrights, trademarks, and patents
in their own cultural and scientific innovations.[35] Strikingly, the traditional advocates for preserving the public domain have flipped. "Native
peoples once stood for the commons,"[36] but with the imbalance of TRIPS
becoming ever more apparent, advocates of the poor are turning their attention to securing affirmative intellectual property rights for their own
cultural and scientific innovations. Paradoxically, however, the concepts of
"traditional knowledge," the "public domain," and "cultural environmentalism" are now proving to be obstacles to understanding poor people's
knowledge *as intellectual property*. Claims by native peoples to hold intellectual property are resisted as threats to the public domain, or as the

false consciousness of neo-liberalism, or as a radical assault on our intellectual property tradition, which encourages and promotes cultivation, not stewardship.[37]

We should be wary of these declarations and "the romance of the public domain" itself.[38] Anupam Chander and I have argued that, while the banner of the public domain is taken up for all of humanity, a binary view of "intellectual property versus the public domain" may not be to the benefit of the world's poor.[39] Often, we have explained, the benefits of an open-access commons go to the richest and the strongest. Differences in wealth, gender, and class determine whether one will in fact be able to convert the riches of the commons into lucrative property. This is what we call the *"romance* of the commons: the belief that because a resource is open to all by force of law, it will indeed be equally exploited by all."[40] Concerns arising from efficiency alone obscure the disparate effects of the commons on the poor. Staying attuned to the distributional effects of the public domain, in contrast, may require thinking about poor people's knowledge in "uncommon property"[41] terms, facilitating their capability to exert greater control over their property and to extract compensation from their knowledge.

The "cultural environmentalism" metaphor reifies the division between "raw" and "cooked" knowledge, a conceptual separation long fundamental to intellectual property law. Ironically, the cultural environmentalism metaphor has fortified the very boundary between authors and raw materials that Boyle himself had begun to tear down. Boyle pulled the rug out from under the romantic author, exposing the equally important role of sources and audiences in the process of innovation. He also underlined the vagaries and cultural bias in intellectual property law's determinations of who were authors and who (Mr. Moore) or what (his spleen) were the mere raw materials of scientific and cultural production. Boyle recognized the problem of "rewarding a narrow set of contributions to world culture and science."[42] But he stopped short of advocating reform of a Western intellectual property tradition that was founded on naturalizing particular distinctions between nature and culture, idea and expression, raw material and innovation. Anchoring his argument in the orthodox language of efficiency, Boyle praised intellectual property's tradition of striking the proper balance between intellectual property and the public domain but argued that the Information Age had upset that balance.

Intellectual property policies could continue to promote innovation, he argued, if it returned to that balance.[43]

Poor people benefited from this approach to the extent that their contributions toward preserving the cultural environment were unrecognized in the past. At the same time, reifying the negative has the perverse effect of congealing poor people's knowledge as the *object* of property, the raw material from which real intellectual property is derived, and obscures its status as the *subject* of property, deserving of the label intellectual property in its own right.

We must consider how law's reification of the negative invents tradition rather than discovers it. The lines between the inputs and outputs of innovation are anything but static. At the end of the last century, we witnessed the migration of many forms of knowledge from the public domain to intellectual property: university research, business methods, and even life forms joined the realm of intellectual property. In truth, our intellectual property traditions are more complex than political campaigns for the public domain allow us to recognize. Viewed in this light, we may begin to see how the invention of traditional knowledge as perennially raw rather than cooked erects a false wall between modernity and tradition. Worse still, it deprives diverse peoples of the world of their humanity and cultural creativity. As the Indian eco-feminist and property theorist Vandana Shiva describes, biodiversity is not simply the bounty "of nature, guided by nothing but Providence." Far from it, "commons are resources shaped, managed and utilized through community control."[44] A quarter-century ago, William Cronon helped give birth to the environmental movement with a similar observation of the active role played by Native Americans in cultivating the New England environment, which colonists had deemed "natural." "One must not exaggerate the differences between English and Indian agricultures," Cronon wrote.[45] As Cronon explained, "[b]y making the arrival of the Europeans the center of our analysis, we run the risk of attributing all change to their agency, and none to the Indians. The implication is not only that the earlier world of 'Indian' New England was somehow static but also that the Indians themselves were as passive and 'natural' as the landscape."[46] Today, when law defines the contributions of the poor as nature rather than culture, the "creativity of both nature and other cultures is negated."[47] Boyle underlined "law and the *construction* of the Information Society."[48] Our understanding of information and knowledge is not preordained but involves political choices. Indeed, this is the insight of Shiva's own political act of defining as "biopiracy" the "patent claims over biodiversity and indigenous knowledge that are based on the *innovations, creativity and genius of the people of the Third World.*"[49] "Since a 'patent' is given for invention," she argues, "*a biopiracy patent denies the innovation embodied in indigenous knowledge.*"[50]

I do not claim that our ability to distinguish the inputs and outputs of innovation is entirely indeterminate. Nor do I advocate for a system of law that would shift continuously according to the changing political strength of either the rich or the poor in these matters. But I do call for legal decision-makers to recognize contingency, bias, and unreasoned orthodoxy in the legal definitions that begin to appear natural. Today we can see how constructing poor people's knowledge as raw materials supports a model of "benefit sharing," permitting local communities to perhaps receive some compensation from Western patents derived from those communities' resources. But this approach rewards the poor only as wardens, not also as cultivators. In some cases, when the poor's innovation is overlooked, benefit sharing may be "the equivalent of stealing a loaf of bread and then sharing the crumbs."[51]

A TRUER MODEL: THE POOR AS CULTIVATORS OF KNOWLEDGE
Today the poor seek to learn how to use the tools of intellectual property to recognize their own cultural and scientific contributions, not just those of the West. "Traditional knowledge" is continually being invented. In Mysore, India, the makers of internationally famous silk sarees have begun offering waterproof sarees. Inlaid marble designers in Agra, home of the Taj Mahal, who for years peddled "hackneyed tourist designs" to visitors, now apply their craft to create "stunning dinnerware" to be served in the finest Indian and Western homes.[52] Traditional people move, intermarry, share ideas, and modify their skills and products to respond to the shifting demands of the market and their culture. These activities are not merely strategic and pragmatic, but are evidence of a healthy and dynamic culture. In short, traditional knowledge is more vibrant and innovative than is acknowledged by the "environmentalism" metaphor, with its emphasis on conservation of nature's raw materials.

Debates over the protection of traditional knowledge, however, often fail to recognize its dynamic character. "Traditional knowledge" typically refers to knowledge handed down from generation to generation. This knowledge includes such forms of cultural expressions as songs, dances, stories, artworks, and crafts, as well as "symbols, marks, and other recurring expressions of traditional concepts."[53] Agricultural, scientific, and medical knowledge is also covered.[54] It is often believed that this knowledge has existed for millennia and, remarkably, that it has remained static over time. We are told that proper authorship cannot be determined because the knowledge has been passed down through an oral tradition and was not written down. Even if inscribed, we may not locate a single author; traditional knowledge is often communally held. Now mix in the historic conception of indigenous and third-world peoples as the anti-West: anti-commodification, anti-property, and anti-markets. The result is that, partly because of the difficulties of fitting poor people's knowledge into Western frameworks and partly because this knowledge is valued *as the opposite of property*, the creative knowledge of the poor, and their capacity for knowledge creation, are often overlooked. Instead, poor people's concerns are addressed by stimulating technology transfer, foreign direct investment, access to Western knowledge, and, at best, equitable benefit sharing. Much less attention is given to how law can tap the innovation and productive knowledge capacities of the poor.

This paradigm is beginning to change. A recent World Intellectual Property Organization (WIPO) report on traditional knowledge finds that, in fact, "much [traditional knowledge] is not ancient or inert, but is a vital, dynamic part of the contemporary lives of many communities today."[55] This finding should not be surprising. Many of the most ancient monuments survived because they remained in use. Traditional knowledge techniques also survive in this way, by continuously evolving as humans innovate around them to meet current needs and solve contemporary problems. Traditional knowledge, WIPO tells us, "is being created every day and evolves as individuals and communities respond to the challenges posed by their social environment. . . . *This contemporary aspect is further justification for legal protection.*"[56]

Return to the example of Mysore silk sarees. The "grand old queen" of Indian silk[57] has had a makeover since obtaining a geographical indication, updating its look with trendy new (but, interestingly, *natural*) colors— "lilac, ecru, coffee-brown and elephant-grey"—and with "contemporary" designs inspired by temple architecture and tribal jewelry.[58] Make no mistake: tradition is hard work. As an executive producer of Mysore silk sarees explained, revamping the designs without losing the sheen of the silk took "months of painstaking research and trials."[59]

Consider another example, closer to home. A San Francisco–based artist trained in the modernist textile tradition of Ray Eames received a felt rug from her Iranian-American husband, which he purchased in 1999 on his first trip back to Iran after the Revolution. The felt rug, the product of a seven-thousand-year-old tradition, inspired the designer to apply her contemporary paintings to the rugs themselves—a collaboration across cultures and generations. This was an idea that the Internet and the Creative Commons could not assist. Indeed, the couple embarked on a four-year journey across Iran to learn more about felt rug making, to find that only a few living felters remain, sprawled all over that country and unconnected to one another. The couple put the felters in touch with each other and established an Iranian factory that employed the best of their techniques, literally reviving an art on the verge of extinction and creating a profitable market for the rugs both within and beyond Iran.[60]

Tradition is cultivated, not discovered. The concept of traditional knowledge, too, is a modern invention. Those studying poor people's knowledge warn of the dangers of "overdrawing the distinction between [traditional knowledge] and modern knowledge."[61] In truth, "no one's life is entirely traditional, and no one's life is entirely modern."[62] Indeed, forcing ourselves to see the modern aspects of traditional knowledge also helps us to view more critically our own romantic notions of Western intellectual property as "new." As Boyle demonstrated so well, the line separating the public domain and intellectual property does not often involve the eureka discovery that the trope of the romantic author suggests.

Developing marketable uses for third-world cultural products is "ultimately perhaps the most effective way to protect their traditions."[63] Increasingly, third-world artisans recognize that "[e]xcept in a museum setting, no traditional craft skill can be sustained unless it has a viable market."[64] And recent activity suggests that many third-world craftspeople and artisans are more accepting of market strategies and practices than is generally acknowledged. We see again that commerce and culture are not necessarily at odds, as demonstrated by the revitalization of Iranian felt rug making by the introduction of global markets, a process that has encouraged preservation through commercialization. And vehicles like geographical indications help preserve geographical diversity.[65] Weavers, artisans, farmers, and the makers of handicrafts do not have to leave their skills or homes for city life. If properly identified, trained, and protected, they can remain at home while participating in a global industry.

In short, applying principles of intellectual property rights to poor people's knowledge will encourage third-world development, and not just in the defensive sense of resisting TRIPS.[66] Partly, the development interest here is economic, although it is unclear how much monetary value is at stake.[67] In 2000, handicrafts alone were estimated to generate nearly $3 billion in annual revenue.[68] The United Nations estimates that developing countries lose about $5 billion in royalties annually from the unauthorized use of traditional knowledge.[69] Poor people's turn to property is surely about economics, but it is about social and cultural values as well. These claims recognize that the relationship between intellectual property and development goes beyond GDP. People, rich and poor alike, want recognition of their creativity and of their contributions to science and culture. This capacity for innovation, work, and cultural sharing is part of what makes us human.

WIPO and TRIPS have focused on teaching the poor how to protect the intellectual property of the West. We need to turn our attention to helping the poor to use intellectual property to protect their own inventions as well. Only some of the people who hold traditional knowledge oppose the commodification of their knowledge on religious or cultural grounds; but *most* are poor, lacking in the infrastructure for production, and are ignorant of intellectual property laws and commercial knowledge of marketing and branding. Intellectual property ownership does not come naturally.

> In many cases . . . poor people's knowledge meets the standard
> of novelty that modern IP law demands. . . . The development
> dimension lies in helping poor people to master the commer-
> cial/legal tools needed to collect the value of their novelty. This
> is about entrepreneurship, about finding clever ways to repack-
> age traditional knowledge into products useful for consumers
> in mass markets, and about developing the capacity to produce
> and deliver these products in sufficient quantity and quality as
> to satisfy such markets.[70]

Increasingly, indigenous people and those in the third world seek "training on IP tools and how to use them."[71] The new Indian Geographical Indications Act offers an example. When the act became effective in 2003, few were aware of its implications. Nongovernmental organizations thus embarked on extensive campaigns to educate local farmers and artisans about geographical indications (GIs).[72]

The TRIPS agreement offers a foundation for international recognition of GIs. It defines GIs as "indications which identify a good as originating in the territory of a Member . . . where a given quality, reputation, or other characteristic of the good is essentially attributable to its geographical origin."[73] "Champagne," "Tequila," and "Roquefort" are examples of the types of goods recognized as GIs. Under TRIPS, member states must provide legal means to prevent uses of a designated GI that either mislead the public as to the geographical origin of the good or constitute "unfair competition" under Article 10bis of the Paris Convention.[74] In addition, TRIPS Article 23 mandates that further protection be extended to GIs for "wines and spirits,"[75] which must be protected even in the absence of consumer confusion.[76]

Two-tiered protection—a higher level of protection for wines and spirits and a lower one for everything else—has been a source of continuing conflict between Europe and the developing world.[77] The conflict is due in part to a perceived inequity in the current TRIPS system, and in part to the fact that GIs are considered to be where much of the wealth of poor people lies: in local production methods and cultural goods, from Darjeeling tea to Mysore silk to basmati rice.[78] The patent provisions of TRIPS have posed clear challenges for developing countries, which typically lack capital for R&D-intensive breakthroughs or manufacturing capacity. GIs, in contrast, are hailed as the poor people's intellectual property rights, tools for ensuring recognition of the knowledge of weavers, farmers, and craftspeople rather than just the high-technology contributions of multinational corporations. The structure of GIs does make them particularly suited to poor people's knowledge. First, GIs recognize collective intellectual property rights; under the Indian GI Act, multiple associations of artisans may be recognized as the authorized producers or users of a GI.[79] GI applications are also relatively cheap, at least for a group of artisans working together. Under the GI Act, it costs a modest five thousand rupees (a little more than $100) to apply.[80]

Although GIs certainly hold promise for the poor, they have limits. The Indian GI Act protects only those goods or processes whose quality or reputation is shown to be "due exclusively or essentially to the geographical environment, with its inherent natural and human factors."[81] GI applications require "proof of origin" and a "historical record"[82] of continuous use of the goods or process. Registrants obtain the exclusive right to use the GI,[83] and licensing of GIs is prohibited.[84]

Such requirements and restrictions take a narrow view of traditional knowledge, linking culture to land. The rule against alienability poses special concerns. Even if this approach may enable people to *remain* within their communities (and preserve the physical environment, as well), what if they move? What rights do traditional weavers from Mysore have if they move to North India—or the United Kingdom?[85] Of course, there are good reasons to prevent the alienation of the GI from the particular geographical community. It prevents the scenario in which a large foreign corporation hires a member of that community away and then begins to produce "authentic" work elsewhere, using that GI—and decimating the livelihoods of the traditional community left behind. At the same time, such a restriction could stifle opportunities for individuals who remain within a traditional community not by choice, but because of economic necessity. People move, intermarry, and change jobs. Culture flows with them. The GI Act does not recognize this dynamic nature of culture; instead it ossifies authentic production in *today's* localities.

Within a recognized "association," traditional leaders may impose their will on members, reifying traditional hierarchies.[86] Elizabeth Povinelli notes that cultural rights often lead to the ironic production of authenticity or indigeneity, which conforms to traditional structures from the past, rather than celebrating cultures as diachronic peoples who are dynamic and heterogeneous.[87]

The GIs also pose economic concerns. While GIs protect Darjeeling tea, for example, they also prohibit the Indian manufacture of Scotch whiskey, driving up the cost of Scotch in India. It is possible that the poor may reap greater economic rewards in a system with fewer production constraints.[88] Boyle's concern about the public domain also applies; at which point does too much intellectual property impede the very processes of cultural sharing and innovation that law ought to promote, especially to aid the little guy in cultural production? These economic concerns raise an important question of liberal strategy. As critical legal theorists have aptly warned, we must stand ready to openly question when and how "rights" might work to the disadvantage of the poor rather than to the poor's benefit.[89]

These concerns notwithstanding, GIs do potentially offer a range of benefits, from recognizing the innovation of collectives, to preserving geographic diversity and stimulating some redistribution of wealth. It may be more important to think of GIs as part of a larger framework in which the poor learn the secrets of Madison Avenue. If one simply produces goods, then any successful product will eventually draw stiff competition from global mass production. But creating a protected *brand* allows one to stave off complete usurpation by mass-produced substitutes. The GI Act works on this principle. It rewards the local community for having created a valued reputation and protects that reputation from the forces of global commerce. It recognizes that consumers everywhere seek authentic products and that they may care about *who* produces something, not just the ultimate product.[90] Fair Trade coffee, Rugmark carpets, and dolphin-safe tuna, for example, appeal to people's desire to consume free from the worry about exploitation in the process of production. In response to the commercialization of ghetto style by white-owned fashion houses, one African American company declares to the consumer its ghetto roots by branding itself "FUBU"—For Us, By Us. Such authenticity marks translate into profits in the marketplace.

The goal is "to help poor people get along in the modern world—to use modern instruments for managing the ownership of knowledge either to collect on the commercial value of that knowledge or to prevent its use in a way that its owners consider inappropriate."[91] New organizations such as Light Years IP are emerging to address this need, specializing in marketing and branding a developing country's intellectual property.[92]

The Danish artists' collective Superflex has pioneered this strategy. The Superflex "Supercopy" art collaboration employs what it calls a "counter-economic strategy" to teach local farmers in the third world how to convert their biodiversity and traditional knowledge into branded end products that can eventually compete with the products of global multinationals. In one ongoing collaboration, Superflex works with a farmers' cooperative in Maués, Brazil. This region in the Amazon is famous for cultivating the guarana berry, prized by the local population for its perceived medicinal and energy-giving properties. The Dutch multinational Ambev and Pepsi Co. have successfully marketed global energy drinks derived from this plant, most notably Ambev's "Antarctica" drink. The local Maués farmers complained that the multinationals have formed a cartel, driving down the price of the guarana berries from $25/kilo to $4/kilo. So the cooperative is fighting back. In collaboration with Super-flex, farmers held brainstorming sessions to begin developing their own product and designing a label for it. One member, for example, suggested a coffee drink called Maués Café, evoking the internationally popular Nescafé drink.

Eventually, the cooperative decided to manufacture and distribute a soft drink: Guaraná Power. Members designed a label for the drink, which comprises a photograph of local farmers affixed atop the familiar Antarctica label. Guaraná Power's marketing slogan? "[O]riginal Maués guarana for energy and empowerment."

The Superflex collaboration turns on a simple idea: empowerment for the poor will entail their learning how to control and market their own knowledge products. In the words of Superflex (appropriated from Ani DiFranco): "Every tool is a weapon if you hold it right."[93] The Maués collective spoke with lawyers about intellectual property rights, raised capital, paired with a production company in Denmark, and searched for global distributors for Guaraná Power.[94] Superflex's Guaraná Power gallery floor reproduces the shop floor, taking visitors on a journey from producing to bottling, labeling, refrigerating, and tasting Guaraná Power.

The poor must be recognized as both receivers and producers of knowledge. Failing to promote poor people's capacity for creative work and their participation in global culture and commercial markets hinders development as freedom. As Sen writes, "the rejection of the freedom to participate in the labor market is one of the ways of keeping people in bondage and captivity."[95] In the Knowledge Age, wealth lies not simply in access to other people's knowledge (although this is certainly important), but also in the ability to produce new knowledge and to benefit from this creation, culturally and economically.

CHAPTER SIX

Bollywood/Hollywood

IN MAY 1967 THE ACCLAIMED Indian director of *The Apu Trilogy*, Satyajit Ray, received a "joyous carillon of a cable"[1] from Hollywood: Columbia Pictures would back *The Alien*. Ray would have a free hand. Both Marlon Brando and Steve McQueen were keen to play a leading role. Saul Bass would mastermind the special effects.[2] And what luck—Peter Sellers was in Hollywood at that very moment, playing an Indian in a comedy, and was anxious to meet Ray for the second time to discuss playing the Indian philanthropist in the film. As Ray later wrote, "With the hum of the machinery in my ears, I arrived in Hollywood on June 1."[3]

By 1967, Satyajit Ray was already widely considered a genius filmmaker and the "father of Indian cinema."[4] His films, rooted in the lives of Bengalis in post-Independence India and filmed in the Bengali language, depict ordinary lives: children fated to die of poverty, women trapped in subservient familial roles, a new generation of middle-class Indians seeking liberation from their elders and the traditions of the past. In his first feature film, *Pather Panchali,*[5] Ray brilliantly directed impoverished Bengali villagers living in the rural countryside in the 1920s. In the film a wrinkled old woman brushes her teeth with her fingers and spits outside the house door; the main character, a young girl named Durga, succumbs to illness because of the family's poverty. The acuity with which Ray cap-tures their humanity is lyrical. Countless filmmakers around the world fondly recall their first viewing of the film.

Needless to say, Ray's films (some thirty-seven in all) bore little resemblance to the grandeur of Hollywood cinema—or, for that matter, to the glitzy, upper-middle-class escapades glorified by escapist Bollywood films. But a chance correspondence between Ray and his friend Arthur C. Clarke, the British science-fiction writer and author of *2001: A Space Odyssey*, put Ray on a fateful journey across the Atlantic in the hopes of partnering with Hollywood to create his first science-fiction film. The film was to be called *The Alien*.[6] The screenplay would be based on a short science-fiction story titled "Bankubabur Bandhu" (translated as "Banku's friend") that Ray had written in Bengali for his family magazine, *Sandesh*, a few years earlier. For most films Ray would not even have considered American backing—but a science-fiction film like *The Alien* would require special effects that Indians could not afford. Indeed, to this day Bollywood avoids the genre because of prohibitive costs. Ray's story revolved around a spaceship that lands in a pond on the outskirts of a Bengali village. Locals begin worshipping it as a temple, which they think has risen from the Earth. The alien befriends a young village boy named Haba, and the story is largely about their friendship, and about the humorous pranks the alien plays on the local villagers, from reviving a farmer's dying crops to pestering a mean farmer by ripening his mango tree out of season.

Fascinated with Ray's idea, Clarke put him in touch with an American friend living in Sri Lanka, Mike Wilson. (Clarke was living in Sri Lanka at the time, as he did for most of his life.) Wilson had just written, directed, and produced a film about a Sri Lankan secret agent—unabashedly named James Banda (this should have been a warning sign to Ray). Wilson took a keen interest in Ray's idea and swiftly flew out to Calcutta, where he propped himself in the renowned director's apartment for two weeks until Ray finished a script. Wilson flew the script to Hollywood and pressed Columbia Pictures to take up the project. By then Ray had become uncomfortable with Wilson's aggressive partnering. Ray traveled to Hollywood in 1967 to discuss the project with Columbia Pictures, but his high hopes were quickly deflated. For starters, mimeographed copies of *The Alien* script were floating around the Columbia Pictures offices emblazoned with the legend "Copyright Mike Wilson and Satyajit Ray."

When Ray confronted Wilson, Wilson insisted that he had put himself on the copyright to protect Ray's interests. Later, Columbia Pictures asked Ray whether he had received any of the $10,000 advance they had given to Wilson for them to share—Ray had not. The relationship between Ray and Wilson further deteriorated, and Columbia Pictures never made the film.

Still, Ray had not completely ruled out *The Alien* project when, in 1982, Steven Spielberg's *E.T.: The Extraterrestrial*[7] premiered. The film, which began as a Columbia Pictures project, bore a striking resemblance to *The Alien*. Most telling, in Ray's words, was that the alien is "small and acceptable to children and possessed of certain superhuman powers—not physical strength but other kinds of powers, particular types of vision, and that it takes an interest in earthly things."[8] Both Ray's and Spielberg's aliens "had a sense of humor, a sense of fun, a mischievous quality. I think mine was a whimsy,"[9] said Ray. Ray's friend, Arthur C. Clarke, also immediately saw the resemblance between the two films, and he urged Ray to write to Spielberg and point out the similarities. "Don't take it lying down," Clarke advised. But while Ray did later say that "*E.T.* would not have been possible without my script of *The Alien* being available throughout America in mimeographed copies,"[10] he did not pursue the matter further. *E.T.*'s release deepened Ray's dismay over the culture of Hollywood. Spielberg himself later denied any suggestion of plagiarism, saying he was in high school when the script had first been circulated in Hollywood. But that is not quite accurate—Spielberg graduated from high school in 1965, and by 1967 (when Ray visited Hollywood) Spielberg was already working in Hollywood, to the extent that he released a short film in 1968 through Universal Studios. By 1969, Spielberg was the youngest director at a major Hollywood studio.[11]

THE BLACK ATLANTIC

As part of his "Black Atlantic" thesis, Paul Gilroy observed how musical influences flowed across the African diaspora. In this chapter, I consider transnational cultural flows influencing films from Bollywood to Hollywood. Just as Gilroy celebrated "the inescapable hybridity and intermixture of ideas"[12] with respect to literary and musical works, so too should we embrace—descriptively and prescriptively—the transcultural flow of ideas regarding the stories we tell in the movies. This chapter flatly rejects those notions of cultural purity and essentialism that would forbid ideas from flowing from East to West, and vice versa. In so doing I adopt an explicitly transcultural and intercultural perspective. Culture will and must be shared widely and freely both across borders and within them.

But in this chapter I consider another view of the black Atlantic, focusing on claims of copyright piracy and exploitation that lurk in the shadows of global cultural exchanges. Simply put, free flows of culture are not always fair flows of culture. Global cultural changes take place against a backdrop of sharp differentials in power and knowledge, which affect the way authors are recognized and rewarded. In this chapter I seek to highlight how global inequalities combined with long-standing cultural biases may impede the free *and fair* exchange of culture.

It is by now a commonplace observation in copyright scholarship that all creativity is derivative. Yet romantic notions of authorship and originality continue to have a strong hold on the imagination. The flip side is also true: the dramatic image of copyright pirates brashly ripping off the masterworks of original creators is equally alluring. One thesis of this chapter is that *cultural stereotypes help feed the myth of the romantic author,* on the one hand, *and that of the inglorious pirate,* on the other. Cultural biases buttress the strong copyright claims of some creators—primarily those in the West who are seen as "creative" and "original"—and undermine claims for cultural dynamism and borrowing made by other creators—primarily those in Asian developing countries, which are thought to breed cultures of slavish imitation and obedience to tradition. These myths mask the underlying dynamic nature of innovation, which relies on transcultural flows of knowledge. More insidiously, these stereotypes help to mask exploitation of the weak by the strong.

One goal of this chapter is to flip some common perceptions about the world's innovators and pirates. A recent spate of copyright suits by Hollywood against Bollywood sounds a familiar theme, denouncing Asians as imitators and accusing them of ruthlessly copying film plots and lifting scenes from American hits such as *Mrs. Doubtfire* and *My Cousin Vinny.*[13] But claims of cultural appropriation go back far, and travel in multiple directions. As we have seen, even the revered American director Stephen Spielberg has been accused of lifting *E.T.* from Satyajit Ray's 1962 script for *The Alien.* Later in this chapter I will recount how Disney's

The Lion King bears striking similarities to the Japanese anime television series *Kimba the White Lion,* directed by Japan's master animator, Osamu Tezuka.[14]

Neither Ray nor Tezuka sued the American filmmakers—and this chapter is by no means an effort to revive any legal case. This is not a brief. Rather, my task is to consider copyright's role in promoting free and fair cultural exchange within a global marketplace of ideas that is marked by sharp differentials in power, wealth, and knowledge. The problem in the cases I will recount is not that ideas and expression flow across state lines. To the contrary, copyright law ought to promote cultural exchange, not stymie it. Yet a free culture ought also to be a fair culture, in which people around the world are fairly recognized and remunerated for their protectable work. In this chapter I show how cultural stereotypes combined with actual inequalities across cultures often thwart mutual recognition of diverse authors and their contributions to our shared culture. In so doing, this chapter considers some of copyright's blind spots to differences in global power, and law's assumptions about culture and authorship.

I first consider the romantic authorial claims of a prime mover in Hollywood: Disney. While Disney has come to stand for the romantic author deserving of near perpetual copyright protection, in fact this animation giant grew by appropriating the master works of others, from Hugo to Kipling, which quickly fell into the public domain when copyright terms were shorter. In other instances, Disney may have flat-out stolen the copyrighted works of foreign authors.[15] Cultural stereotypes of the Western creator as an "original genius" help to mask Disney's own cultural borrowings and appropriations.

In stark contrast, Bollywood filmmakers are frequently charged as brashly pirating the screenplays of their Hollywood counterparts. I suggest, however, that while Hollywood films certainly influence the plot of a number of Bollywood films, many Bollywood films are original, and those that do appropriate are far from simple copies. In short, culture does not accurately tell us who is innovative and who is uninspired. At the same time, culture does play a part in explaining how and why people appropriate others' cultural works. Cultural appropriation helps to understand the life of another; putting oneself in another's shoes reveals both what makes us similar and how we stand apart.

Animating this chapter is an understanding of copyright in broader terms than the traditional, narrow vision of law as merely a tool for incentivizing the innovation of cultural products. Copyright is far more than that. Copyright governs the creation, distribution, and participation in culture and art, which John Dewey memorably described as "the most effective mode of communication that exists."[16] Critics today are appropriately questioning the narrow economic incentive thesis, exploring the plural motivations that spur creativity.[17] In this book, I have argued that the very essence of culture is sharing meaning with others and promoting mutual understanding. Consequently, we must take *participation* in cultural production more seriously, so that our law will not just incentivize the production of more cultural goods, but also promote global participation in making our cultural world, from music to film to stories.

Cultural pluralism—a global culture in which all peoples have an opportunity to be creative authors of their own lives and of our world— is both an end in itself, and a means to economic development in the Knowledge Age. Cultural pluralism is an end of freedom in the sense that making and sharing meaning with others—from singing together to recounting stories—is fundamentally what human freedom is *for*. The cultural sphere of life encompasses those joys and relationships that make a human life truly worth living.[18] At the same time, participation in cultural production today has significant social and economic effects. Promoting the recognition of diverse authors and creators of cultural works fosters dignity and respect for others as creative intellectuals and as fellow human beings with worthy stories to tell. What's more, in today's Knowledge Age, substantial revenues flow from the production and control of cultural goods exchanged through global markets. Finally, cultural pluralism promotes mutual understanding through cultural exchanges. As Dewey eloquently put it, "The art characteristic of a civilization is the means for entering sympathetically into the deepest elements in the experience of remote and foreign civilizations."[19] Today, the arts remain central to the project of fostering mutual understanding of and sympathy for others. The 2008 Academy Award–winning film *Slumdog Millionaire*[20] put people around the world into the shoes of three impoverished and orphaned children born in the slums of Bombay. Literature and films help convey tragedy through comedy, humanize those born on far sides of the Earth, and reveal what is common in our sentiments and aspirations. As Martha Nussbaum writes, "We do not automatically see another human being as spacious and deep, having thoughts, spiritual longings, and emotions. It is all too easy to see another person as just a body—which we might then think we can use for our ends, bad or good. It is an achievement to see a soul in that body, and this achievement is supported by poetry and the arts, which ask us to wonder about the inner world of that shape we see—and, too, to wonder about ourselves and our own depths."[21]

Martin Scorsese, for example, recounts seeing Satyajit Ray's film *Pather Panchali* in New York City in the early 1960s: "I was 18 or 19 years old and had grown up in a very parochial society of Italian-Americans and yet I was deeply moved by what Ray showed of people so far from my own experience." Scorsese "was very taken by the style of these films—at first so much like the Italian neo-realist films, yet surprising the viewer with bursts of sheer poetry."[22] Scorsese later helped convince the Academy of Motion Picture Arts and Sciences to award Ray an honorary Oscar. The Academy finally did give Ray the honor, in 1991, just before his death at the age of seventy.[23] Ray called the Oscar "the best achievement of my movie-making career,"[24] equating it with a Nobel Prize for filmmakers. What most touched Ray is that audiences and critics worlds apart could appreciate his art. "The most distinctive feature [of my films]," said Ray, "is that they are deeply rooted in Bengal, in Bengali culture, mannerisms, and mores. What makes them universal in appeal is that they are about human beings."[25]

And yet, much art today is not so transcendent. Hollywood is criticized as being all too parochial in its choice of subjects. Worse still, at the dawn of the twenty-first century, there is still too much art that demonizes rather than humanizes the other. Heroes are white and villains are black, Asian, or Middle Eastern. Women are objects, not subjects, still largely seen as the ultimate trophy in a contest among male protagonists. Bollywood fares no better. Often these films depict women as being pure as the Goddess Sita, long-suffering and sexually objectified (wet saree scenes are abundant).[26] Such problems are not limited to popular culture. Even great literature is rife with gross imbalances and, indeed, racist mischaracterizations, as we learned with Margaret Mitchell's *Gone with the Wind*.[27] In short, art can insult, mischaracterize, colonize, and provoke misunderstanding.

Copyright relations, too, can upend cultural production and further the divide between East and West, North and South, rich and poor. That is, copyright can help to promote either recognition or misrecognition of global others. The special effects that Satyajit Ray, one of the greatest film-makers of all time, sought to include in his science-fiction film were out of reach of Indian production budgets; he needed a Hollywood partner. Yet his encounter ultimately led to disappointment. Indeed, the exploitation of Ray's copyright from the beginning of the project dissuaded him from becoming involved in the project altogether. Poor copyright relations meant Ray's film never got made.

There is a connection between the depiction of Indians in Hollywood films at the time and Hollywood's treatment of Ray himself. Ironically, on Ray's visit to Hollywood in 1967, Peter Sellers invited Ray to watch him on the set, where he was playing "an Indian in a Hollywood setting" in the film *The Party.*[28] Indeed, Ray had initially tapped Sellers for *The Alien*[29] because he had seen Sellers play an Indian before, in *The Millionairess.*[30] A Hollywood-financed movie would need a big-name actor like Sellers to seal the deal, and Sellers was keen to play a role in *The Alien,* telling Ray that a fortuneteller had told him to take the part; it was "fate."

Yet Sellers evinced a great naiveté about his own role in perpetuating negative stereotypes of Indians abroad. Watching Sellers filming *The Party,* Ray began to question Sellers's judgment. As Ray recounts, he witnessed "quite the most tasteless, heavy-handed caricature of an Indian ever put on the screen."[31] "I was so disgusted that I would in any case have found it most difficult to work with him,"[32] Ray later said of Sellers. A year later Ray watched a screening of *The Party* while on tour in Sydney and took Sellers's depiction as a personal insult. In *The Party,* Sellers plays a two-bit Bollywood actor who is mistakenly invited to an A-list Hollywood party. At the party, the Indian ogles a big-breasted blonde; she takes a fancy to him and invites him home. But standing at the door of her apartment, he declines to enter.[33] Ray recounts the film's end: "I'm sorry," says Bakshi to the girl who has taken a fancy to him and has asked him into her flat. "I'm sorry, but I must go back to my monkey." "Monkey!" "Yes. My pet monkey, Apu."[34] Ray believed the name of the monkey, Apu, was not mere coincidence (Ray's celebrated troika of films chronicling the life of one boy, beginning with *Pather Panchali,*[35] is called *The Apu Trilogy*). His Hollywood experience, Ray later wrote in a letter, was "the beginning of a period of profound uneasiness. . . . I was too *deeply* disturbed, and for another—I was in a strange sort of way *fascinated* by the sinister turn of events and waited to see which way and how far it would go."[36]

HOLLYWOOD

Examples of global cultural borrowing and appropriation abound. Consider the classic case of the romanticized "author"—Disney. Disney's mega-hit animated film *The Lion King*[37] has earned over a billion dollars thus far and is one of the most beloved animated films in the Disney canon. *The Lion King* musical won several Tony awards and is one of the longest-running shows on Broadway. What is far less known, however, is that the film has been beset by allegations of piracy from global creators. As we have already seen, recently Disney paid a hefty settlement to the heirs of Solomon Linda, the late South African musician who composed the film's musical hit, "The Lion Sleeps Tonight" (originally titled "Mbube") in 1939. Linda and his family received virtually nothing for the song until a *Rolling Stone* journalist revealed the song's origins in 2000, together with the sordid history of exploitation of Linda's copyright across the "Black Atlantic," from Africa to the United Kingdom to the United States.[38]

But charges of plagiarism had been leveled at Disney well before the Linda family's suit. On the heels of the film's release in 1994, well-known Japanese manga (comic) artists and fans organized public protests against *The Lion King*, which bears a striking resemblance to the popular television series *Kimba the White Lion*[39] by the master Japanese animator Osamu Tezuka.[40] Tezuka has long been hailed as the father of Japanese anime and the "Walt Disney of Japan." His well-known anime series *Kimba the White Lion*, based on his manga serial *Jungle Emperor*[41] of the early 1950s, aired as the first color animated television series in Japan in the early 1960s and circulated widely among animation buffs internationally. English and Spanish versions of the series were created in 1966, and *Kimba the White Lion* was aired as a syndicated program by NBC in the United States for more than a decade.[42] (Other Japanese anime programs on American television at that time include *Speed Racer* and Tezuka's own *Astro Boy*, which aired in primetime on NBC.[43]) Tezuka reportedly spent a year researching Africa before penning *Jungle Emperor*, which he considered his crowning achievement.[44] As one scholar writes, "There is not a single Japanese who does not know Tezuka and *Jungle Emperor*."[45]

(The claim may not be overblown: comics penetrate more broadly in Japan than in the West. It is frequently said that everyone reads comics in Japan.[46]) Tezuka's own admiration for Disney had been great, so much so that upon hearing the allegations that creators of *The Lion King* had copied from Tezuka, the president of Tezuka Productions said the revered Japanese artist would have been flattered if that were the case.[47] (Tezuka died in 1989, before *The Lion King* was made.)

Devotees of Tezuka are less sanguine about the similarities, which are abundant:[48]

- The basic story plot and setting are the same: an African emperor lion dies early, leaving a young cub. The son struggles with himself over his responsibilities to lead the animal kingdom. The son eventually returns from exile and overthrows the evil lion who has usurped power in the son's absence.
- Nearly every animal character in *Kimba the White Lion* has an analogue in *The Lion King*. For example, in both versions a baboon serves as an old sage, the henchmen for the evil lion are hyenas, and the hero lion's adviser is a parrot.
- The evil lion in *Jungle Emperor*, "Claw," is blind in one eye; the evil lion in *The Lion King*, "Scar," has a scar across one eye.[49]
- In both stories the lion cub doubts his ability to lead his people and his father comes to him as a vision in the moon to embolden him.
- The names of the leading lion cubs are similar—Kimba and Simba.
- Both lion cubs eventually grow up and mate with their childhood playmate, a lioness cub.
- The setting of the film and the television series is similar—a rocky terrain, not the more common desert habitat that lions roam.
- Both Kimba and Simba become vegetarian and eat insects to help save the other animals.
- A stampede scene during the lion cubs' early years is a pivotal moment in the cubs' lives.
- In both the TV series and the later film, a lightning bolt starts a forest fire and rain puts it out.

• Most importantly, there are several scenes of nearly identical cine-
  matic and artistic expression in the films.[50]

The similarities even inspired a *Simpsons* parody of *The Lion King*'s Mu-
fasa, which appears in a cloud and says to Lisa, "You must avenge my
Death Kimba . . . I mean Simba!"[51]

To be sure, there are differences between the *Kimba* series and *The
Lion King*. Most notably, humans played a significant role in the *Kimba*
story, which considered the benefits of human civilization over the law
of the jungle. Indeed, just as Ray's original *The Alien* was inspired by the
Bengal famine of 1943, *Jungle Emperor* had a particularly local focus on
the costs and benefits to Japan of modernization and Westernization. *The
Lion King*, in contrast, has no humans or similar themes. Nonetheless,
observers call the similarities "striking."[52] The *San Francisco Chronicle*
reported that Tezuka Productions had "received calls of congratulations
from several people who assumed the firm had licensed the project to
Disney."[53] In 1994, Machiko Satonaka, a well-known Japanese comic artist,
published in a major Japanese daily newspaper an open letter signed by
two hundred Japanese animation artists, who claimed that "[s]imilarities
between *The Lion King* and *Jungle Emperor* cannot be dismissed as mere
coincidence," and that as Japanese who respect Walt Disney, they were
"saddened by such similarities."[54] To the outrage of Tezuka fans, Disney
not only denied lifting any of the plot or characters from *Jungle Emperor*
or *Kimba*, but went even further, claiming not to have even heard of
Tezuka or *Kimba the White Lion*. "Frankly, I'm not familiar with [the
TV series]," stated Rob Minkoff, co-director of *The Lion King* with Roger
Allers, in response to the allegations.[55] Fans in Japan and the United
States were angry, not at Disney's being inspired by Tezuka's work, but by
Disney's failure to acknowledge Tezuka and his influence. To make matters worse, *The Lion King* was billed as the first Disney animated feature
that presented an *original* story.[56] Former Disney studio chair (now CEO
of Dreamworks Animation) Jeffrey Katzenberg called the film Disney's
"first cartoon feature not based on a fable or a literary work."[57] The film's
creators say the story was inspired by Joseph and Moses in the Bible and
Shakespeare's *Hamlet*.[58]

Animation experts and historians have argued that Disney's claim
of ignorance of Tezuka is likely disingenuous, given the prevalence of

the master animator's work in the United States from the late 1960s on and the frequency of Disney's own executives' travel to Japan, including to Tokyo Disneyland.[59] *The Lion King*'s co-director Roger Allers himself lived in Tokyo and worked in animation there in the 1980s, during which time Tezuka was alive and already well known as "Japan's Walt Disney." A remake of *Jungle Emperor* aired in prime time on Japanese television contemporaneously.[60] Alternatively, some argue that Disney's purported ignorance of Tezuka at the very least undermines its claims of superior knowledge of all things animation.[61] Anime historian Fred Patten concludes that at least some people working on *The Lion King* knew about *Kimba the White Lion*.[62] Patten surmises that these animators either subconsciously copied, or paid silent homage to, Tezuka's work with in-group references to it in *The Lion King*.[63]

Few stories of artistic inspiration and cultural appropriation are simple or unidirectional. Tezuka, who died in 1989 at the age of sixty, met Walt Disney and describes his own artistic debt to Disney in his autobiography. Tezuka describes the arrival of *Bambi*[64] to Japan after World War II, and admits traveling from Osaka to Tokyo and staying in a hotel near the theater so he could see *Bambi* "over one hundred times."[65] Subsequently Tezuka licensed the rights to Disney's *Bambi* to make his own adaptation. At a comics festival in Los Angeles in 1978, Tezuka described *Jungle Emperor* as both an homage and a critique of *Bambi*, which Tezuka believed did not sufficiently consider the possibility of mutual recognition between animals and humans.[66] Perhaps, then, similarities between *Kimba the White Lion* and *The Lion King* derive from their both being based on Disney's own *Bambi*[67] (hence the similarities to Tezuka's work may reflect the "circle of creativity"). Two or more original works may have much in common because each borrows from the same works in the public domain. In this case, both *Kimba the White Lion* and *The Lion King* have their source in *Bambi*, common folktales, and the story of *Hamlet*. In short, as in so many other cases, the search for authorship of *The Lion King* may resemble a vain "search for the source of the Nile and all its tributaries."[68]

Notably, in all three cases—*The Alien, Kimba the White Lion,* and "The Lion Sleeps Tonight"—new works in the United States appear to have been derived not from the work of unknown foreign artists, but from the artistic expressions of great masters: Ray, Tezuka, and Linda, respectively.

Ray was already an internationally recognized and award-winning film director by the time he made the acquaintance of Hollywood. Tezuka, the creator of yet another well-known anime classic, *Astro Boy* (recently remade by Hollywood in 2009), created Japan's first television animation studio in 1961[69] and is often referred to as the "Godfather of Anime," as well as "Japan's Walt Disney." The creator of more than seventy titles and 150,000 pages during his lifetime, Tezuka was the subject of a retrospective at the Asian Art Museum of San Francisco in 2007 (the first ever such exhibit outside of Japan), titled *Tezuka: The Marvel of Manga*.[70] And Linda's original composition, "Mbube," was recorded and had become Africa's first pop hit.[71]

These stories resemble the case in which Italian director Sergio Leone took in broad daylight the copyrighted work of Japanese filmmaker Akira Kurosawa, another great auteur of the twentieth century (Kurosawa, too, received an Oscar for lifetime achievement).[72] Kurosawa's films document well the mutual influence of global artists. Kurosawa himself was highly influenced by the American Westerns of John Ford, as well as the literature of Shakespeare and Dostoevsky. In offering his own perspective on the Western in films like *Seven Samurai* and *Yojimbo,* Kurosawa transformed the genre. Yul Brynner, who starred in the Hollywood adaptation of *Seven Samurai*,[73] *The Magnificent Seven*,[74] identified *Seven Samurai* as "one of the great Westerns of all time, only it was made by the Japanese, in the Japanese medium."[75] Many sought permission to remake Kurosawa's works, but when Leone copied *Yojimbo*[76] and remade it as *A Fistful of Dollars*[77] without permission, Kurosawa protested. In a letter to Leone, Kurosawa wrote of *A Fistful of Dollars,* "It is a very fine film, but it is my film. Since Japan is a signatory of the Berne Convention on international copyright, you must pay me." An out-of-court settlement determined that Kurosawa would receive 15 percent of *Fistful*'s worldwide receipts, with a guarantee of around $100,000.[78] Ironically, the reworking of the American Western by a Japanese director not only recast the Western itself, but also inspired the creation of another genre, the "Spaghetti Western," for which Leone is most well-known. Furthermore, some remakes such as *The Magnificent Seven* and *A Fistful of Dollars* became iconic films themselves and made stars of actors like Steve McQueen and Clint Eastwood, both of whom became icons of American manliness.

There are many charges that Bollywood has appropriated Hollywood hits in broad daylight—what one observer wryly describes as "(re)making hay while the sun shines."[79] But examples of allegations against Hollywood for similar activity are less familiar. What about our conceptions of originality and romantic authorship leads us to more easily view some cultures as creative and original, and others as appropriators and copiers? Disney has long been considered the epitome of the romantic author: a wholly "original" genius. But the world's most famous copyright owner has often made a fortune by mining the works of past creators that have passed into the public domain. "There would hardly be a Disney at all if not for the works by Rudyard Kipling, H. C. Andersen, Victor Hugo, and Robert Louis Stevenson, all of whom make it possible for Disney to make animated features of wolf-boys, mermaids, hunchbacks, and Long John Silver,"[80] Eva Hemmungs Wirtén reminds us. Wirtén criticizes Disney's hypocrisy for benefiting from iconic works that quickly fell into the public domain under old copyright laws with short copyright terms, while holding its own works tightly and nearly into perpetuity. If current law had governed when Disney made *The Jungle Book*,[81] the corporation would have had to either wait another forty years before releasing the film or negotiate permission from Kipling's heirs.[82]

My point is not that Disney erred in producing new works based on the old. To the contrary, this is a natural part of the creative process and should be encouraged. Enabling individuals in the present to interact with cultures of the past leads to rich rewards for all cultures, ranging from fostering communities with shared values to allowing current generations to critically reconsider the values of the past. At the same time, we ought to reconsider biases in our understanding that lead us to more readily recognize some creators as original thinkers and others as slavish imitators. Walt Disney and the Disney Corporation have been romantically embraced as epitomizing creativity and originality. Yet some have accused Disney of plagiarism, not of works in the public domain, but of foreign copyrighted work. Furthermore, we ought to pause and consider how cultural stereotypes may lead copyright law to misrecognize altogether some "foreign" authors whose contributions to world culture are more readily ignored—or at least not granted attribution and royalties.

How do differences in power and knowledge affect people's willingness to share culture? Global inequalities render some more vulnerable to exploitation of their rights. Fear of exploitation may discourage people from sharing and distributing their knowledge, be it music and literature or local knowledge of the medicinal properties of plants. The University of California, Berkeley, historian of science Abena Dove Osseo-Asare documents how those with knowledge of traditional medicine in Ghana, for example, have kept that knowledge close for fear of being exploited.[83] Modern global copyright law must confront this reality of difference in the world and explore creative legal tools that would incentivize people to share across cultures, class divides, and colonial histories. Promoting fairness among global creators makes for good innovation policy, fosters free speech, and encourages better cultural and social relations. Modern intellectual property law ought to be attentive to crafting rules that promote the ethical extraction of knowledge. In our global Knowledge Economy, both economic and human development depend on fair cultural exchanges in global markets.

Considerations of global justice and fairness may shed light on our traditional understanding of incentives themselves within copyright law. We have come to believe that property rights in intellectual creations are there simply because they incentivize creative activity. But there is an older understanding that flows out of notions of unfair competition and more visceral feelings of justice. It is now commonplace that in fact people create without exclusive property rights—as evidenced by open-source software, fan fiction, and user-created mash-ups. But behavioral economists have identified a natural sense of justice that may lead people to "irrational" decisions if they feel that they are being treated unfairly.[84] Even the premise of the "intellectual property as incentives" thesis can be understood as responding to the "vulnerability" of the creator in the absence of intellectual property rights, given the often high costs of production and the typically low costs of copying.[85] Studies show it is not necessarily true that individuals will refuse to create without incentives, but it may well be the case that creators will not innovate or share if they are continually treated unjustly in an unregulated marketplace.

The next section examines some of the dynamics of cultural borrowing in the other direction, from Hollywood to Bollywood. Stereotypes of Asian "pirates" permeate and Bollywood itself is plagued with a reputation for mimicry, not creativity. But sometimes the claims of piracy may be overblown. Furthermore, global borrowing by Bollywood from Hollywood must be understood in the context of cultural hegemony and resistance.

BOLLYWOOD

Bollywood is the world's largest film industry,[86] and Bollywood films are "the most-seen movies in the world."[87] Some one thousand films are produced annually in Bombay and other major film centers in India; Bollywood films enthrall moviegoers not only all over India and among the Indian diaspora, but also "in such unlikely places as Russia, China, the Middle East, the Far East, Egypt, Turkey, and Africa."[88] The industry earns more than $2 billion annually.[89] Handsome dancing heroes like Amitabh Bachchan and Shahrukh Kahn and Ms. Universe–worthy starlets from Aishwarya Rai Bachchan ("the world's most beautiful woman"[90]) to Madhuri Dixit shake their hips and entertain literally billions. In 2001 when U.S. troops drove the Taliban out of Kabul after the September 11 attacks, the first film to play in that city was a Bollywood epic.[91]

Cinema was born in India, in Bombay, roughly contemporaneously with its birth in other parts of the world. In 1896 the first "cinematographe" show premiered on the Indian subcontinent at the Watson's Hotel in Bombay, just three months after a premier in Paris. "The marvel of the century" proclaimed the *Times of India*.[92] But only British elites attended the premiere, because the hotel barred Indians. Shows were first screened to Indians a week later at the Novelty Theatre in Bombay. Later, Bombay also became the site of one of the first films made in India. Bombay's position as a gateway for commerce and trade created by the British East India Company made it a natural portal for the reception of film technology. The city's own access to capital and vibrant creative culture of theater groups and writers made it fertile ground for the eventual development of a full-fledged indigenous film industry,[93] now oft-referred to as "Bollywood" (though the city has now shed its British name of Bombay in favor of the Indian "Mumbai").

The visionary idea of an indigenous Indian film industry came from the early and influential film pioneer Dhundiraj Govind Phalke. In 1910 he watched the film *Life of Christ* in a Bombay theater and had a transformative experience. "While the life of Christ was rolling before my physical eyes, I was mentally visualizing the Gods, Shri Krishna, Shri Ramachandra, their Gokul and Ayodhya," Phalke recounts, continuing: "I was gripped by a strange spell. I bought another ticket and saw the film again. This time I felt my imagination taking shape on the screen. Could this really happen? Could we, the sons of India, ever be able to see Indian images on the screen?"[94] Phalke openly linked the creation and sustenance of an indigenous film industry with nationalism and self-determination. Home Rule depended on Indian support of this industry, Phalke said.[95] In 1913 his first film, *Raja Harishchandra*,[96] debuted in Bombay. The story was based on the Indian epic poem the *Mahabharata,* and the film was advertised as "the first film of Indian manufacture."[97] The film was silent; sound and music did not arrive to the Indian cinema until 1931. But its focus on Indian stories had a profound and lasting influence.

The organization and structure of the Indian film industry in Bombay are distinct from those of the mega–production studios in Hollywood. Unlike Hollywood, where big motion picture studios finance everything from production to film distribution, Bollywood is a fragmented industry. Independent entrepreneurs finance Bollywood films, while others pay for the rights to distribute and exhibit them. During World War II, illicit war profiteers looking to invest their black-market fortunes began an unholy alliance between the underworld and Bollywood. Mobsters still serve as a significant (though declining) source of the financing for Bollywood films, creating instability, lawlessness, and violence in the industry. Mob influence even affects the artistic content of the films. Some consider Bollywood's inclination to remake Hollywood hits—rather than experiment with original stories—to be a direct result of mafia pressure for surefire hits.[98]

On paper, Indian copyright law is not much different from the law of Western countries. Indian copyright law traces its origins to the British Empire. The first copyright laws developed in India under British rule substantially paralleled Britain's copyright law of 1911. India's first copyright act after Independence, the Copyright Act of 1957, retained many of the prior provisions. India's most recent amendment to its Copyright Act, in 1999,[99] brought the law in line with the Agreement on Trade-Related Aspects of Intellectual Property (TRIPS).[100] Despite the laws on the books, however, the lack of enforcement of copyright laws is a continuing complaint and source of strain on India's trade relationship with the United States, prompting the United States to place India on the Section 301 "watch list" for lax enforcement of copyright.

For its own part, Bollywood appears to be of two minds about copyright. On the one hand, Bollywood filmmakers rely on copyright law to protect against video piracy. Pirated DVDs of Bollywood films are freely available in India and abroad, with resulting losses to the industry that some claim are at least $80 million a year.[101] With the advent of cable television, pirated copies of films have been shown on television, sometimes on the very day the films were released in movie theaters. Still, enforcement of copyright claims is lax because such claims remain a low priority for the police and the courts.[102]

In contrast to Bollywood's stance against video piracy, many charge that the industry has not been respectful of the copyright claims of artists within or outside of the industry. Actors, directors, and writers frequently work without any written contracts. Scripts are few and far between, and directors develop films on the fly. Musicians have been particularly vocal about the unjust appropriation of their work, claiming, "Plagiarism is routine."[103] One Bollywood director, when scolded for such copying in the industry and when asked "Where is your artistic skill?" replied, "My skill is knowing what to steal."[104]

In recent years, since 2000 when the Indian government granted industry status to Bollywood, filmmakers have been able to seek more secure sources of funding, from banks, foreign investors, and India's own corporate titans such as the $8 billion Tata Group and the $13 billion Reliance Industries. In 2011 Indian billionaire Anil Ambani of Reliance Industries invested some $825 million in Steven Spielberg's DreamWorks SKG Studios.[105] The huge sums now available within India for investment in Bollywood could potentially transform the Indian film industry. Recall, for example, that Ray initially reached out to Hollywood because he lacked the technology and funds necessary to make a successful science-fiction film—indeed, Indians have continued to avoid this genre of films and others, including animation, for the same reasons. New sources of funding offer new creative opportunities.

Major Hollywood studios, including Warner Bros., Sony Pictures, Twentieth Century Fox, and Disney, are also now investing in Bollywood. This comes as no surprise—Hollywood has long sought, albeit unsuccessfully, to tap into the vast film market of India, where movies are as much a national pastime as cricket. Strikingly, Hollywood, which controls a whopping 80 to 90 percent of the European film market, has failed to penetrate the Indian market with its own films. Hollywood films make up only 10 percent of the Indian film market.[106] This surprisingly low level of penetration is the result of neither quotas nor nationalist censor boards. Hollywood films simply do not seem to appeal to Indian moviegoers. Hollywood films released in India with straight-up dubbing have flopped.[107] As one Bollywood director puts it, "Hollywood films are considered 'dry' here."[108]

Hollywood's new strategy? Invest in Bollywood films instead. In 2009, Warner Bros. released *Chandni Chowk to China,*[109] only the third Bollywood/ Hollywood collaboration in history. But the film, starring Bollywood megastar Akshay Kumar, was a box-office flop. A comedy about an Indian vegetable seller from New Delhi's Chandni Chowk neighborhood who ends up in China (Hollywood's ambition appeared to be to tap two of the world's largest moviegoing markets with this one film),[110] it did not draw anywhere near the audiences that Hollywood had hoped it would.[111]

Hollywood executives recognize that Indian movie audiences are growing quickly; indeed, before the recent global economic downturn, Indian domestic box-office returns were growing at a rate of 15 percent, compared to a 2 percent growth rate in the United States during the same period.[112] One result of such new alliances, of course, is that more Bollywood profits will now flow back to the West rather than remain at home. Another result of American alliances is increased pressure on Bollywood to clean up its act with respect to copyright. Hollywood began paying close attention to Bollywood several years ago, with the success of Mira Nair's *Monsoon Wedding*[113] and Aamir Khan's *Lagaan,*[114] which in 2002 was nominated for an Oscar for Best Foreign Film. The attention has not all been positive, as Hollywood directors soon realized that Bollywood has been appropriating ideas from Hollywood in their own films. Bollywood adaptations include *Deewana*[115] (similar to *Sleeping with the Enemy*[116]), *Akele Hum Akele Tum*[117] (resembling *Sleepless in Seattle*[118]), *Chachi 420*[119] and *Aunty No. 1*[120] (both similar to *Mrs. Doubtfire*), and *Ghajini*[121] (an homage to *Memento*[122]). But these resemblances do not always violate copyright. Indian copyright law, like copyright law everywhere, protects original expression but not ideas. Directors of Indian films based on Hollywood hits claim their films are "inspired" by the ideas in the Hollywood films, but that their own expression of the idea is unique. The film *Chachi 420,* for example, is similar to *Mrs. Doubtfire* only in plot (an estranged father dresses as a nanny to spend more time with his child), but no original expression is taken from the Hollywood film. Says Bollywood director Subhash Ghai: "There are only 36 plots in the world drama, and you can make 36,000 stories out of those. So stories don't change; science changes, times change and values change."[123]

The critical and box office success of *Slumdog Millionaire*, in particular, has piqued Hollywood's interest in Bollywood once more.[124] Though *Slumdog Millionaire* was not technically a Bollywood movie (the film's director, Danny Boyle, is British), it succeeded internationally by employing typical Bollywood themes of urban poverty and corruption, staged with Indian actors, Bollywood-style melodrama, and stop-action dance numbers set to the music of acclaimed Bollywood musical director A. R. Rahman. Again, however, the attention has meant a spate of copyright claims by Hollywood against Bollywood. Recently Hollywood ran ads in the *Times of India* warning Bollywood not to go through with a rumored Indian version of *The Curious Case of Benjamin Button*.[125] The actual similarities between the recently released Bollywood film *Paa* and *Benjamin Button* are trivial.[126] The film *Benjamin Button* is adapted from a 1922 short story of the same name written by F. Scott Fitzgerald, which tells the tale of a man who ages backward. *Paa*, in contrast, is a literal story of a boy with progeria, the disease many believed inspired the *Benjamin Button* story, but which is never expressly mentioned in Fitzgerald's tale or the Hollywood version of it. *Paa* trades largely on the gimmick of having Bollywood's most famous actor, Amitabh Bachchan, play the child afflicted with progeria, while his real-life son, Abishek Bachchan, plays the child's father.

Recently, the Delhi High Court threw out another case, by Warner Bros. against the producers of the Bollywood film *Hari Puttar: A Comedy of Terrors*,[127] finding the film bore little resemblance to the *Harry Potter* series.[128] This was not a copyright case but a trademark dispute. Warner Bros., which owns a trademark in Harry Potter, argued that the name Hari Puttar was confusingly similar to the Harry Potter mark and threatened to dilute the famous original mark. But the Delhi High Court ultimately agreed with the defendants that the name, which referred to a Punjabi boy whose full name was Hariprasad Dhoonda ("Hari" is a common short form for Hariprasad and "Puttar" means son in Punjabi), would not likely be confused with J. K. Rowling's famous boy Potter. Notably, the court found that the difference in the class, language, and exposure of the audiences for the Potter films and the Puttar film were relevant, supposing that "an illiterate or semi-literate movie viewer, in case he ventures to see a film by the name of Hari Puttar, would never be able to relate the same with a Harry Potter film or book. Conversely," the court continued, "an educated person who has pored over or even browsed through a book on Harry Potter or viewed a Harry Potter film, is not likely to be misled . . . for, in my view, the cognoscenti, the intellectuals and even the pseudo-intellectuals presumably know the difference between chalk and cheese or at any rate must be presumed to know the same."[129]

But a settlement for $200,000 in the summer of 2009, awarded to Twentieth Century Fox from the Bollywood producer of *Banda Yeh Bindaas Hai*,[130] accused of stealing from *My Cousin Vinny*,[131] seems to have sent a strong signal to Bollywood. Now two Indian producers have bought the rights to the two Hollywood films they want to copy (including a license from Orion Pictures to remake the Hollywood film *Wedding Crashers*[132]), a move largely unheard of before. Many in Bollywood welcome the idea of paying royalties to Hollywood.[133] The acclaimed musical director A. R. Rahman, who composed the original music for *Slumdog Millionaire* and scores of Bollywood films, opined that "it's high time everyone cleaned up his act and people started getting fair to creative people."[134]

Bollywood ought to play by the rules: remakes that take original, protectable expression and that are not fair use should be licensed. Yet we may also ask whether claims of piracy by Bollywood may not at times be overblown, if not also partially misconceived. Consider the following:

1. *The most influential films in post-Independence Indian cinema are not remakes.* Of the top-ten-grossing Bollywood films in 2008, only one or two are remakes of Hollywood hits. The top-grossing *Ghajini*, starring Aamir Khan, has a plot nearly identical to the American film *Memento;* another, titled *Race*,[135] admits inspiration from the 1998 Hollywood film *Goodbye Lover*.[136] But most of that year's blockbuster films were not expressly or obviously derivative of earlier American works (for example, *Singh Is King* and *Jodhaa-Akbar*—with the latter, starring Hrithik Roshan and Aishwarya Rai Bachchan, the sixteenth-century love story between the great Mughal emperor, Akbar, and a Rajput princess, Jodha).[137] Indeed, the most influential Hindi films have had expressly Indian storylines: *Devdas* (1935, remade in 2002, about star-crossed lovers torn asunder by class differences); *Mother India* (1957, in

which a poor peasant woman, Radha, raises two sons and over-comes her difficulties against all odds); *Guide* (1965, the story of a clever village tour guide mistaken for a holy man); *Sholay* (1975, marking the advent in Hindi films of the "angry young man" who grows up in poverty and avenges the murders of family members killed by underworld bandits); and *Lagaan* (2001, chronicling how Indian villagers in nineteenth-century India rose up against crippling colonial taxation).[138]

2. *Remakes are common in both Hollywood and Bollywood.* Bolly-wood is not alone in turning to remakes as a guarantor for finan-cial success. Hollywood, too, equally driven by concerns for the bottom line, frequently turns to remaking classics, local and global. As mentioned earlier, in 2009 Hollywood offered an of-ficial remake of Osamu Tezuka's *Astro Boy*. Recall, too, that re-makes may themselves later become iconic "classics," from *The Magnificent Seven* to *A Fistful of Dollars*. These and even more recent examples also challenge the conception that it is only American culture that influences the rest. Clearly Asian film has had a strong influence on Hollywood as well. To take another example, Martin Scorsese's Academy Award–winning film *The Departed* (starring Leonardo DiCaprio and Matt Damon) was a remake of the Hong Kong crime film *Mou Gaan Dou* (2002), known by the English translation *Internal Affairs*.[139] *The Departed* won the Oscar for Best Picture in 2006. And the 2002 Holly-wood horror film *The Ring* is a remake of the 1998 Japanese horror film *Ring*.[140]

3. *Learning through pastiche.* Writers, musicians, and filmmakers practice their craft, and eventually develop their own voice, by adapting existing works. Today, new technologies from digital video recorders to the Internet make the art of filmmaking acces-sible even to the poor in the developing world, democratizing not only broader consumption of cultural goods, but cultural produc-tion as well. Notably, indigenous film industries have grown through the fruitful combination of cheap technological infra-structure and a rich creative heritage—often Bollywood films—from which to adapt more local stories. Nigeria now boasts one of the world's largest film industries (earning it the nickname

"Nollywood"), largely through perfecting this very modus operandi, that is, by combining cheap video technologies and "a creative history of appropriation and localization of Bollywood films."[141]

The Indian scholar Lawrence Liang describes a similar phenomenon in India, where an alternative film industry has emerged in the unlikely small town of Malegaon, located some eight hours away from Mumbai. Several years ago a local entrepreneur in this town of predominantly migrant Muslim loom workers found himself with a case of empty videocassettes. Deciding the cassettes would be more valuable with content on them, he made a "local" version of a well-known Bollywood film.[142] The concept took off and now the town is famous for a fledgling film industry that thrives on making local adaptations of Bollywood hits. Where the Oscar-nominated film *Lagaan* focused on oppressive taxes under the British Raj, for example, the Malegaon adaptation confronts issues of local access to city services.[143] Far from criticizing the Malegaon copy, Aamir Khan, the director of *Lagaan,* has praised the use of "video theaters as a film school."[144]

4. *Copying requires creativity.* Imitation is often a more creative act than we recognize. Take again the example of the fledgling Malegaon film industry. Liang lauds the creativity of the poor, who remake Bollywood films but on shoestring budgets of a mere $1,000 per film.[145] One film, for example, reshot a helicopter scene in a Bollywood movie using a plastic toy helicopter that cost less than a dollar. The Malegaon example, Liang argues, suggests that the "creativity that goes into the making of the remakes lies as much in the way that the film is made, as in the content of the film."[146]

5. *"Indianized" Hollywood films have minimal effect on the market for the originals because Indian audiences do not otherwise see the Hollywood films.* Bollywood filmmakers often seek to retell a Hollywood film story, but in a way that appeals to Indian audiences. Usually this is done by "adding emotions," family relationships, and an extra hour of song and dance numbers. Bollywood

film writer Anjum Rajabali emphasizes the difference in genres this way: "Relationships! That seems to be the primary criteria when Indianising a subject. Lots of strong, close, intense relationships that will have interesting moving stories/graphs of their own. Adding family is one important thing. That is why I think subjects like James Bond, detective stories, westerns and the like don't work as they are here. Who were James Bond's parents? Does Clint Eastwood of *The Good, The Bad, & Ugly* love anyone? What about his brothers or sisters?"[147]

Perhaps this overstates cultural differences between India and the United States. More persuasively, Indian directors argue they are offering a remake because Indians are simply not going to see the original Hollywood film. The Indianized remake, then, allows these audiences "to see a great story in their own language."[148]

6. *Bollywood remakes stave off Hollywood cultural imperialism.* Perhaps more controversially, copyright law may give some consideration to the ways in which local adaptations of dominant, global cultural works from Hollywood enable local communities to resist cultural hegemony and talk back to the dominant Hollywood culture. Recall that women, gays, and minorities in the United States and elsewhere actively remake dominant cultural stories from Harry Potter to Star Trek through writing and sharing practices (such as fan fiction) so as to bring their own subjectivity to bear on the traditional tales.[149] The process of "Indianizing" a Hollywood film is a similar practice.

Some argue that Bollywood should make its own original stories and not engage with those of the West. But as Liang argues, they assume that poor countries can afford to "disavow the global," which he says they cannot. "[I]n many countries," writes Liang, "the very question of what it means to be modern has always been defined in relation to an idea of the global."[150] Thus, for countries to be modern, they have no choice but to engage with the West. At the same time, viewing Western films forces poor audiences "to confront their physical and cultural marginality every time they attend the cinema," writes Liang.[151] Preparing local adaptations of Hollywood films, by contrast, allows Indians to experience a "global" story or phenomenon, but on more locally relevant and palatable terms. The nationalist vision that inspired Indian film pioneer Phalke thus continues to play a role in Bollywood's continued success. Phalke's concern was for the psychology of a nation that sees itself represented on-screen.[152] The message? A white English boy cannot always be the hero.

COPYRIGHT AND ASIAN VALUES

The current legal claims against Bollywood echo a long-standing meme about Asians as copiers, and Asian culture as one more suited to imitation than innovation. In the influential book by William P. Alford, *To Steal a Book Is an Elegant Offense: Intellectual Property Law in Chinese Civilization* (1995), Alford attributes the long absence of intellectual property law in China to the country's unique civilization and Confucian values. "Lying at the core of traditional Chinese society's treatment of intellectual property was the dominant Confucian vision of the nature of civilization and of the constitutive role played therein by a shared and still vital past," Alford writes, continuing: "Only through encountering the past—which provided unique insight into the essence of one's own character, relationships with other human beings, and interaction with nature—could individuals, guided by nurturing leaders, understand how properly to adhere to those relationships of which they were a part."[153] Alford concludes that this understanding of the moral foundation played by the past confounded intellectual property protection in China: "The indispensability of the past for personal moral growth dictated that there be broad access to the common heritage of all Chinese."[154] Alford points out that Chinese engagement with the past did not necessarily mean lack of originality in new works.[155] Yet he still contends that "interaction with the past is one of the *distinctive* modes of intellectual and imaginative endeavor in traditional Chinese culture."[156] He concludes that, "in the Chinese context," use of the past "was at once both more affirmative [than in the West] and more *essential*."[157] Alford describes as "Confucian" scholars' "disdain for commerce" and the idea that they "wrote for edification and moral renewal rather than profit."[158]

But let us examine these claims further. Is the past not just as important for self-understanding beyond China's borders? And are Chinese scholars really unique in their altruistic desire to create knowledge for others? In fact, cultural stereotypes have the effect of buttressing arguments for strong copyright (Westerners are profit maximizers who will only create for monetary reward) and weakening arguments for limits (Westerners are relationally unconnected and have no need to access the past). In contrast, those who value community, shared meaning, and knowledge creation to benefit the public are cast as foreign and premodern.

Civilizational views about copyright are misleading because they elide the plural values in all cultures, which rightfully recognize the values of innovation and participation, as well as of shared meaning and common heritage. The Nobel laureate Amartya Sen has highlighted how cultural stereotypes about Asians have been wrongly used to justify a denial of human rights in Asian countries. As Sen points out, the mistaken idea that Asians do not value human rights is voiced by authoritarian Asian leaders and skeptical Westerners alike. In so doing, Westerners inadvertently buttress Asian authoritarians. More perniciously, civilizational rhetoric elides plural, critical traditions committed to freedom, rationality, equality, and tolerance that have long been present in Asian histories. As Sen demonstrates, Asian nations, religions, and traditions are rife with conflicting and diverse views on these topics.[159] He points out, for example, that scholars often cite Confucian values when considering China, but seldom invoke Buddhist philosophy. Great Indian leaders such as Ashoka and Akbar championed and practiced pluralism in governing their vast empires long before those values were adopted in the West. As Sen concludes, "so-called Asian values that are invoked to justify authoritarianism are not especially Asian in any significant sense."[160]

Something similar is true in the case of copyright and so-called Asian values. As one scholar has recently argued, Chinese commitments to access to knowledge are influenced by Buddhist enlightenment philosophy, not just Confucian commitment to tradition and authority.[161] Read in this light, the focus on public access to knowledge may be understood as part of a larger endeavor to promote enlightenment and freedom, not just as obedient acquiescence to authoritarian elders. Recognition of each culture's plural traditions and values is crucial because it offers a more critical lens with which to assess our own societies. If access to shared culture is understood only as being fed by authoritarian values, we will naturally reject a robust public domain in the name of freedom. But if we understand diverse motivations, including those stemming from universal concerns for enlightenment and access to knowledge, then such

commitments cannot easily be cast aside. Furthermore, claims that intellectual property laws are more "foreign" on some soils than others
understate the extent to which intellectual property is something we must
all be taught—it does not come naturally. Indeed, today in the United
States copyright industries expend great effort and money to teach (or
indoctrinate) young children about the wrongs of piracy. And American
university academics continue to resist encroaching norms that pit the
pursuit of knowledge for the benefit of the public against the stepped-up
efforts of university technology transfer offices to teach researchers to
patent their inventions.

Some have suggested that China now has an "innovation deficit"[162]
and needs to develop its own creative industries. While rates of innovation
may indeed vary across the world, this may reflect a variety of factors,
including access to knowledge, capital, education, and markets. These
varying rates may also reflect culture, but we should be careful not to
paint culture with too broad a brush, identifying one group as natural
innovators and another as natural copyists. In fact, there is a great deal
of creative activity taking place in Asia, not just in film, but in every area
from computer gaming to fashion. For example, *Farmville*, "the most
popular game on Facebook," with over 45 million unique monthly players, admittedly "rips off *Happy Farm*, a hugely popular online game in
China."[163] Each season, fashion industry buyers from the United States
and Europe travel to Tokyo, whose youth are "trailblazers of street fashion"
and "the envy of Western designers," "to buy up bagfuls of the latest hits.
The designs are then whisked overseas to be reworked, resized, stitched
together and sold under Western labels."[164] If innovation and progress are
our ultimate goals, we must take greater care to recognize how differences
in global power and knowledge, combined with cultural stereotypes, affect
the production and distribution of culture today.

The effects of today's global copyright laws extend well beyond incentives
to create. Copyright law implicates mutual recognition or misrecognition
of others. Furthermore, this law determines who will benefit from the
wealth deriving from knowledge production today. In short, copyright
law has both dignitary and distributive effects. Arguments to buttress
the intellectual property rights of Western creators typically presume
these creative professionals are more deserving of protection than others

because their creations are "original," while those of developing (especially Asian) countries are derivative. But this distinction overlooks the extent to which much of human creativity is derivative (recalling Paul Gilroy's description of culture as "routes," not "roots"[165]). More importantly, the distinction elides the extent to which all humans are creative and active producers of knowledge of the world. Cultural stereotypes about originality and piracy do a disservice to our understanding of the universal aspects of human creativity and the ways in which power may upend the ultimate goals of promoting cultural exchange and mutual understanding. We need to take into account the ways in which actual global inequalities, combined with long-standing cultural biases, may impede the free and fair exchange of culture.

CHAPTER SEVEN

An Issue of Life or Death

THEMBISA MKHOSANA HAS AIDS. If she lived in the West, this diagnosis would likely not be life-threatening. Advances in antiretroviral treatments today mean that patients who can afford to pay for the treatments can live a healthy, full, and long life with the disease. But Thembisa, a mother of two living in a village on the outskirts of Cape Town, South Africa, will likely die from her illness. While miracle medicines exist, she cannot afford them. She is hardly alone. Few in Africa, where the majority of HIV/AIDS patients in the world live, have the resources to buy the most effective antiretroviral medicines on the free market. The medicine that Thembisa needs to live costs $10,000 a year, a price that neither she nor her government can afford.

Thembisa has been lucky until now. Since 2003, when she was first diagnosed with the disease, she has been treated at a Doctors Without Borders clinic. Born out of relief efforts by French physicians in Biafra and a cyclone in East Pakistan (now Bangladesh) in 1970, Doctors Without Borders has long provided medical help in the aftermath of tsunamis, wars, and pandemics. Today it treats over a hundred thousand HIV-positive patients in the developing world, administering first- and second-line antiretroviral treatments. Thembisa initially responded well to these treatments. They enabled her to go back to work and, most importantly, care for her two children. But now she has developed resistance to the drugs.

Indeed, most AIDS patients develop resistance within five years of starting these treatments. And while third-line ARV treatments are available in Europe and the United States, they are not available in South Africa, where few could afford them.

Why does Doctors Without Borders offer only the first- and second-line retrovirals and not the third-line antiretroviral treatments that might save Thembisa? The first-line and second-line drugs cost a relatively small $80 per person annually. They are out of patent, while the third-line (and fourth-line and fifth-line) drugs remain in patent—that is, the drugs are still under the control of companies, which have not yet offered the medicine under terms that would bring continued treatment within her reach. The result is that while AIDS is a treatable, chronic condition in the developed world, in the developing world, second-line treatments are the end of the line. The World Health Organization antiretroviral therapy guidelines offer a grim suggestion in cases like Thembisa's: "If a patient has exhausted all available antiretroviral . . . treatment options . . . it becomes reasonable to stop giving ARVs and to institute an active palliative and end-of-life care plan."[1] Thembisa's caregivers from Doctors Without Borders feel defeated. "Seeing a patient you have been treating since 2003, and now this patient is failing on her second combination, you feel you are a failure," says Mpumi Mantangana. Thembisa's only concern is her family. "I know that I'm going to die," she says, but "who is going to look after my children?"[2]

Not too long ago, an HIV-positive diagnosis was tantamount to a death sentence—for people in the East and the West, in the South and the North. The drug companies that perfected the antiretroviral therapies invested princely sums to find these miracle cures. To justify their investment, they rely on the promise of a patent—the twenty-year exclusive right to make, use, and sell an invention that is novel, non-obvious, and useful. The patent allows the drug company to charge high sums for the medicine, and thereby recoup its enormous investments in scientists and drug trials, while also turning a profit for shareholders and investing in research toward future breakthrough drugs. Thus patents have saved countless lives, including Thembisa's thus far.

But this structure has its limits. Indeed, the evidence is mounting that in crucial ways patents fail to promote the health of people in the developing world, and in some cases in the developed world as well.[3]

First, the exclusive patent right allows a monopoly on the production of the drug, which generally leads to higher prices for the cure. The enormous differences in price—$80 per annum compared to an annual per person cost of $10,000 in the case of Thembisa's medicines—creates vast inequities between those who are wealthy enough to purchase the cure (or to have one purchased for them by their government), and those who must suffer, often knowing that a cure exists but lies beyond their means.

Some will say that Thembisa cannot be worse off for the patent because but for the patent, there would be no drug that she was struggling to obtain. But this denies that patents are but one among many alternatives for stimulating and rewarding innovation, including prizes and subsidies. Furthermore, drug companies often benefit from enormous public investment, including basic research conducted in universities and research supported by nonprofit foundations and governments. I will explore these points further in this chapter.

Second, patents do save lives, but primarily only the lives of those who are willing and able to pay. In truth, drug companies do not target entire populations of developing countries. To the contrary, they quite openly identify a market in only a small portion of a developing country's population. One major Western drug company calculates the effective drug market in India to be seventy to eighty million people—that is, less than 10 percent of that country's population. An anonymous pharmaceutical executive put it in these terms: "There could easily be 70 to 80 million people [in India] who can afford expensive medicines, just as they go out and buy expensive cars, branded clothes and consumer goods. . . . That is equal to the size of a UK or a Germany."[4]

The third point is related to the second: the patent system skews innovation to serve rich-country markets. The result is that Western drug companies are not producing the medicines most needed in the developing world, where few can afford to pay. As a 2006 World Health Organization study showed, intellectual property is not a significant factor in contributing to innovation for diseases that disproportionately affect developing countries, such as malaria and tuberculosis. A *Lancet* study concluded that only 1 percent of the 1,556 drugs developed in the last twenty-five years targeted so-called neglected diseases such as malaria and tuberculosis, even though these diseases account for over 10 percent of the global disease burden.[5] Indeed, these diseases have earned the name "neglected diseases" because so little of the world's proportion of R&D dollars is dedicated to them.[6] Global diseases are generally categorized as Type I (diseases spread evenly through the developed and developing worlds); Type II (diseases that are predominantly in the developing world but on which a substantial proportion of R&D sums are spent—the sole example here being AIDS), and Type III (diseases for which 95 percent of the global burden falls in the developing world, and little if any global R&D funds are spent).[7] As a recent World Health Organization report on patents and incentives concluded, "There is no evidence that the implementation of the TRIPS agreement in developing countries will significantly boost R&D in pharmaceuticals on Type II, and particularly Type III diseases,"[8] explaining that "[i]nsufficient market incentives are the decisive factor."[9]

The failure to develop an AIDS treatment for children serves as a glaring example of this lacuna in the incentive theory underlying patents. There are 2 million children with HIV in the world and 90 percent of them live in sub-Saharan Africa. Without treatment, a third of those children with the virus will die before their first birthday. And in fact, few if any have access to treatment, not simply because treatments are unaffordable, but also because Big Pharma has not found it profitable to develop pediatric treatments for this primarily poor group.

Fourth, patents only incentivize drug production in countries that already have the necessary technical capacity and capital investment for breakthrough research. Indeed, in countries with lesser technical capacity, patents may impede their ability to gain technical knowledge by copying more advanced industries abroad. Simply put, the elusive promise of a patent will not spur the creation of new treatments if a country lacks technical know-how. Thus patents in the developing world not only inhibit technology transfer to poor countries; they also engender dependence on developed countries and their drug companies—companies that, as we have seen, are not particularly interested in serving the populations of the developing world.

Fifth, the economic incentive theory does not justify worldwide recognition of a patent. In Thembisa's case, for example, the existence of U.S. and European patents was enough to spur the creation of drugs that could save her life. Under the incentive theory, the incentives existed for these drugs to save European and American lives. The fact that Thembisa's life has been saved thus far is only incidental. So why don't the companies that hold the patents on the third-line treatments donate the medicines to the world's poorest nations at cost? Are they really hoping to make money from these people? There are some likely reasons that companies have been slow to offer their drugs at a fraction of the cost they charge in the wealthier parts of the world. First, as we have seen, drug company executives hope to profit by catering to the small markets of the very rich in these places. Second, these executives worry that low prices in the developing world will call into question monopoly prices in the developed world. Moreover, they are concerned about grey-market reimportation of the cheaply produced drugs into richer countries. Yet the hope of catering to a sliver of the developing world market ought not to prevent the use of mechanisms such as compulsory licenses for generic drug production to service the majority of the poor. In fact, the creation of generic drug markets for the poor ought not significantly impact the bottom line of Big Pharma, which derives only 5 to 7 percent of its profits from this part of the world. The grey-markets concern is a valid one—but, as we shall see, the World Trade Organization has begun to craft creative solutions to this problem (requiring generic drugs made for developing world markets to be distinctively labeled, for example).

Patents are a question of life *and death*. In the developed world, effective markets spur the investment of billions of dollars in R&D, leading to the creation of breakthrough drugs. As a 2006 World Health Organization report on intellectual property and public health concluded, "Intellectual property rights have an important role to play in stimulating innovation in health-care products in countries where financial and technological capacities exist, and in relation to products for which profitable markets exist." But in the developing world, patents actually impede the distribution of drugs to the poor. In the words of one observer: Innovation is meaningless if newly developed products remain out of reach. Furthermore, patents do little to spur cures for the ills that affect the poor; neither do patents incentivize domestic production where local industry lacks technological capacity, basic research, and the capital required for breakthrough innovation. That is, according to the same World Trade Organization report, in developing countries "the fact that a patent can be obtained may contribute nothing or little to innovation if the market is too small or scientific and technological capability inadequate."[10]

In 2005 the Nobel Prize–winning relief organization Doctors Without Borders put the matter more starkly, warning the WTO that when monopoly pricing takes medicines fully out of the reach of the poor, patents can kill.[11] The result? We have a global patent system that works some of the time and in some parts of the world. But in critical humanitarian and economic respects, our patent system is broken.

PATENTS, PARTICIPATION, AND DEVELOPMENT

These are powerful critiques of the economic incentive theory of patents: Patents fail to incentivize research that addresses poor people's diseases; patents offer little incentive for R&D in poor countries, which lack basic technological capacity; the patented drugs produced by multinationals are priced out of reach of the poor; and finally, Big Pharma will not allow generic drug production in the developing world, even though doing so would not adversely affect its incentives. But there are additional critiques of our current patent system that we may articulate and consider, critiques that expand our response to Thembisa and her tragic situation beyond the success or failure of intellectual property rights *as incentives.*

In this book I have emphasized cultural participation as both a means and an end of development. Producers of music, art, and scientific innovations today seek economic development in the sense that they are asking for fair remuneration for their intellectual production from global markets. At the same time, participation in the production of the world's knowledge is an end in itself. All human beings seek to "think for themselves," to apply their ingenuity to better their own lives and the lives of those around them. This is *what development is for.* Amartya Sen's agency-oriented conception of development as freedom recognizes that individuals in the developing world do not simply wish to sit back and be the "beneficiaries of cunning benefit programs," but rather seek to enhance their capacity to live a life that is happy and fulfilling, to care for themselves, and to interact with others, near and far.

Patents are crucial to realizing this vision of participatory democracy and development. At the most basic level, patents on medicines affect individuals' capacity to live "a human life of normal length," which Nussbaum places at the very top of her list of central human capabilities. Health without fear of dying prematurely is the essential foundation on which a full life can be built. With access to effective and affordable medicines (themselves spurred by patents), Thembisa can care for her children and be a productive participant in her community and national economy. But let me be clear: we are not interested only in Thembisa's potential contributions, seeing her as a means and not an end, or simply in the economic costs to society of her illness. The "[e]conomic effects of the AIDS epidemic are important not so much on their own but primarily because of their consequences on human lives and happiness and freedoms," Sen reminds us.[12] Most importantly, we must be concerned when patents impose significant costs on Thembisa's happiness, thwarting her hopes of raising her children and living a full and independent life of her own making.

It must be acknowledged that patents are not the lone culprit in keeping medicines from the poor. The point is often made that a vast majority of essential drugs are off patent, and yet these remedies nonetheless fail to get distributed to the destitute because of poor mechanisms for delivery and use of the drugs, inadequate treatment facilities, and lack of patient education. Yet we cannot ignore the role of patents. As I have detailed, the effects of patents on the poor's access to medicines range from neglecting diseases of the developing world like malaria and tuberculosis to ratcheting up the costs of medicines so that they are simply out of reach.

Patents are constitutive of cultural democracy and development in another fundamental way. Patent law is a critical tool for structuring a society's capacity to innovate. Nations have long understood that their patent policy has helped determine the success or failure of their indigenous creative industries and the social welfare of their people. Indeed, for most of world history patent systems were tailored to the developmental needs of each nation, with even many European countries enacting weak patent laws in their early days in order to borrow and copy freely from more advanced nations abroad. Switzerland, for example, protected its successful watch-making industry with patents in mechanical inventions, while simultaneously seeking to copy and learn from the more advanced German chemical industry by excluding patents in chemical products.[13] India famously overhauled its patent laws in 1970 after a 1959 study concluded that the old law, a remnant of colonial days, "has failed in its main purpose, namely, to stimulate invention among Indians" and "to secure the benefits thereof to the largest section of the public."[14] The study, led by a commission under Supreme Court Justice Rajagopal Ayyangar, concluded that the inherited British patent law—which recognized sixteen-year patents in most inventions, including pharmaceutical drugs—was remarkably unsuited to a newly independent India, which lacked the technological know-how to spur indigenous scientific industry, and whose population was too poor to pay the high prices for medicines that such a patent regime engendered. The Ayyangar report found that the main beneficiaries of the old patent law were foreigners, not Indians—indeed, 91 percent of patents owned in India by the end of 1958 were held by foreigners.[15]

Notably, the report's main recommendation, that India retool its patent law to weaken patent protection—particularly with respect to food and drug products—in order to stimulate indigenous industry and facilitate cheaper medicines for all, drew largely from the actions of many European governments at the time. Germany, the report noted, recognized patents in chemical processes but not products—thus allowing multiple companies to produce the same drug product. Observing that European countries of the time enacted patent laws that promoted their own industrial and social interests, the Ayyangar report concluded that India ought to do the same. In particular, the report recommended amending the patent law by:

> 1. Defining with precision those inventions that should be patentable and by rendering unpatentable certain inventions for which the grant of patents would retard research or industrial progress or be detrimental to national health or well-being;
> 2. Expanding the scope of "anticipation" so as to comprehend not merely what is known or published in this country, but also that which is known or published outside India;
> 3. Providing remedies for the injustices that India, like other countries, experiences from foreign-owned patents that are not employed within the country, but which are held either to block the industries of the country or to secure a monopoly of importation;
> 4. Including special provisions regarding the licensing of patents for inventions relating to food and medicine; and
> 5. Offering remedies for other forms of abuse resorted to by patentees, to secure a more extended monopoly or a monopoly for a longer duration than what the statute grants.[16]

The Indian Patent Act of 1970 adopted many of the Ayyangar report's suggestions. The crucial distinction made in the Indian Patent Act of 1970 was to recognize patents in pharmaceutical processes but not products. So long as a company could develop an alternate way of producing a drug, it was legal. In addition, process patents were relatively short—five years from the date of grant or seven years from the date of filing, whichever was earlier—and an automatic "licence of right" was to be available three years after the grant of the patent. This legal framework, along with government investment into laboratories, allowed Indian pharmaceutical companies to reverse-engineer nearly every drug produced by foreign multinational companies. A booming generic drug industry in India ensued. Competition from generics in turn drastically lowered drug prices and facilitated access to medicines for the poor—not just in India, but also in poor export markets, from Asia to South America to Africa. Because India had been one of the few countries with the ability to manufacture generics not only for its domestic population, but also for other developing countries, competition from India's generic producers lowered prices dramatically throughout the developing world. Over a ten-year period, the introduction of Indian generics in Africa reduced the price of AIDS treatments from $15,000 to $200 annually, bringing life-saving treatment within the ordinary person's reach. Indian pharmaceutical companies quickly became "the pharmacy of the developing world." Doctors Without Borders estimates that over 80 percent of the antiretrovirals it prescribes to over 100,000 patients in the developing world are generics made in India. Indeed, by 2005, India had the fourth largest pharmaceutical industry in the world, from which it earned $3 billion annually.[17] As Tanuja Garde concludes, the Indian Patent Act of 1970 "arguably achieved the goals of the Ayyangar Report's recommendations: the number of licensed drug manufacturers in India increased from 2,237 in 1969–70 to around 16,000 in 1992–93," and "while multinational corporations enjoyed about 80–90 percent of the pharmaceutical market around 1970, by 1993, Indian firms accounted for over 60 percent of the market."[18]

The nation-specific approach to intellectual property was premised on the conventional wisdom that strong intellectual property rights are beneficial for countries that are primarily producers of knowledge—that is, the developed world. Similarly, this conventional wisdom recognized that intellectual property rights would not benefit the developing world, which was primarily a net importer of knowledge. Thus, developing countries followed a minimalist approach to intellectual property in the interest of promoting their ability to borrow and build on the knowledge of the developed world. Indeed, in the case of copyrights even the United States took a minimalist approach to intellectual property protection during its first hundred years. It was in our best interest to freely copy the knowledge of the richer parts of the globe—we could not have so quickly built our own knowledge industry had the rules been otherwise. In India's case, its ability to produce generics and to learn through this process has helped to lay the foundation for several of its pharmaceutical companies to become global players today. The United States is now the biggest market for Ranbaxy, India's largest pharmaceutical company. Most of Ranbaxy's production is either drugs licensed from foreign pharmaceutical companies or generics of off-patent drugs. India's second largest pharmaceutical company, Dr. Reddy's, similarly found success by providing cheap generics to developed world markets as well as to developing world governments seeking to address their public health woes. The formula was simple, and it worked: minimalist intellectual property regimes allowed developing countries to stand on their own feet, develop indigenous knowledge and industry, and meet the needs of their own people without being dependent on foreigners.

But this conventional wisdom about intellectual property and development was turned on its head at the end of the last century. In 1995, with the establishment of the World Trade Organization, intellectual property rights were for the first time considered an international trade issue, and came to be governed by a new international law, the Agreement on Trade-Related Aspects of Intellectual Property, otherwise known as the TRIPS agreement. The TRIPS agreement imposed, for the first time in history, high minimum standards for intellectual property protection that *all members of the WTO were required to recognize and enforce, on pain of trade sanctions.* The upshot is that today 90 percent of the world's countries must follow a one-size-fits-all approach to intellectual property, regardless of the country's level of development. The agreement represents a radical departure from a centuries-old approach that had allowed countries to develop intellectual property rules conducive to their particular developmental needs.

Among other things, the TRIPS agreement now requires its members to recognize patents in all areas of technology, including in processes *and products,* for twenty years (the only exception being for the least developed countries, which have until 2016 to implement patents in drug products if they had no such law in the past). Thus, whereas countries such as India were free to make generic drugs prior to 2005—to serve India's own population and much of the developing world's populations, as well—the legality of much of India's past generic production is now uncertain. And while the TRIPS agreement provides for compulsory licenses to address public health needs and in the case of national emergencies (which I will describe shortly), the procedures required to exercise such options are sometimes onerous, and the political pressure on nations not to issue compulsory licenses is immense.

There are some salutary aspects of this situation. As the incentives for India's pharmaceutical industry likely shift to promoting the creation of new, innovative drugs rather than generic versions of existing drugs, the Indian pharmaceutical industry may move more into knowledge production, not just its circulation (although Indian companies have not had any successful breakthrough invention thus far). But the hope that this industry may better address developing world diseases may be overly optimistic. Indian pharmaceutical companies will face the same market pressures as Western pharmaceutical companies: to produce drugs for the markets that can pay the largest sums—which has historically meant developed world markets.

In immediate terms, the added delays and demanding criteria for creating generic versions of new drugs will mean that AIDS patients who develop resistance to older drugs will not have cheap access to newer AIDS drugs as they become available. In fact, Thembisa and tens of thousands of poor people like her who benefited from India's patent law prior to 2005 may be unable to access such drugs for the period of the patent, that is, twenty years.

This tragic result illuminates how tying countries' hands in this way—and in particular, tying the hands of developing countries—thwarts democratic participation and development in the most fundamental sense. First, a one-size-fits-all approach to patent protection conflicts with nations' particular constitutional and fundamental normative commitments. The Indian Patent Act of 1970, for example, reflected more than just a utilitarian calculus regarding good innovation policy. More fundamentally, the law bore in mind a national, democratic commitment to the principle of access to medicines for all. As Indira Gandhi articulated it, Indians envisioned a nation in which "medical discoveries would be free of patents and there would be no profiteering from life or death."[19] Today nations have much less room than ever before to adjust their intellectual property laws to promote their democratically deliberated interests and commitments.

Nevertheless, a number of countries are courageously striving to be TRIPS compliant without compromising democracy at home. One way countries can still seek to meet their basic constitutional and fundamental obligations is by adopting stringent patenting standards; another is utilizing the "flexibilities" or exceptions built into the TRIPS agreement, especially those allowing for compulsory licensing to promote public health. India, for example, which recognizes a "right to life" in article 21 of its constitution, has recently witnessed a spate of high court cases that pit its new TRIPS-compliant patent law against this constitutional commitment. Thus far, the high courts have sided with the constitution, reading limitations in the new patent law in light of that country's constitutional commitment "to provide easy access to the citizens of this country to life saving drugs and to discharge the Constitutional obligation of providing good health care to its citizens."[20] Brazil and Thailand have effectively used compulsory licensing to meet the needs of their respective national health programs (I will discuss their efforts shortly). Yet despite working within the TRIPS framework, these countries have been sued by multinationals and pressured and threatened by Western governments for defending the rights of their citizens against Big Pharma. In short, the "one-size-fits-all" approach to patent law threatens democracy itself.

FROM MARKET FAILURE TO MORAL FAILURE

The current international regime governing access to medicines must be fundamentally reconsidered. The first step, which the World Health Organization and other international actors have recently begun, is to reevaluate whether patents really are the best or even a good comprehensive innovation policy. As we have seen, the evidence suggests grave limits to relying solely on patents to promote innovation that benefits rich and poor alike. In the next section I outline some important alternative innovation policies that may do a better job of promoting medical research relevant to the poor, and which ought to facilitate generic drug production enough to bring medicines within reach of the poor. In this section I consider how the very means for evaluating the effectiveness and justness of our patent regime must also expand beyond simply calculating outputs.

We have been here before. In 1971, the New Jersey Supreme Court declared that property rights could not stand in the way of the health and well-being of the poor. In *State v. Shack,* a farmer employed migrant workers for his seasonal needs, housing them at a camp on his property. Defendant Tejeres sought out a migrant worker who needed the removal of twenty-eight sutures. Shack, an attorney, sought to discuss a legal problem with another migrant worker. Tejeres and Shack insisted on delivering their aid and information to the workers in the privacy of the workers' living quarters. When they entered the property, however, the owner called on a state trooper to evict them. The New Jersey Supreme Court held that the owner's rights in his land could not "stand between the migrant workers and those who would aid them."[21] Memorably, the court declared: "Property rights serve human values."[22]

State v. Shack sits firmly in the property law canon. It represents property law's "social enlightenment"—the recognition that in a complex and increasingly interconnected society, property rights will inevitably conflict with other vital interests, from the property rights of others, to health, to speech, to civil rights. And like landlord/tenant cases such as *Javins v. First National Realty Corp.,* which responded to the civil rights struggles of the previous decade, *Shack* paid heed to social facts about the plight of migrant farmworkers. The court in *Shack* was openly moved by governmental recognition of the poor living and social conditions of the nearly one million migrant farmworkers arriving as seasonal workers to the United States. The court noted that private property rights could not be used to prevent this "highly disadvantaged segment" of society, which was "rootless and isolated . . . unorganized and without economic or political power," from accessing the assistance to which the state held they were entitled.[23]

Fast-forward thirty years: in the new millennium, the world's attention has again turned to poverty and social relations between the first and third worlds. Today, the Internet and digital technology enable information to trespass legal and technical barriers, and social workers such as Doctors Without Borders seek to bring medicines to those suffering from

AIDS and other illnesses in the third world. Again, property rights would stop them, although this time they are copyrights and patents rather than rights in land. And again, we witness a social movement articulating fundamental rights to health and well-being—and the tragedy of property rights thwarting them. This movement has gathered pace since poor countries signed onto TRIPS in 1995, which, again, requires all WTO member states to recognize patents in everything from medicines to seeds.

Today, estimates are that approximately ten million people die needlessly every year because they cannot access existing essential medicines and vaccines. The WTO has recognized this humanitarian crisis and, to its credit, has declared that the TRIPS agreement must be interpreted in a way to protect public health and promote development. Recognizing "the gravity of the public health problems afflicting many developing and least-developed countries, especially those resulting from HIV/AIDS, tuberculosis, malaria and other epidemics,"[24] in November 2001, with the commencement of the "Development Round" of World Trade Organization negotiations, member countries adopted the groundbreaking "Declaration on the TRIPS Agreement and Public Health." The "Doha Declaration" unequivocally holds that patent rights cannot trump the rights of millions of people to health and dignity, or the rights of states to meet the humanitarian needs of their peoples. Significantly, it clarifies that TRIPS "does not and should not prevent members from taking measures to protect public health."[25]

The Doha Declaration on TRIPS and Public Health comes closest to offering a *State v. Shack* for intellectual property. Affirming that TRIPS "can and should be interpreted and implemented in a manner . . . to protect public health and . . . to promote access to medicines for all,"[26] the Doha Declaration began a process of social enlightenment of intellectual property. With it, the WTO announces that intellectual property, too, serves human values. The declaration acknowledges that incentives are necessary to stimulate pharmaceutical production because they enable the drug companies to recoup their research and development costs, but it also recognizes that the strict patent regime imposed by TRIPS—twenty-year terms on patents in all technologies—will lead to hikes in the prices of drugs and limited access to life-saving treatments for the poorest people. The Doha Declaration reaffirms that developing countries can exercise flexibilities built into the TRIPS agreement to meet the public health needs of their citizens, in particular highlighting that any member state has a right to grant compulsory licenses on medicines—essentially reverting that country's patent law to pre-TRIPS days—so as to allow the production or importation of cheap generic drugs. The declaration assures that each member state has "the freedom to determine the grounds upon which such licenses are granted"—stipulating that this includes but is not limited to cases of national or medical emergency—and there is no exhaustive list as to which diseases can be treated.[27]

Furthermore, the Doha Declaration recognized that not all countries were equally positioned to issue compulsory licenses. Noting "that WTO members with insufficient or no manufacturing capacities in the pharmaceutical sector could face difficulties in making effective use of compulsory licensing under the TRIPS Agreement," the Doha Declaration recognized that the least developed nations are dependent on other countries, like India, for the supply of cheap generic drugs.[28] The declaration directs the TRIPS Council to ensure that countries can use compulsory licenses not only to produce drugs, but also to import them, and a subsequent amendment to the TRIPS agreement in 2005 sought to promote just this sort of endeavor (although the effectiveness of this amendment is as yet unclear, as I will discuss shortly).[29]

The Doha call for limiting patent holders' rights in drugs to accommodate public health crises cannot be explained by traditional law and economics analysis. The Doha Declaration permits compulsory licenses to correct a moral failure, not a market failure. If only economics are considered, there is no failure: medicines are already reaching those needy people willing and able to pay. According to such logic, it is perfectly fine that nearly the entire continent of Africa is priced out of some drugs. But the Doha Declaration makes a different assessment, arguing that intellectual property holders' rights do not include the ability to preclude access to essential medications for millions.

I offer *State v. Shack* as an important precedent, but not as a perfect analogue. Furthermore, I recognize that in intellectual property law circles there is understandable discomfort with the property metaphor. Property rights are relative in theory but absolute in the popular consciousness. Even so, today intellectual property rights may be limited in theory, but they are succumbing to a more absolutist conception in fact. The social movement to limit intellectual property rights to serve human values confronts the increasing absolutism of intellectual property rights. The movement also calls attention to the need to analyze intellectual property in various contexts: when a life depends on immediate access to essential medicines, for example, twenty-year patents *are* perpetual. Most importantly, the social movement to bring essential medicines to the poor harbors all the same basic insights of *Shack:* it recognizes that the poor are disparately affected by intellectual property rights, that there is a real and growing conflict between the fundamental right to health and claims of intellectual property, and that intellectual property rights may be respected without sacrificing other fundamental values. To that end, and as mentioned earlier, the Doha Declaration clarifies that TRIPS allows for each member state to grant compulsory licenses in the event of a national emergency or a public health crisis—that is, the right of a state to impose a license on an essential drug for a "reasonable royalty" to the patent owner.

Unfortunately, in the decade since the adoption of the Doha Declaration, several first-world members of the World Trade Organization have taken actions against the spirit of the agreement, threatening the ability of developing countries to reconcile their TRIPS obligations with their constitutional and democratic commitments to the health and well-being of their people. The United States and the European Union have entered into bilateral free trade agreements with developing countries that impose intellectual property obligations more stringent than those in TRIPS (called "TRIPS-Plus"). In addition, countries such as Brazil and Thailand, which have exercised compulsory licenses wholly consistent with the TRIPS agreement, have nevertheless been criticized and threatened with trade sanctions for doing so. In the face of such pressures, it is worth reviewing some of the strategies available to developing countries seeking to improve access to medicines post-TRIPS.

STRATEGIES FOR PROMOTING GLOBAL PUBLIC HEALTH
Patents have proven to be a poor mechanism for distributing and delivering drugs that treat common diseases, such as AIDS or cancer, to those too poor to pay. Patents have also proven to be inadequate tools for spurring research into what are known as neglected diseases, such as malaria and tuberculosis, which predominantly afflict the poor. As the economist Jagdish Bhagwati puts it, the market-based intellectual property system

has thus far failed because in poor countries there is "need but no effective demand," where demand is defined as willingness and ability to pay.[30]
What tools are available to help address the gaps in access and incentives
produced by the current legal and policy environment?

Access-Enhancing Tools
Compulsory licenses. The Doha Declaration recognizes that countries have
the "right to grant compulsory licenses," and "the freedom to determine
the grounds upon which such licenses are granted."[31] In fact, the declaration simply reaffirmed nations' rights already outlined in the TRIPS
agreement. In particular, article 31 of the TRIPS agreement allows member states to grant compulsory licenses to authorize the making of generic
drugs in the event of "national emergency" or "extreme urgency," or in
the context of "public non-commercial use"[32]—that is, where a government distributes medicines under a national health policy. In all three
cases, TRIPS requires governments to first engage patent holders, for a
reasonable amount of time, in negotiations over drug pricing. Yet this
requirement may be waived at the discretion of the member state.[33] Notably, and contrary to popular perception, the TRIPS agreement does not
limit states' use of compulsory licenses to any particular diseases, such
as HIV/AIDS or malaria. Neither does TRIPS direct that compulsory
licenses may be used only to access "essential" or "life-saving drugs."
To the contrary, member states have broad flexibility to use compulsory
licenses to meet their public health needs as they themselves determine
these needs. The declaration reaffirms "the right of WTO Members to
use, to the full, the provisions in the TRIPS Agreement, which provide
flexibility for this purpose."[34]

In 2007 the Thai government sought to exercise these flexibilities to
meet its obligations under its national health plan. Thailand's national
health scheme covers 80 percent of its total population—that is, some 63
million people. Like most low- and middle-income countries, Thailand's
number one killer is not AIDS, but heart disease. Using the discretion
afforded to its government under TRIPS, Thai authorities issued a compulsory license on the antiplatelet drug clopidogrel, which is used to treat
heart disease. With the compulsory license, the drug price fell from two
dollars a pill to two cents per pill—a savings of 99 percent. This is far
lower than any discounted price the government would have been able to

negotiate with the patent owner. Thailand also issued compulsory licenses to authorize generic production of the heart medication Plavix and the AIDS drug Kaletra. Uproar from Western governments ensued. Critics argued that compulsory licenses ought to be limited to AIDS drugs alone. But in fact no such limitation exists under TRIPS. In fact, the World Health Organization has recognized heart disease as the leading cause of death for adults, with 80 percent of these deaths occurring in low- and middle-income countries. The Thai government was simply acting to meet the public health needs of the Thai people. Furthermore, Thai democracy is itself at stake—Thailand's constitution guarantees citizens an "equal right" to receive health services. Thus while a small minority of Thai citizens can and do pay the monopoly drug prices charged in the developed world, the vast majority of the nation's people must depend on the state for their health care, including medicines.

For such compulsory licenses to be effective, of course, there must be a generic drug industry ready to make the drug. In the case of clopidogrel, there was robust competition among generic drug makers in India, because India did not recognize drug patents when the drug was introduced in 1987. As a result, more than forty Indian firms were producing the drug in 2007, and fierce competition among them forced the drug price down dramatically.[35] The scope for continued generic production of new drugs introduced after 2005 remains unclear because of international patent obligations. But as we will see, governments like India and Brazil have nonetheless sought to limit new patents by adopting high patent-ability standards as well as procedures for contesting patent applications, all within the framework of TRIPS. The leaders of these countries hope to exclude from patentability those innovations that are not truly novel and thus preserve room for continued generic drug production, albeit on a more limited basis.

Brazil has also taken a lead in using or threatening to use compulsory licenses to provide access to medicines for its citizens. The Brazilian government is recognized the world over for its public health program to combat AIDS—the state provides free treatment to all who need it. An estimated 600,000 Brazilians are infected with AIDS, and the nation's program is credited with maintaining the life of some 170,000 AIDS patients annually. But the government has only been able to meet the public health needs of its citizens through the repeated use or threat of compulsory licenses on patented AIDS drugs. In recent years the country's president has himself issued a compulsory license on AIDS drugs in the hopes of treating afflicted Brazilian patients.

Some express the concern that compulsory licensing will adversely affect pharmaceutical companies' incentives. Generic drug prices available under compulsory licenses are certainly far lower than specially negotiated prices with drug companies would be. Yet studies suggest that the incentive effect of compulsory licenses on drug companies is in fact negligible because profits from poor populations in countries such as Thailand and Brazil rarely enter into Big Pharma's expected profit calculations in the first place. By and large, Big Pharma ignores these markets altogether, catering only to the rich minority populations in these places. As James Love, an advocate for global access to medicines, argues, there is little to no incentive effect of using compulsory licenses "where consumption of high priced patented medicines [is] basically zero."[36] This was the case for Plavix in Thailand—the drug simply was not available to those under the national health scheme—and has been the case for AIDS drugs in Thailand, Brazil, and South Africa. Love concludes, "In these and in countless other cases, the harm from the lack of access is huge, and the incentive effects are incredibly small. These empirical realities are quite important in evaluating the trade-offs."[37]

It is important to note here that compulsory licenses are in fact a common tool used in the context of patents even in the developed world; they are by no means limited to use by the developing world. The U.S. government has famously issued compulsory licenses—from the early twentieth century when it broke the Wright Brothers' patent in the airplane in order to build fleets of planes during World War I, to the beginning of the new millennium when it threatened to break the pharmaceutical company Bayer's patent in the medication Cipro during the anthrax scare. Notably, the U.S. Supreme Court recently opened the door even further to compulsory licenses with its 2006 opinion in the case of *eBay v. MercExchange*. The Court in that case held that a finding of patent infringement does not automatically demand an injunction to stop infringement. In cases where equity demands it, a compulsory license may be the better remedy. In the United States, compulsory licenses have been invoked to balance the equities and further the public interest, even where incentives and markets would be substantially affected.

Compulsory licenses for least developed countries. TRIPS Article 31(f) requires that compulsory licenses be used for the supply of a country's "domestic market" only.[38] Yet as the Doha Declaration recognized, the least-developed countries could not take advantage of the compulsory licensing provisions in TRIPS because they lack the manufacturing capability to produce generics in their home countries. As mentioned earlier, in 2003 the WTO temporarily resolved this conundrum through a waiver agreement allowing countries such as India to use compulsory licenses for export markets as well. But the waiver (now an amendment to the TRIPS agreement) has so far largely failed to move drugs to the poorest countries—indeed, to date it has only been invoked one time. In 2007 Rwanda issued a compulsory license to import an AIDS drug manufactured by a Canadian pharmaceutical company; per the waiver's procedural requirements, Canada also issued a compulsory license to produce and export the drug. Such cumbersome procedures—requiring both the exporting and importing countries to issue compulsory licenses—have stalled the effective use of this tool by some of the countries that need it the most.

High patentability standards and progressive procedures. The success of compulsory licensing depends on having countries that can produce generic drugs. The Indian Patent Act of 1970 allowed India to produce generic drugs for its own population and for the rest of the developing world. But the introduction into all WTO countries of TRIPS standards, which went into effect in 2005 in all but the least developed countries, puts considerable pressure on generic drug industries in countries like India. Since that date, India has had to recognize patents in novel and nonobvious processes *and products in all fields of technology.* In amending its patent law in 2005 to be TRIPS compliant, however, Indian legislators wisely introduced progressive provisions into its law—both substantive and procedural—that maximize their ability to reject non-novel patents, thus opening the door to future generic medicines. For instance, one important substantive provision in India's new patent law is section 3(d), which prohibits a practice pejoratively known as "evergreening," where drug companies seek to extend the life of current patented products by seeking to patent slight modifications to existing drugs. A common evergreening practice, for example, is to seek a patent on a salt form of a drug. Salt forms typically have no added therapeutic value, but they do extend the shelf life of a drug. Brazil has a similar provision against evergreening in its new patent law, and recently both Brazil and India have rejected patents on various "new" first- and second-line HIV treatments, arguing that the patent applications showed no improved therapeutic effect.

An important procedural addition to India's amended patent law is its provision for both pre-grant and post-grant opposition to a patent. Notably, "any person" can challenge either a patent application before it is granted, or a patent after it is granted. Brazilian patent law has similar provisions. These procedural rules have opened the door for civil society groups such as patients' rights advocates to directly challenge patents that affect millions of lives. The combination of the anti-evergreening provision and pre-grant opposition has led to some notable successes in both India and Brazil. A recent case brought by a coalition of AIDS patients to the Delhi Patent Office resulted in a statement by the patent office that it must "give a strict interpretation of patentability criteria" because a decision in this matter "shall affect the fate of people suffering from HIV/AIDS for want of essential medicine."[39] In 2007 Novartis sought an Indian patent in imatinib mesylate, a salt form of imatinib, a cancer drug that sold under the brand name Gleevec. There, too, a plaintiff group representing cancer patients challenged the law under section 3(d), and in June 2009 the Indian Intellectual Property Appellate Board rejected the patent, holding that Novartis was unable to show increased "efficacy" in the salt form. An Indian high court also held that the new patent act must be interpreted in such a way as to uphold India's constitutional right to health.

Improved technical assistance. The Doha Declaration extends the date of implementation to 2016 for the world's least developed countries. If such countries have not already recognized patents in pharmaceutical drugs, they have until 2016 to enact legislation recognizing such patents. Despite this safety hatch, however, the United States and other countries have pressured some least developed countries to hasten their adoption of patents for drugs.[40]

An important step for preserving access to medicines in these poorest countries of the world is for intellectual property authorities, particularly the World Intellectual Property Organization (WIPO), to provide balanced "technical assistance" to the developing and least developed countries regarding how they can tailor their intellectual property systems to promote local developmental needs while still complying with TRIPS. The new patent laws in Brazil and India, with their anti-evergreening and patent opposition procedures, may serve as models for progressive patent legislation in this regard.

Leveraging publicly funded research to promote the public interest. Eight years ago, several Yale University students turned an insight into a tool that could promote access to medicines for millions. They recognized that a patent held by Yale University on a crucial AIDS drug could be used as leverage to force downstream pharmaceutical companies to ensure access to the drugs in poor countries. The students' insight was this: universities, which are openly dedicated to serving the public interest, are important players in the access-to-drugs dilemma. As a matter of fact, university research is essential to drug development. A U.S. Senate committee report in 2000 found that university research was "instrumental" in developing fifteen out of the twenty-one drugs considered by experts to have had the highest therapeutic impact.[41]

Recognizing that research universities with patentable knowledge were a powerful tool, the students launched a student movement known as Universities Allied for Essential Medicines, or UAEM. As part of this movement, they also developed an even more powerful tool—called the Equitable Access License (EAL)—that universities can use to negotiate access rights for the poor when they sell or license their patents in upstream research to private drug companies, which in turn use this knowledge to develop medicines. The EAL proposes that universities license their knowledge to private companies in exchange for an agreement that third parties can engage in generic drug production in developing countries, regardless of those countries' patent laws or whether the owner of the drug files a patent in those countries. Just as in the copyright field lawyers have shown how, through the use of Creative Commons licenses, copyright owners can donate portions of their works to the public (for example, for noncommercial use), UAEM encourages universities to use licenses to enable generic drug production in the developing world, much as was done prior to TRIPS.

Rolling back TRIPS. The TRIPS agreement has a distasteful history. It is now well known and accepted that the TRIPS agreement was not freely negotiated between the developing and developed world, but rather was a result of coercion and a WTO bargaining process that lacked transparency and favored a privileged few. A common critique of the agreement—that intellectual property rights disproportionately favor knowledge-rich countries and disfavor knowledge-poor countries—is bearing out in the flows of cash from the developing world to the developed world after TRIPS was signed. In 1999 alone, well before full compliance with TRIPS was mandatory, the developing world paid some $7.5 billion more in royalties and license fees than it received. In short, TRIPS triggered a massive transfer of wealth from poorer to richer states. Worse still, "TRIPS-plus" standards imposed by bilateral free trade agreements impose intellectual property obligations on countries well beyond those set out in the TRIPS agreement, obligations that have cut significantly into the flexibilities provided in TRIPS. Brazil, for example, was pressured into recognizing drug patents even before 2005, the deadline given it by the TRIPS agreement, and its government spent approximately $420 million in higher drug prices between 2001 and 2005 because of the preponement. Not surprisingly, Brazilian civic groups are challenging the validity of this law.[42]

Innovation-Centered Tools
Thus far I have considered mechanisms for promoting access to existing medicines under the current international patent system. But access is only part of the problem of our current exclusive reliance on patents for promoting innovation. The patent system has also failed to incentivize socially beneficial innovation where there are no effective markets—that is, where the poor have a need but are unable to pay to meet it. As more and more economists, philosophers, and legal experts have come to recognize this glaring gap in global innovation policy, highlighting the world's "missing knowledge," alternatives to patents for promoting socially beneficial innovation are emerging.

Prizes. Government-awarded prizes would be funded by taxpayers in the developed world and would be targeted to addressing pressing social needs, such as the need to cure the neglected diseases of the poor. Prize systems have several immediate benefits over patents. First, R&D for drug innovation would be delinked from drug price. Government-sponsored prizes would incentivize innovation and compensate drug companies for conducting research and holding clinical trials as part of their efforts to treat neglected diseases. Such a system may prove cheaper than the patent system, because the prize would be calculated to reward social benefit in terms of lives saved or enhanced, unlike a patent system that arbitrarily allows drug owners to charge monopoly prices for the period of the patent, regardless of social cost or benefit. Second, payment would not fall on the sick themselves (a double burden on the sick poor) but would come from better-off citizens in the developing world. While some would object, arguing that prizes create a tax on the rich to benefit the poor (and worse still, that this tax is to benefit foreigners), this is in fact not unlike the current patent system, where R&D is largely funded by citizens in the developed world. Third, prizes help to more closely direct innovation that is socially beneficial and addresses unmet needs—unlike patents, which currently skew incentives to favor therapies for the rich (like cures for baldness) over other therapies. Finally, prizes are a good tool for promoting access to medicines. Unlike patents, which create exclusive rights and monopoly prices that few can afford, developers of new drugs under a prize system would receive a lump-sum reward and no exclusive rights to control price, leaving the medicines themselves to be free for generic production and thus facilitating widespread access to them. Medicines developed under a prize regime would be owned by the people.

Granted, there are serious concerns about prizes, and some areas in which prizes do not significantly present an improvement over the patent system. Both patents and prizes, for example, introduce potential redundancy of efforts among competing firms, whereby too many firms work toward the same goal, but with the possibility of only one winner. The question of how to reward follow-on inventors is also difficult under both patent and prize systems. But these hurdles may be overcome. The legal scholars William Fisher and Talha Syed suggest, for example, capping the number of firms permitted to work simultaneously on a disease treatment.[43] Finally, there is the difficult question of what research to incentivize with a prize. The patent system does not require state coordination of innovation—private companies determine what to research. Surely we ought to be concerned about the myopia of states with respect to directing innovation too closely. But a prize system alongside a patent system would at least help states direct innovation toward social causes that are clearly both desirable and overlooked by the current patent system.

Patent pools. I have mentioned the lack of pediatric AIDS drugs because Big Pharma sees no effective market for them—yet another example of what the World Health Organization calls the "missing knowledge" that gets passed over by the market-based intellectual property system. Patents pose a further burden in such cases because follow-on creators are stymied by the existence of patent thickets, where overlapping patents in the underlying technology exist and must be overcome in order to develop a pediatric drug. In the case of a patent thicket, even if a subsequent drug developer sought to license technology from one or two patent holders, they would still face potential lawsuits from several other patent holders —and thus may back down from their effort completely. To address such patent thickets with respect to AIDS therapies and pediatric doses, in particular, UNITAID, a French health funding agency, has established a patent pool of the key pharmaceutical companies holding AIDS treatment technologies. With the aid of groups such as Doctors Without Borders, UNITAID has publicly asked nine companies to contribute patents for twenty-one products and their combinations into a pool to facilitate research for fixed-dose therapies and pediatric treatments. Like in a typical patent pool, relevant patent holders agree to license their technologies to both facilitate innovation and generate revenue. Royalty fees go to a pool manager, who divides the proceeds among the pool members. Thus far, the U.S. National Institutes of Health and Gilead Sciences have donated patents to the pool.

A Health Impact Fund. A recent proposal by philosopher Thomas Pogge and economist Aidan Hollis seeks to enhance pro-poor medical care through a market-based solution. Their proposed Health Impact Fund would create a fund from donations from world governments—ideally, every government would contribute .03 percent of their gross national income to the fund. Firms that register a patent with the fund agree to sell their drug globally at cost, in exchange for a share of the fund, for a limited period, in proportion to the drug's assessed health benefit. The guaranteed benefits from the fund would serve as a market incentive to Big Pharma to develop novel drugs for the poor; at the same time, the fund's commitment to at-cost distribution would provide access to the new medicines for the poor. While the Health Impact Fund has been widely praised and is getting serious attention in global circles, some concerns about the fund remain, including whether the potentially high costs of the fund are the best way for nations to spend their money.

In 1952 Jonas Salk developed the world's first safe and effective polio vaccine. Today it seems unthinkable to innovate without the promise of a patent, but just sixty years ago, one of the most important humanitarian

innovations of the twentieth century was the result of the tireless commitment of Salk, a medical researcher at Pennsylvania State University who
labored single-mindedly for seven years with the sole purpose of playing
a significant role in the eradication of a global plague. That year polio had
reached its height in the United States, affecting some 52,000 people. The
most famous victim of the disease was President Franklin D. Roosevelt,
who initiated an organization focused on developing a cure for the disease.
What inspired Salk's innovation was not the dream of a property right,
but rather an eleemosynary interest in applying his ingenuity to better-
ing humankind. When a television news reporter asked him whether he
owned the patent in the vaccine, a mystified Salk replied, "Who owns the
patent? The people do." Salk could not imagine claiming an exclusive
right on knowledge so important to humanity, replying, "Could you patent the sun?" Since then, hundreds of millions of people have received a
polio vaccine, and today, the disease has been largely eradicated.

Our theories of innovation and creativity matter. Our two-dimensional
theory of intellectual-property-as-incentives has, in just several decades'
time, come to influence the way many scientists and artists alike engage
the world. Standing in sharp relief from the public commitment and
meaningful work of Salk sixty years ago, today many do not think twice
about the claims from Big Pharma that they will not innovate at all, or
worse still, that they will not share their drugs in markets like Thailand
that issue compulsory licenses. We need to probe these incentive arguments on their own terms. In fact, the evidence shows that patents offer *no
incentive* for developing drugs for neglected diseases that predominantly
afflict the poor. Additionally, compulsory licenses in developing countries
do little harm to innovation, because drug companies do not sell to those
markets in the first place. But the problem lies much deeper than this. The
legal philosopher Seana Shiffrin condemns a legal system that condones
a situation where "talented people ransom their talents, withholding their
creative products in order to demand greater compensation." Shiffrin
asks whether a legal system that acquiesces to such immoral demands
is not itself unjust.[44]

A one-size-fits-all patent system for drugs in the developing world
is unjust on additional grounds, beyond incentives. Patents that impede
access to the poor thwart both local democracy and human development.
Nations must have the freedom to democratically construct patent poli-

cies to meet their humanitarian needs. For centuries countries had this freedom—nations from Germany to Switzerland took advantage of their freedom to ignore patents and copy freely knowledge that came from other parts of the globe. Indeed, the self-determination to construct one's own patent law reflects more than a simple utilitarian calculus to promote indigenous innovation. Patent policy affects the ability of a country to stand on its own two feet, independent of foreign knowledge and industry.

Economists call the millions of people who need a drug but cannot afford it "dead weight loss." But the millions who die needlessly because of the patent system are more than an inefficiency in the system. This loss of *human lives* fundamentally thwarts human development at the most basic level. Furthermore, lack of access to essential medicines is patently unjust because it is preventable. Wholly unlike physical property, which will naturally lose its value if overrun by large numbers, the unique property of knowledge is that *its value is not diminished by greater use*—far from it, the knowledge value only grows as it is used by more people, in additional, different ways. As Thomas Jefferson wrote so eloquently centuries ago, "He who receives an idea from me, receives instruction himself without lessening mine, as he who lights his taper at mine, receives light without darkening me."[45] We must both adopt alternative mechanisms for developing and distributing medicines to the poor (including prizes), and fully support the use of compulsory licenses by developing countries to treat their sick poor. Patent law cannot draw the line at rectifying market failure. Our law must contend with moral failure as well.

ACKNOWLEDGMENTS

THIS IS A BOOK ABOUT *BRICOLAGE*—how we create our lives from the diverse range of material around us. The creation of a book is no different, and for each page I can recall the varied conversations with colleagues, exchanges with my students, and experiences with my children that shaped the contents herein. Popular culture and politics, too, profoundly affected this work. During the writing of this book, the United States elected its first black president, after a campaign that employed YouTube and social networks. Decades-long dictatorships in the Middle East were brought to their knees by Internet activists informing and coordinating those who marched in the streets. Michael Jackson died. I joined Facebook. And my babies began growing up, working their way through the fantasy world of *Winnie the Pooh* and later, *Harry Potter*. I watched them build new worlds with wood blocks, Legos, and the Wii. So much has changed even during their short lives so far. While my daughter's first word was "dog," my son's first word just a few years later was "pbskids.org."

I was traveling for much of the writing of this book, because my husband and I were invited to be visiting law professors at the Yale Law School and the University of Chicago Law School. Traveling, as James Clifford suggests, can be culturally productive. My encounters with the faculty and students of the Yale Law School were particularly helpful as I began formulating this book. It was a lunch conversation with Bruce

Ackerman that pointed me toward Habermas and a chat with Jack Balkin that led me to conclude, in his words, that "Kant Can't Dance"—that is, that modern social theory has not adequately taken account of dance and cultural performance. So Michael Jackson and Jack Balkin together influenced sections on dance in this book. (Talk about a mash-up.) Jack's helpful observation, and reminder, that this is a book about "culture, not intellectual property" provided a valuable guidepost throughout my journey. Bob Ellickson counseled against the narcissism of the new "i" and "My" generation, keeping me alert to the repercussions, good and bad, of Web 2.0. Akhil Amar and Amy Chua gave generous advice about book publishing. Laura DeNardis, Lea Shaver, and the Yale Information Society Project (ISP) provided a wonderful intellectual breeding ground for the early days of this project. Harold Koh, then dean of the Yale Law School, continues to be a mentor extraordinaire.

At the University of Chicago, I had the fortune to work with Martha Nussbaum, whose scholarship has long been an intellectual inspiration. Martha's imprint can be seen throughout this book—not just her theory of human capabilities, but also her engagement with dance, music, and drama as a vehicle to freedom and equality. She generously read several chapters and has advised me on many levels throughout the writing of this book. We discussed Rawls and Habermas on the top of Mount Tamalpais, and performance theory on the Tahoe Rim Trail. Emily Buss heightened my sensitivity to copyright's effects on children, and conversations with her led me to study more closely the relevance of theories of child development to intellectual property law. The manuscript started to take real shape in Chicago and I gained tremendously from the critical insights of so many on the faculty there, especially Daniel Abebe, Rosalind Dixon, Lee Ann Fennel, Tom Ginsburg, Aziz Huq, Saul Levmore, Richard McAdams, Randy Picker, Julie Roin, Adam Samaha, Omri Ben-Shahar, Lior Strahilevitz, and David Weisbach. Jonathan Masur's invitation to host a mob blog debate on the University of Chicago Law faculty blog on "cultural versus economic theories of intellectual property" gave me a further opportunity to explore and develop the broad themes of the book with invited scholars, including Robert Merges of UC Berkeley, Rochelle Dreyfuss of NYU, Graeme Dinwoodie of Oxford, and Mario Biagioli— then of Harvard, now my colleague at UC Davis. All of these wonderful interlocutors helped me to revise and refine my arguments.

It was back at my home, at the UC Davis School of Law, where I finally finished this book. I am grateful to my colleagues at UC Davis, who have made the Martin Luther King, Jr. Hall an exceptional intellectual environment for me. I cannot imagine a dean more supportive than Kevin Johnson. My beloved colleague, the late Keith Aoki, was a constant source of ideas and support. If I had only known my time with him would be so limited, I would have spent every day talking to him to learn from that brilliant mind. Tom Joo did the Herculean task of closely and critically reading a number of draft chapters, for which I am so thankful. Peter Lee is always ready to chat about IP, and Jack Ayer and Joel Dobris provide me a constant stream of fresh examples from the news and the Net. Mario Biagioli's arrival at UC Davis, and with him a new Center for Science and Innovation Studies (CSIS), has had a transformative effect already on our campus and on my thinking. Through the CSIS I have already learned much from my newly discovered colleagues across the Quad, especially Marisol de la Cadena, Joe Dumit, and Kriss Ravetto. Kelly Twibell at the Center for Child and Family Studies at UC Davis supplied insights into the role of play in child development.

Above all, this book is a conversation with my mentors and colleagues in the intellectual property academy, to whom I owe my greatest debt. Indeed, the book began the day in 2006 when Larry Lessig asked me to write a paper reflecting on the ten-year anniversary of James Boyle's public domain scholarship. The paper I wrote for that celebratory event, "Cultural Environmentalism @ 10," held at the Stanford Law School, appears here as Chapter 5. The gathering was a veritable "Who's Who" of intellectual property scholars and I gained much from my exchanges there, especially those with Yochai Benkler, Jamie Boyle, Maggie Chon, Terry Fisher, Mark Lemley, and Peggy Radin. The influences of all of these giants in the field can be seen throughout this book.

Maggie Chon, Anupam Chander, and I were together in Geneva in 2007 when the World Intellectual Property Organization (WIPO) adopted a revolutionary "development agenda" to reorient its practice to promote human development. I have learned much from both of them about the meaning of development, as I have also learned from James Love and Thiru Balasubramaniam of Knowledge Ecology International, who kindly allowed us access to WIPO during this critical period. Intellectual property scholars in India have also become my colleagues over this period, in particular Anil Gupta, V. K. Unni, Sudhir Krishnaswamy, and V. C. Vivekanandan.

Participants at workshops around the world were generous with ideas and encouragement. The Fordham University School of Law's Center for Law and Information Policy brought in a dream team of commentators—Shyam Balganesh, Julie Cohen, Jamela Debelak, Deven Desai, Sonia Katyal, John Palfrey, Joel Reidenberg, and Thane Rosenberg—for a workshop on my draft manuscript in New York. The book benefited from presentations at the UCLA School of Law, the Loyola–LA Law School, Santa Clara Law School, the "Copyright Culture, Copyright History" conference at the Tel Aviv University Law School, the annual Conference of the Asian Pacific American Law Faculty, and the Progressive Property Scholars Workshop hosted at McGill University Law School. So many individuals provided valuable feedback in these fora, but a few stand out for taking the time to correspond with me further about the project, and for this I thank especially Jade Eaton, Doug Lichtman, and Jennifer Rothman.

I received fabulous research assistance at a number of schools. Special thanks to Mytili Bala, Amy Benford, Krista Celentano, Sheirin Ghoddoucy, Roya Ladan, Rabia Paracha, and Dominick Severence. I have always been able to rely on UC Davis librarian Erin Murphy to track down even the most obscure requests.

A special shout-out goes to my friend Shyam Balganesh, who read the entire manuscript from cover to cover and provided invaluable advice and criticism. Ongoing conversations with my longtime mentors, Rich Ford and Janet Halley, have braced me in the writing process. I am grateful to Aruna and Hima Dasika, who read the manuscript with an eye to making it more accessible for a general audience. I received generous research support from the UC Davis School of Law, the University of Chicago Law School, Yale Law School, and the Carnegie Corporation. Though I was named a Carnegie Corporation Scholar to support my work on Muslim women's reinterpretation of Islam in equality-promoting ways, that research influenced my thinking on law and culture here. For artistic inspiration (and copyright permissions), I thank the Indian artist Mohan Sivanand and the Danish super-group Superflex: Bjorn Christiansen, Jakob Fenger, and Rasmus Nielsen. My parents, family, and friends have been a constant source of encouragement—and my dad, a provider of much needed prodding with his relentless query, "Is the book finished yet?"

Chapters and portions of chapters of this book were published earlier in law reviews. The broad themes of the book were first explored in "IP3," published in 2006 in the *Stanford Law Review,* and sections of that paper reappear here, as do portions of "Foreword: Is Nozick Kicking Rawls's Ass?" co-authored with Anupam Chander, which appeared in 2007 in the *UC Davis Law Review* (vol. 40, pp. 563–79, copyright 2007 by The Regents of the University of California. All rights reserved. Reprinted with permission). Much of Chapter 4 was co-authored with Anupam Chander and originally published in 2007 in the *California Law Review* as "Everyone's a Superhero: A Cultural Theory of 'Mary Sue' Fan Fiction as Fair Use." An earlier version of Chapter 5 was published in 2007 in *Law & Contemporary Problems* under the title "The Invention of Traditional Knowledge." And much of Chapter 6 first appeared in 2011 in *Theoretical Inquiries in Law* as "Bollywood/Hollywood."

I am grateful to Michael O'Malley, my acquisitions editor at Yale University Press, for his unwavering confidence in this project. And thanks to Piyali Bhattacharya, Julie Carlson, Niamh Cunningham, and Alison MacKeen, who have proven to be an especially valuable team of editors.

Finally, I thank my husband, colleague, and co-author in life, Anupam Chander. In this case, Anupam literally co-wrote Chapter 4, which we originally published together. But that is just the smallest evidence of his collaboration. With Anupam, I have learned that life itself is a work of art.

NOTES

INTRODUCTION

1. Martha Nussbaum, *Women and Human Development* 5 (2000).
2. Rian Malan, *In the Jungle* 7 (2003).
3. World Health Organization, *Declaration of the TRIPS Agreement and Public Health*, para. 4 (2001) [hereinafter Doha Declaration], available at http://www.wto.org/english/thewto_e/minist_e/min01_e/mindecl_trips_e.htm (last visited Aug. 8, 2011).
4. *The 45 Adopted Recommendations Under the WIPO Development Agenda*, para 45, (2007), available at http://www.wipo.int/ip-development/en/agenda/recommendations.html (last visited Aug. 8, 2011).
5. This is the classic account of copyright and patent rights. See William M. Landes and Richard A. Posner, *The Economic Structure of Intellectual Property Law* 37–165, 294–333 (2003). Recent understandings of trademark also encompass a version of the incentive rationale (at 166).
6. "Statement of Progressive Property Scholars," 94 Cornell L. Rev. 743–44 (2009).
7. Joseph Singer, "Democratic Estates: Property Law in a Free and Democratic Society," 94 Cornell L. Rev. 1009, 1020 (2009).
8. Michel Foucault, "What Is Enlightenment?," in *The Foucault Reader* (P. Rabinow, ed. 1984).
9. Nussbaum, *Women and Human Development* 78 (2000).
10. These are excerpts from Nussbaum's elaborated list of central human capabilities; see *id.* at 78–80.
11. Michel Foucault, "What Is an Author?," in *Language, Counter-Memory, Practice: Selected Essays and Interviews* 118 (Donald F. Bouchard, ed., 1977).
12. See Andrew Keen, *The Cult of the Amateur* 4 (2007), where Keen decries

user-created content as mediocre, uninformed, inferior, inaccurate, inane, tasteless, embarrassing, unreadable, and shameless.

13. Amartya Sen, "Cultural Liberty and Human Development," in *Human Development Report, 2004: Cultural Liberty in Today's Diverse World* 13 (2004).

14. Antje Gimmler, "Deliberative Democracy: The Public Sphere and the Internet," 27 Philosophy and Social Criticism 21, 22 (2001).

15. President Barack Obama, Inaugural Address, Jan. 20, 2009.

16. Mary Hohmann and David P. Weikart, *Educating Young Children: Active Learning Practices for Preschool and Child Care Programs* 59 (2002).

17. John Dewey, *The Later Works, 1925–1953*, vol. 10: *Art as Experience* 335 (2008).

18. Salman Rushdie, "Excerpts from Rushdie's Address: 1,000 Days 'Trapped Inside a Metaphor,'" N.Y. Times, Dec. 12, 1991 at B8 (excerpts from speech delivered at Columbia University).

19. Immanuel Kant, "An Answer to the Question: What Is Enlightenment?," in *Perpetual Peace and Other Essays on Politics, History, and Morals* 41 (Ted Humphrey, trans., 1983 [1795]).

20. Zadie Smith, "Generation Why?," N.Y. Review of Books, Nov. 25, 2010 at 57.

21. Cass Sunstein, *Republic.com* (2001).

22. Keen, *Cult of the Amateur* 7 (where he complains that rather than using the Internet "to seek news, information, or culture, we use it to actually BE the news, information, the culture").

23. Virginia Heffernan, "The Many Tribes of YouTube," N.Y. Times, May 27, 2007.

24. Henry Smith, "Mind the Gap: The Indirect Relation Between Ends and Means in American Property Law," 94 Cornell L. Rev. 959, 970 (2009) (responding to Gregory S. Alexander, "The Social-Obligation Norm in American Property Law," 94 Cornell L. Rev. 745 [2009]).

25. United Nations Development Programme, *Human Development Report, 2004: Cultural Liberty in Today's Diverse World* 6 (2004).

26. Robert S. Boynton, "The Tyranny of Copyright?," N.Y. Times, Jan. 25, 2004 at 40.

27. Michel Foucault, "What Is Enlightenment?," in *The Foucault Reader* 32, 42 (Paul Rabinow, ed., 1984) ("Modern man . . . is not the man who goes off to discover himself, his secrets and his hidden truth; he is the man who tries to invent himself").

CHAPTER 1. BEYOND INCENTIVES

1. See James Boyle, *Shamans, Software, and Spleens: Law and the Construction of the Information Society* 44 (1996) (characterizing economic incentives as a common justification for intellectual property); William Fisher, "Theories of Intellectual Property," in *New Essays in the Legal and Political Theory*

of Property 168, 169 (2001) (describing utilitarian theory as the "most popular" theory of intellectual property); Mark A. Lemley, "Property, Intellectual Property, and Free Riding," 83 Tex. L. Rev. 1031 (2005) ("Intellectual property protection in the United States has always been about generating incentives to create"); Jed Rubenfeld, Professor, Yale Law School, Remarks at the Duke Conference on the Public Domain (Nov. 9–11, 2001), available at http://www.law.duke.edu/pd/realcast.htm (last visited Aug. 8, 2011, calling economic analysis of intellectual property the "ruling paradigm" in the field); *cf.* William W. Fisher III, "Property and Contract on the Internet," 73 Chi.-Kent L. Rev. 1203, 1214 (1998) (writing that while the judicial and scholarly writings on intellectual property are "rife with invocations of [the utilitarian] ideal," the theoretical bases of intellectual property are contested). Even the scholarship championing the public domain relies largely on incentives arguments regarding the importance of the public domain to the process of creation. I have critiqued that scholarship's failure to integrate concerns for distributive justice. See Anupam Chander and Madhavi Sunder, "The Romance of the Public Domain," 92 Cal. L. Rev. 1331 (2004); Madhavi Sunder, "The Invention of Traditional Knowledge," 70 Law & Contemp. Probs. 95 (Spring 2007).

2. William M. Landes and Richard A. Posner, *The Economic Structure of Intellectual Property Law* 424 (2003). Posner and Landes conclude that "there is no basis for confidence that the existing scope and duration of either patent or copyright protection are optimal" (at 422). They clarify that "The doubt is not whether the protection is too meager but whether it is too great, imposing access and transaction costs disproportionately to the likely benefits from enhancing the incentives to produce socially valuable intellectual property" (at 422).

3. Mark A. Lemley, "Property, Intellectual Property, and Free Riding," 83 Tex. L. Rev. 1031, 1075 (2005); see also Robert S. Boynton, "The Tyranny of Copyright?," N.Y. Times, Jan. 25, 2004, at 40 (pronouncing the same).

4. See Brief for George A. Akerlof et al. as Amici Curiae Supporting Petitioners at 2, *Eldred v. Ashcroft,* 537 U.S. 186 (2003) (No. 01–618), 2002 WL 1041846 (emphasis mine). See also *Eldred v. Ashcroft,* 537 U.S. 186, 254 (2003) (Breyer, J., dissenting) (saying of the Copyright Term Extension Act of 1998 that "no one could reasonably conclude that copyright's traditional economic rationale applies here"); *id.* at 257 ("[I]n respect to works already created . . . *the statute creates no economic incentive at all*"). Judge Posner has also agreed that "tacking on years at the end of an already long copyright term has only negligible effects on the incentive to create a copyrighted work in the first place." Richard A. Posner, "Eldred and Fair Use," 1 The Economists' Voice 1, 1 (2004).

5. *Metro-Goldwyn-Mayer Studios Inc. v. Grokster, Ltd.,* 125 S. Ct. 2764 (2005).

6. Brief for Kenneth J. Arrow, Ian Ayres, Gary Becker, William M. Landes, Steven Levitt, Douglas Lichtman, Kevin Murphy, Randal Picker, Andrew

Rosenfield, and Steven Shavell as Amici Curiae Supporting Petitioners at 8, *Metro-Goldwyn-Mayer Studios Inc. v. Grokster, Ltd.*, 125 S. Ct. 2764 (2005) (No. 04–480), 2005 WL 176441.

7. Brief for Internet Law Faculty as Amici Curiae Supporting Respondents at 2, Metro-*Goldwyn-Mayer Studios Inc. v. Grokster, Ltd.*, 125 S. Ct. 2764 (2005) (No. 04–480), 2005 WL 508098.

8. Shyamkrishna Balganesh, "Foreseeability and Copyright Incentives," 122 Harv. L. Rev. 1569 (2009).

9. *State Street Bank & Trust Co. v. Signature Financial Group, Inc.*, 149 F.3d 1368 (Fed. Cir. 1998).

10. *Bilski v. Kappos*, 130 S.Ct. 3218 (2010).

11. *Ebay Inc. v. MercExchange*, LLC, 547 U.S. 388 (2006).

12. See Emmanuelle Fauchart and Eric A. Von Hippel, "Norms-Based Intellectual Property Systems: The Case of French Chefs," MIT Sloan working paper no. 4576–06 (Jan. 2006), available at http://ssrn.com/abstract=881781 (last visited Aug. 8, 2011). See also Dotan Oliar and Christopher Jon Sprigman, "There's No Free Laugh (Anymore): The Emergence of Intellectual Property Norms and the Transformation of Stand-Up Comedy," 94 Va. L. Rev 1789 (2008); Kal Raustiala and Christopher Jon Sprigman, "The Piracy Paradox: Innovation and Intellectual Property in Fashion Design," 92 Va. L. Rev. 1687 (2006).

13. See Fauchart and Hippel, "Norms-Based Intellectual Property Systems." See also Oliar and Sprigman, "There's No Free Laugh (Anymore)"; Raustiala and Sprigman, "The Piracy Paradox."

14. See Mark A. Lemley, "The Modern Lanham Act and the Death of Common Sense," 108 Yale L. J. 1687 (1999). See also Boyle, *Shamans, Software, and Spleens;* Lawrence Lessig, *Free Culture: How Big Media Uses Technology and the Law to Lock down Culture and Control Creativity* (2004).

15. Information about the Founders' Copyright is available at http://creative commons.org/projects/founderscopyright (last visited Aug. 8, 2011).

16. Landes and Posner, *The Economic Structure of Intellectual Property Law* ("there is much more to economic analysis of intellectual property than a concern with providing incentives to create such property").

17. See Fisher, "Property and Contract on the Internet," 1203, 1215–1218.

18. Landes and Posner, *The Economic Structure of Intellectual Property Law* at 420 ("Economics is a great simplifier of law").

19. In fact, the majority relied in part on Judge Pierre Leval's arguments put forth in Pierre N. Leval, "Toward a Fair Use Standard," 103 Harv. L. Rev. 1105 (1990), which argued for a broader assessment of fair use than that focused merely on market failure. Justice Kennedy's concurrence cites Richard A. Posner, "When Is Parody Fair Use?," 21 J. Legal Stud. 67 (1992).

20. See, e.g., Robert P. Merges, "Are You Making Fun of Me? Notes on Market Failure and the Parody Defense in Copyright," 21 Am. Intell. Prop. L. Ass'n. Q.J. 305 (1993).

21. Posner, "When Is Parody Fair Use?," 67, 71.

22. *Id.* at 72.

23. Henry Jenkins, *Convergence Culture* 198–99 (2006).

24. *Id.* at 198.

25. A snapshot of the original webpage is on file with the author. The website was quickly taken off the Internet after Dangermouse received a cease-and-desist letter from EMI.

26. Carly Carioli, "Black + White = The Grey Album" *Portland Phoenix,* Mar. 5–11, 2004.

27. Henry Louis Gates, Jr., *Figures in Black: Words, Signs, and the "Racial" Self* 235–36 (1987) ("Signification is a theory of reading that arises from Afro-American culture; learning how to signify is often part of our adolescent education"); see also Thomas G. Schumacher, "'This Is a Sampling Sport': Digital Sampling, Rap Music and the Law in Cultural Production," 17 Media, Culture & Soc'y 253, 267 (1995); Joanna Demers, *Steal This Music: How Intellectual Property Law Affects Musical Creativity* (2006).

28. Jenkins, *Convergence Culture* at 199.

29. Similar conclusions are offered in the Ford Foundation–sponsored *Code of Best Practices in Fair Use for Online Video* (2008), available at http://www .centerforsocialmedia.org/fair-use/related-materials/codes/code-best-practices-fair-use-online-video (last visited Aug. 8, 2011).

30. Michel Foucault, "What Is an Author?," in *Language, Counter-Memory, Practice: Selected Essays and Interviews* 118 (Donald F. Bouchard, ed., 1977).

31. Paul Oskar Kristeller, "'Creativity' and 'Tradition,'" 44 J. Hist. Ideas 105, 107 (1983).

32. In contrast, Neil Netanel values parody because speech outside the original copyrighted work would be "far less effective, far less believable, and of far less value to the intended audience without reproducing substantial portions of the author's work." Neil Netanel, *Copyright's Paradox* 112 (2008).

33. See generally Jürgen Habermas, *The Theory of Communicative Action,* vols. 1 and 2 (1981).

34. Madhavi Sunder, "Cultural Dissent," 54 Stan. L. Rev. 495, 564–65 (2001).

35. Linda Civitello, *Cuisine and Culture: A History of Food and People* 64 (2008).

36. Janet Adamy and Roger Thurow, "Ethiopia Battles Starbucks over Rights to Coffee Names," Wall St. J., March 5, 2007.

37. The parties entered a five-year nonexclusive license, under which Starbucks (and, in separate licenses, other roasters) agree in good faith to advertise the brand to consumers. See Trademark License Agreement, http:// www.ethiopiancoffeenetwork.com/downloads/US_Trademark_License _Agreement.pdf (last visited Aug. 8, 2011).

38. Benoît Daviron and Stefano Ponte, *The Coffee Paradox: Global Markets, Commodity Trade and the Elusive Promise of Development* 160 (2005).

39. Adamy and Thurow, "Ethiopia Battles Starbucks over Rights to Coffee Names."

40. Amartya K. Sen, *Poverty and Famine* (1983).
41. "Struggle over Hoodia Patent Continues," Business Day (Johannesburg), Jul. 12, 2006 at 6.
42. European Patent Office, *Scenarios for the Future* at 9 (2007) (emphasis in original).

CHAPTER 2. BESPOKE CULTURE

1. This is a story told by Clay Shirky. See Web 2.0 Conference, San Francisco 2008, available at http://video.google.com/videoplay?docid=-2708219 489770693816# (last visited Aug. 8, 2011, declaring that "a screen that ships without a mouse ships broken" and sharing his own motto for Web 2.0: "We're looking for the mouse."). On the generation that is "born digital," see John Palfrey and Urs Gasser, *Born Digital: Understanding the First Generation of Digital Natives* (2008); "Born Digital: Children of the Revolution," Wired, Sept. 2002.
2. I use the word "culture" to describe both artistic and scientific knowledge, the production of which is the express purpose of Constitutionally mandated copyright and patent in the United States. See generally the U.S. Const., art. 1, §8, cl. 8, empowering Congress "To promote the Progress of Science and useful Arts, by securing for limited Times to Authors and Inventors the exclusive Right to their respective Writings and Discoveries."
3. Seth Schiesel, "All Together Now: Play the Game, Mom," N.Y. Times, Sept. 1, 2009 at AR1.
4. John Hartley, "Uses of YouTube: Digital Literacy and the Growth of Knowledge," in Jean Burgess and Joshua Green, *YouTube: Online Video and Participatory Culture* 130 (2009).
5. Janet Halley, "Culture Constrains," in *Is Multiculturalism Bad for Women?* (Princeton University Press, 1999).
6. Kwame Anthony Appiah, *In My Father's House* 141 (1992).
7. Arjun Appadurai, "Disjuncture and Difference in the Global Cultural Economy," 2 Pub. Culture 1, 18 (1990).
8. Edward B. Tylor, "Primitive Culture," in *High Points in Anthropology* 6 (Paul Bohannan and Mark Glazer, eds., 2d ed. 1988).
9. Bronislaw Malinowski, "Culture," in *Encyclopedia of the Social Sciences* 4:621 (1931).
10. Ruth Benedict, *Race: Science and Politics* 13 (1959 rev. ed.).
11. Margaret Mead, *Cooperation and Competition Among Primitive Peoples* 17 (1937).
12. Edward T. Hall, *The Hidden Dimension* 177 (1966).
13. Emile Durkheim, *The Division of Labor in Society* 79–80 (1933).
14. *Merriam Webster Dictionary*, available at http://www.merriamwebster.com/dictionary/culture (last visited Aug. 8, 2011).
15. Clifford Geertz, *The Interpretation of Cultures* 4 (1973).

16. *Id.* at 5.

17. James Clifford, *The Predicament of Culture* 10 (1988).

18. C. W. Mills, *The Power Elite* (1956).

19. Jürgen Habermas, *The Theory of Communicative Action* 390 (1981).

20. Jürgen Habermas, *The Structural Transformation of the Public Sphere: An Inquiry into a Category of Bourgeois Society* 160 (1962) ("The public sphere in the world of letters was replaced by the pseudo-public or semi-private world of culture consumption").

21. *Id.* at 164, 168.

22. *Id.* at 164.

23. *Id.* at 165 ("mass culture has earned its rather dubious name precisely by achieving increased sales by adapting to the need for relaxation and entertainment on the part of consumer strata with relatively little education").

24. *Id.* at 166.

25. *Id.* at 172.

26. *Id.* at 175.

27. *Id.* at 249.

28. *Id.* at 246.

29. Julian Dibbel, "We Pledge Allegiance to the Penguin," Wired, Nov. 2004, available at http://www.wired.com/wired/archive/12.11/linux.html (last visited Aug. 8, 2011).

30. Habermas, *The Structural Transformation of the Public Sphere* 247.

31. Paul E. Bierley, *John Philip Sousa: American Phenomenon* 19 (2001).

32. John Philip Sousa, *Congressional Testimony* (1906).

33. John Philip Sousa, "The Menace of Mechanical Music," Appleton's Magazine (1906).

34. *Id.*

35. "Canned Music," N.Y. Times, December 13, 1907.

36. Burgess and Green, *YouTube: Online Video and Participatory Culture* 43.

37. OECD, *Participative Web: User-Created Content* 22 (2007).

38. *Id.* at 24.

39. Burgess and Green, *YouTube: Online Video and Participatory Culture* 43.

40. See A. Michael Froomkin, "Habermas Toward a Critical Theory of Cyberspace," 116 Harv. L. Rev. 749, 855–71 (2003).

41. *Reno v. ACLU,* 521 U.S. 844, 870 (1997) (quoting *Reno v. ACLU,* 929 F. Supp. 824, 842 [E.D. Pa. 1996]).

42. See Anupam Chander, "Whose Republic?," 69 U. Chi. L. Rev. 1479, 1488–89 (2002).

43. Tim Berners-Lee, *Weaving the Web* 57 (1999).

44. Technorati, *State of the Blogosphere 2008,* available at http://technorati.com/blogging/state-of-the-blogosphere/ (last visited Aug. 8, 2011).

45. *Wikipedia,* available at http://en.wikipedia.org/wiki/Wikipedia (last visited Aug. 8, 2011).

46. See, e.g., Thomas Wuil Joo, "A Contrarian View of Copyright: Hip-Hop, Sampling, and Semiotic Democracy," 44 Conn. L. Rev. (forthcoming 2012).

47. Human Rights Watch, "Egypt: Investigate Beating of 'Facebook' Activist," May 10, 2008, available at http://hrw.org/english/docs/2008/05/10/ egypt18800_txt.htm (last visited Aug. 8, 2011).

48. Burgess and Green, *YouTube: Online Video and Participatory Culture* 83.

49. John Rawls, "The Idea of Public Reason Revisited," 64 U. Chi. L. Rev. 765, 768–769 (1997).

50. *Id.* at 768 (1997) ("The idea of public reason does not apply to the background culture with its many forms of nonpublic reason nor to the media of any kind").

51. John Rawls, "Political Liberalism: Reply to Habermas," Journal of Philosophy 132, 134, vol. 92 (March 1995).

52. Jürgen Habermas, *Between Facts and Norms: Contributions to a Discourse Theory of Law and Democracy* xli (William Rehg, trans., 1996).

53. Michel Foucault, "What Is Enlightenment?," in *The Foucault Reader* 32 (Paul Rainbow, ed., 1984).

54. *Id.* at 38, 42.

55. *Id.* at 35.

56. *Id.* at 50.

57. Balkin defines a "democratic culture" as one in which "everyone—not just political, economic, or cultural elites—has a fair chance to participate in the production of culture, and in the development of the ideas and meanings that constitute them and the communities and subcommunities to which they belong." Jack M. Balkin, "Digital Speech and Democratic Culture: A Theory of Freedom of Expression for the Information Society," 79 N.Y.U. L. Rev. 1, 3–4 (2004).

58. *Id.* at 39.

59. Salman Rushdie, "Excerpts from Rushdie's Address: 1,000 Days 'Trapped Inside a Metaphor,'" N.Y. Times, Dec. 12, 1991 at B8 (excerpts from a speech delivered at Columbia University).

60. Martha Nussbaum, "Democracy, Education, and the Liberal Arts: Two Asian Models" 44 U.C. Davis Law Rev. 735, 747 (2011).

61. "Glee—Single Ladies—Kurt Version," available at http://www.youtube .com/watch?v=-JccaNIAynI (last visited September 14, 2011).

62. Martha Nussbaum, *Women and Human Development* 5 (2000).

63. Stuart Hall, "Notes on Deconstructing the 'Popular,'" in *Cultural Theory and Popular Culture: A Reader* (John Storey, ed., 2009) at 518.

64. Michel de Certeau, *The Practice of Everyday Life* xi–xxiv (1984).

65. *Id.*

66. *Id.*

67. John Dewey, *Art as Experience* 281 (1934).

68. *Id.* at 281–82.

69. *Id.* at 282.

70. Martha Nussbaum, *The Clash Within: Democracy, Religious Violence, and India's Future* 134 (2007).

71. J. K. Rowling, *Harry Potter and the Sorcerer's Stone* 20 (1997).

72. The Harry Potter Alliance, "What We Do," available at http://thepalliance .org/what-we-do (last visited Aug. 8, 2011).

73. The Harry Potter Alliance, "Banned Books Week 2009," available at http:// thehpalliance.ning.com/profiles/blogs/banned-books-week-2009 (last visited Aug. 8, 2011).

74. *Id.*

75. Henry Jenkins, "What Happened *Before* YouTube," in Burgess and Green, *YouTube: Online Video and Participatory Culture* 115.

76. *Id.* at 116.

77. Hanna Arendt, *On Revolution* 264 (1990).

78. Amartya Sen, "Cultural Liberty and Human Development," in *Human Development Report, 2004: Cultural Liberty in Today's Diverse World* 18 (2004).

79. Foucault, "What Is Enlightenment?," 35.

80. For some recent literature, see Astrida Seja Kaugars and Sandra W. Russ, "Assessing Preschool Children's Pretend Play: Preliminary Affect in Play Scale–Preschool Version," Early Education & Development 733, 734 (Sept. 1, 2009) ("pretend play is considered integral to pre-school children's development since it represents an intersection of cognitive processes, affective processes, and interpersonal processes").

81. See *id.* at 738–39 ("Children who engage in social fantasy play have more often [sic] been found to be more socially competent"); *id.* at 751 ("Children who expressed more affect in their play and who played with ease demonstrated desirable levels of socioemotional adjustment and low levels of behavior problems"). See also Paul Tough, "Can the Right Kind of Play Teach Self Control?," N.Y. Times Magazine, Sept. 27, 2009 at MM31.

82. See Kaugars and Russ, *Assessing Preschool Children's Pretend Play* 733, 739 ("boys and girls who engaged in high levels of pretend play performed better on a task assessing understanding of emotions").

83. Nelson D. Schwartz, "Turning to Tie-Ins, Lego Thinks Beyond the Brick," N.Y. Times, Sept. 6. 2009 at B1.

84. Andrew Adam Newman, "Lego Rejects a Bit Part in a Spinal Tap DVD," N.Y. Times, Aug. 11, 2009 at B3.

85. "Lego Weapon Store," available at http://www.youtube.com/watch?v= RjLR6JYVC9E (last visited Aug. 8, 2011).

86. "Legos Gone Wild," available at http://www.youtube.com/watch?v=7pUdD DFOjG8 (last visited Aug. 8, 2011).

87. Newman, "Lego Rejects a Bit Part in a Spinal Tap DVD" at B3.

88. Schiesel, "All Together Now."

89. On this point, see generally Cornelia J. Homburg, *The Copy Turns Original* (1996).

90. Daniel Radosh, "While My Guitar Gently Beeps," N.Y. Times Magazine, August 16, 2009 at 26, 31.

91. Jürgen Habermas, "Reconciliation Through the Public Use of Reason: Remarks on John Rawls's Political Liberalism," vol. 92, no. 3, The Journal of Philosophy 109, 127 (March 1995).

92. Antje Gimmler, "Deliberative Democracy, the Public Sphere and the Internet," vol. 27, Philosophy and Social Criticism 21, 22 (2001).

93. Burgess and Green, YouTube, 79.

94. *Id.* at 77.

95. Dewey, *Art as Experience* 332.

96. *Id.* at 286.

97. Milan Kundera, *Identity* 45–46 (1999).

98. Burgess and Green, YouTube, 87.

99. David Browne, "Harry Potter Is Their Peter Pan," N.Y. Times, July 22, 2009 at E1.

100. Michael R. Dove, "Dreams from His Mother," N.Y. Times, August 11, 2009 at A17.

101. Schwartz, "Turning to Tie-ins" at B1.

102. See Kaugars and Russ, *Assessing Preschool Children's Pretend Play at* 737–38 ("children who experience affect themes and experience emotions in play may be more likely to develop a broad repertoire of the associations needed in creative activities"); and at 750 ("The affective dimensions of play and a greater number of pretend play intervals were significantly related to creativity").

103. Jürgen Habermas, "Political Communication in Media Society: Does Democracy Still Enjoy an Epistemic Dimension? The Impact of Normative Theory on Empirical Research," Communication Theory ISSN 1050–3293 (2006), William M. Landes and Richard A. Posner, *The Economic Structure of Intellectual Property Law* 423–24 (2003).

104. Cass Sunstein, Republic.com (2002).

105. Anupam Chander, "Whose Republic?," 69 U. Chi. L. Rev. (2002) (reviewing Sunstein's book and arguing that the Internet allows minorities to find and create supportive communities, both national and transnational).

106. Andrew Keen, *The Cult of the Amateur* 204 (2007) ("I believe that our real moral responsibility is to protect mainstream media against the cult of the amateur. We need to reform rather than revolutionize an information and entertainment economy that, over the last two hundred years, has reinforced American values and made our culture the envy of the world").

107. Rob Merges, "IP: Social and Cultural Theory," available at http://uchicago law.typepad.com/faculty/2009/03/ip-social-and-cultural-theory.html (last visited Aug. 8, 2011).

108. Keen, *The Cult of the Amateur* 4.

109. Rob Merges, "IP: Social and Cultural Theory," faculty blog, March 11, 2009,

http://www.facebook.com/note.php?note_id=67830477287 (last visited Aug. 8, 2011).

CHAPTER 3. FAIR CULTURE

1. Sharon LaFraniere, "In the Jungle, the Unjust Jungle, a Small Victory," N.Y. Times, March 22, 2006 ("Music scholars say the 78 r.p.m. recording of "Mbube" was probably the first African record to sell 100,000 copies").
2. Rian Malan, *In the Jungle* 3 (2003).
3. Mr. Linda received 10 shillings—about 87 cents today—when he signed over the copyright of "Mbube" in 1952 to Gallo Studios, the company that produced his record. He also got a job sweeping floors and serving tea in the company's packing house.
4. Lawrence Lessig, *Free Culture: How Big Media Uses Technology and the Law to Lock Down Culture and Control Creativity* (2004).
5. William Landes and Richard Posner similarly conclude that "expanding intellectual property rights can actually reduce the amount of new intellectual property that is created by raising the creators' input costs, since a major input into new intellectual property is existing such property." See William M. Landes and Richard A. Posner, *The Economic Structure of Intellectual Property Law* 422 (2003).
6. Suzanne Scotchmer, *Innovation and Incentives* (2004).
7. Michael Heller, *Gridlock Economy: How Too Much Ownership Wrecks Markets, Stops Innovation, and Costs Lives* (2008) (describing the possibility that licensing rights needed for downstream production might be so cumbersome as to stop such production); Landes and Posner, *The Economic Structure of Intellectual Property Law* at 422 (expressing concern over raising creators' input costs through overbroad intellectual property rights).
8. Lessig, *Free Culture* at 94.
9. *Cf.* Yochai Benkler, *The Wealth of Networks* (2006) (recognizing that better distributive mechanisms—for example, the Internet—enable more productive and democratic use of information in the public domain).
10. Anupam Chander and Madhavi Sunder, "The Romance of the Public Domain," 92 Cal. L. Rev. 1331 (2004).
11. Matt Haughey, "Developing Nations Copyright License Frees Creativity Across the Digital Divide," Creative Commons Blog, Sept. 13th, 2004, available at http://creativecommons.org/press-releases/entry/4397 (last visited Aug. 9, 2011).
12. Lawrence Lessig, "Retiring Standalone DevNations and One Sampling License," Creative Commons Blog, June 4th, 2007, available at http://creativecommons.org/weblog/entry/7520 (last visited Aug. 9, 2011).
13. Lessig, *Free Culture* at xv.
14. James Boyle, *Shamans, Software and Spleens: Law and the Construction of the Information Society* (1996).

15. "Mbube" itself was copyrighted as "Wimoweh" under the alias composer "Paul Campbell." Malan, *In the Jungle* at 22.
16. *Id.* at 21.
17. *Id.* at 24.
18. *Id.* at 31.
19. Charles Seeger, "Who Owns Folklore? A Rejoinder," 21 Western Folklore 93, 97 (1962).
20. I thank Richard McAdams for bringing to my attention a more recent example of a copyright wrong made right. In 1959 Mr. James Carter was serving time in a Mississippi prison when Alan Lomax, "the pioneering collector of American folk songs," appeared on the scene and began tape-recording the songs sung by prisoners to keep up their morale on hard days chopping wood along highways and railroad lines. As an obituary for Carter in the *L.A. Times* recounts: "One of the songs Lomax recorded that hot September day was 'Po' Lazarus,' a melancholy tune about a man who is hunted and gunned down by a sheriff with a .44-caliber revolver. The rhythmic thump of the prisoners' axes provided the only accompaniment. . . . The song left a lasting impression. 'They were 50 black men who were working under the whip and the gun and they had the soul to make the most wonderful song I'd ever heard,' Lomax told National Public Radio in 2002, shortly before his death." Carter, who was the lead singer for the song "Po' Lazarus," likely knew little of the recording. But decades later, "Po' Lazarus" found its way into the Hollywood hit film, *O Brother, Where Art Thou?* directed by Joel and Ethan Coen and starring *George Clooney*. The soundtrack to the film became a surprise hit, selling millions of copies. Lomax's daughter searched for months for Carter to share the spoils, finally appearing on the doorstep of his humble home in Chicago with a royalty check for $20,000 "and a platinum CD bearing his name." Carter "took his first-ever plane ride to Los Angeles with his family" to attend the Grammy Awards that year, where the soundtrack for *O Brother, Where Art Thou?* won album of the year. By the time Carter died, he had received nearly $100,000 in royalties. Dennis Mclellan, "James Carter, 77; Singer in Chain Gang Found Fame," L.A. Times, Dec. 8, 2003.
21. H. Koivunen and L. Marsio, "Ethics and Cultural Policy," *D'Art Topics in Arts Policy* no. 24, April 2008, available at http://www.ifacca.org/topic/ethics-in-cultural-policy (last visited Aug. 9, 2011).
22. Amartya Sen, *Development as Freedom* 18 (1999).
23. A recent submission to the Committee on Economic, Social, and Cultural Rights by the Yale Law School Information Society Project (ISP) argues that "take part in" highlights that "participation is the essence of the right." Moreover, it is a "right of everyone to take part in culture," which "requires the elimination of discriminatory barriers, and special measures to prevent barriers of geography, language, poverty, illiteracy, or disability from blocking full and equal participation." See "Access to Knowledge and the Right

to Take Part in Cultural Life," Submission by the Information Society Project at Yale Law School to the Committee on Economic, Social, and Cultural Rights, 41st sess., November 3–21, 2008, at 2–3.

24. See, e.g., Article 27 of the Universal Declaration of Human Rights, which states: "Everyone has the right freely to participate in the cultural life of the community, to enjoy the arts and to share in scientific advancement and its benefits. Everyone has the right to the protection of the moral and material interests resulting from any scientific, literary or artistic production of which he is the author." Universal Declaration of Human Rights, G.A. Res. 217A, art. 27, U.N. GAOR, 3d sess., 1st plen. mtg., U.N. Doc. A/810, Dec. 12, 1948. See also International Covenant on Economic, Social, and Cultural Rights art. 15, opened for signature Dec. 19, 1966, 993 U.N.T.S. 3 (recognizing "the right of everyone . . . [t]o benefit from the protection of moral and material interests resulting from any scientific, literary or artistic production of which he is the author"); see also Draft Declaration on the Rights of Indigenous Peoples, U.N. Doc. E/CN.4/Sub.2/1994/2/Add.1 (1994) (declaring rights to artifacts, designs, ceremonies, technologies, traditional medicines and health practices). A November 2005 document elaborating on the meaning of this provision in the ICESCR concludes: "intellectual property is a social product and has a social function." See also U.N. Econ. & Soc. Council [ECOSOC], Comm. on Econ., Soc. and Cultural Rights, General Comment no. 17 at 9, U.N. Doc. E/C.12/GC/17, Jan. 12, 2006 ("The right of everyone to benefit from the protection of the moral and material interests resulting from any scientific, literary or artistic production of which he or she is the author").

25. Sen, *Development as Freedom* at 4.

26. Academics are just now beginning to pay greater attention to the links between culture and development. See, e.g., *Culture and Public Action* (Vijayendra Rao and Michael Walton, eds., 2004).

27. *SunTrust Bank v. Houghton Mifflin Co.*, 268 F.3d 1257 (11th Cir. 2001).

28. Manohla Dargis and A. O. Scott, "How the Movies Made a President," N.Y. Times, Jan. 16, 2009. *Cf.* Russell Robinson, "Casting and Caste-ing: Reconciling Artistic Freedom and Antidiscrimination Norms," 95 Cal. L. Rev. 1 (2007).

29. Charles Taylor, "The Politics of Recognition," in *Multiculturalism* 25 (Amy Gutmann, ed., 1994).

30. Salman Rushdie, "Excerpts from Rushdie's Address: 1,000 Days 'Trapped Inside a Metaphor,'" N.Y. Times, Dec. 12, 1991 at B8 (excerpts from speech delivered at Columbia University).

31. For other challenges to identity politics, see generally Cass Sunstein, Republic.com (2001) (arguing that Internet communities breed factionalism); Elizabeth A. Povinelli, *The Cunning of Recognition* 17, 33 (2002) (expressing concern that communities may conform themselves to rigid legal definitions, stifling cultural dynamism); K. Anthony Appiah, "Identity, Authen-

ticity, Survival: Multicultural Societies and Social Reproduction," in *Multiculturalism* 149, 162–63 (Amy Gutmann, ed., 1994) (asking whether, identity politics does not replace "one kind of tyranny with another"); Susan Moller Okin, "Is Multiculturalism Bad for Women?," in *Is Multiculturalism Bad for Women?* 7 (Amy Gutmann, ed., 1994) (arguing that multiculturalism does not promote the best interests of women and children).

32. Iris Marion Young, *Inclusion and Democracy* 105 (2000).

33. Arjun Appadurai, "The Capacity to Aspire: Culture and the Terms of Recognition," in *Culture and Public Action,* 59, 62–63 (Vijayendra Rao and Michael Walton, eds., 2004).

34. Nancy Fraser and Axel Honneth, *Redistribution or Recognition? A Political-Philosophical Exchange* 8 (Joel Golb et al., trans., 2003).

35. U.N. Dept. of Econ. & Soc. Affairs, *Understanding Knowledge Societies,* U.N. Doc. ST/ESA/PAD/SER.E/66 (2005), available at http://unpan1.un.org/intradoc/groups/public/documents/UN/UNPAN020643.pdf (last visited Aug. 9, 2011) at 141, 150.

36. Malan, *In the Jungle* at 3.

37. *Id.* at 7. Malan powerfully describes the universal allure of this song (at 16): "We're talking a pop song so powerful that Brian Wilson had to pull off the road when he first heard it, totally overcome; a song that Carole King instantly pronounced a 'motherfucker.'"

38. Chander and Sunder, "The Romance of the Public Domain" at 1351–54 (describing reasons that developing world companies might find it difficult to exploit resources from their home states to sell globally).

39. In 1999, developing countries paid some $7.5 billion more in royalties and license fees than the royalties and license fees they received. See *id.* at 1354.

40. Madhavi Sunder, "Intellectual Property and Development as Freedom," in *The Development Agenda: Global Intellectual Property and Developing Countries* (Neil W. Netanel, ed., Oxford University Press, 2008).

41. To see Mr. Saidullah explain the inspiration for his amphibian bicycle, watch http://www.youtube.com/watch?v=REx9rMDbqRg (last visited Aug. 9, 2011).

42. Daniel Kahneman et al., "Fairness and the Assumptions of Economics," 59 J. Bus. S285, S299 (1986) ("A realistic description of transactors should include the following traits. [1] They care about being treated fairly and treating others fairly. [2] They are willing to resist unfair firms even at a positive cost. [3] They have systematic implicit rules that specify which actions of firms are considered unfair").

43. See, e.g., Seana Valentine Shiffrin, "Intellectual Property," in *A Companion to Contemporary Political Philosophy* 661 (Robert Goodin et al., eds., 2007) ("once a work is created . . . it is often relatively easy and inexpensive for others to copy and use the work. This makes it easy for competitors [and consumers] to 'steal' a work and undercut the creator's price. This *vulnera-*

bility may deter creators from generating intellectual works."). (Emphasis mine.)

44. See Pam Samuelson, "Copyright and Freedom of Expression in Historical Perspective," 10 J. Intell. Prop. L. 319–27 (2003) (detailing historical focus of copyright law, since the Statute of Anne, on public access to knowledge).

45. I thank Martha Nussbaum for raising this issue.

46. See, e.g., Mark A. Lemley, "Property, Intellectual Property, and Free Riding," 83 Tex. L. Rev. 1031 (2005).

47. See, e.g., Kal Raustiala, "Density and Conflict in International Intellectual Property Law," 40 U.C. Davis L. Rev. 1021 (2007). Raustiala expresses the concern that human-rights-based claims for intellectual property "will serve to wall off still more from the public domain" (at 1033). He cautions that "the risk is that the language and politics of human rights, as it filters [*sic*] into the language and politics of IP rights, will make it harder for governments to resist the siren songs of those seeking ever more powerful legal entitlements" (at 1037).

48. See Neil Weinstock Netanel, *Copyright's Paradox* (2008).

49. For the argument that most subject areas of law should ignore distributional consequences in favor of direct redistribution through the tax system, see generally Louis Kaplow and Steven Shavell, *Fairness Versus Welfare* (2002).

50. Mike Miller, "At 85, Pete Seeger Still Hammers Out Justice," Reuters, May 12, 2004.

CHAPTER 4. EVERYONE'S A SUPERHERO

1. Paula Smith, "A Trekkie's Tale" (1974), reprinted in Camille Bacon-Smith, *Enterprising Women: Television Fandom and the Creation of Popular Myth* 94–95 (1992).

2. See Jed Rubenfeld, "The Freedom of Imagination: Copyright's Constitutionality," 112 Yale L.J. 1, 8 n.34 (2002) (offering examples of retellings from a different character's perspective, including Tom Stoppard's *Rosencrantz and Guildenstern Are Dead,* a play on *Hamlet;* Jean Rhys's *Wide Sargasso Sea,* a play on *Jane Eyre;* and Henry Fielding's *Joseph Andrews,* a play on *Pamela*).

3. Pat Pflieger, "Too Good to Be True: 150 Years of Mary Sue," paper presented at the American Culture Association conference (March 31, 1999), available at http://www.merrycoz.org/papers/MARYSUE.HTM (last visited Dec. 18, 2005).

4. Wikipedia, "Mary Sue," available at http://en.wikipedia.org/wiki/Mary_Sue (last visited April 30, 2009).

5. Keidra Chaney and Raizel Liebler, "Me, Myself & I—Fan Fiction and the Art of Self-Insertion," *Bitch Magazine* 52 (Winter 2005).

6. Cheryl Harris, "A Sociology of Television Fandom," in *Theorizing Fandom:*

Fans, Subculture and Identity 41, 42 (Cheryl Harris and Alison Alexander, eds., 1998).

7. See Justin Hughes, "'Recoding' Intellectual Property and Overlooked Audience Interests," 77 Tex. L. Rev. 923, 940–66 (1999).

8. See Arjun Appadurai, "Introduction: Toward an Anthropology of Things," in *The Social Life of Things: Commodities in Cultural Perspective* 3, 30 (Arjun Appadurai, ed., 1986).

9. *SunTrust Bank v. Houghton Mifflin Co.*, 268 F.3d 1257 (11th Cir. 2001).

10. John Fiske, *Television Culture* (1990).

11. Yvonne Fern, *Gene Roddenberry: The Last Conversation* 107 (1994) (quoting Roddenberry: "One of the things Star Trek says is that when the future comes, we will have successfully dealt with all of those issues of race and sex and class, and we will have evolved").

12. BBC UK, "Black History Month: 1969," available at http://www.bbc.co.uk/1xtra/bhm05/years/1969.shtml (last visited June 16, 2006).

13. "In his role as Sulu, [George] Takei challenged convention by being one of the first Asian American television icons to speak without an accent, without exotic costume, without any of the burden of the stereotypes that encumbered earlier TV portrayals. In doing so, he helped to make the idea of 'Asian as normal' possible." Jeff Yang, "Out, Beyond the Stars," S.F. Gate, Nov. 10, 2005, available at http://sfgate.com/cgi-bin/article.cgi?f=/g/a/2005/11/10/apop.DTL (last visited Aug. 9, 2011). Takei observes that his role served another purpose, to counter images of Asians as the enemy during the Vietnam War: "On the 6 o'clock news, every night you saw people with the same kind of face that I have wearing black pajamas, who were being shot up, who were being characterized as the hoard that was dangerous in the jungles of Vietnam." That was followed by this counter-balancing image of Sulu, something that never existed in American media. Asian Week, Sept. 23, 1994 at 11.

14. BBC UK, "Lt. Uhura," available at http://www.bbc.co.uk/cult/st/original/uhura.shtml (last visited Dec. 18, 2005; the kiss "essentially takes place off-screen, because of the network's concerns about upsetting viewers in the southern states").

15. StarTrek.com, "Deep Space Nine Cast," available at http://www.startrek.com/startrek/view/series/DS9/cast/69054.html (last visited June 16, 2006).

16. Star Trek.com, "Voyager Cast," available at http://www.startrek.com/startrek/view/series/voy/cast/69079.html (last visited June 16, 2006).

17. Children Now, *Fall Colors: 2003–04 Prime Time Diversity Report* at 11, available at http://www.childrennow.org/index.php/learn/reports_and_research/article/216 (last visited Aug. 9, 2011).

18. *Id.* at 7.

19. *Id.* at 8.

20. *Id.* at 1.

21. *Id.* at 2.
22. *Id.* at 4.
23. *Id.* at 6.
24. *Id.* at 3. The Children Now report does not break down roles according to the intersection of race and gender.
25. I*d.* at 2.
26. See Media Action Network for Asian-Americans, "A Memo from MANAA to Hollywood: Asian Stereotypes," available at http://www.manaa.org/ asian_stereotypes.html (last visited Dec. 19, 2005). See also David L. Eng, *Racial Castration: Managing Masculinity in Asian America* 15–19 (2001) (describing the feminization of the Asian-American male in the U.S. cultural imagination); Gina Marchetti, *Romance and the "Yellow Peril": Race, Sex, and Discursive Strategies in Hollywood Fiction* 2 (1993) (noting that Asian men are depicted as either "rapists or asexual eunuch figures," while Asian females are depicted as "sexually available to the white hero"); Darrell Y. Hamamoto, *Monitored Peril: Asian Americans and the Politics of TV Representation* 6–31 (1994) (discussing how racist images have been imposed on Asian Americans on television); Peter Kwan, "Invention, Inversion and Intervention: The Oriental Woman in the World of Suzie Wong, M. Butterfly, and *The Adventures of Priscilla, Queen of the Desert*," 5 Asian L. J. 99 (1998).
27. Dana E. Mastro and Bradley S. Greenberg, *The Portrayal of Racial Minorities on Prime Time Television,* J. Broad. & Elec. Media 690, 691 (2000). One website community titled "DeadBroWalking" hosts a "people of color deathwatch," with entries critical of the representation (or absence) of minority characters in popular media, available at http://community.live journal.com/deadbrowalking (last visited Aug. 9, 2011).
28. Robert M. Entman and Andrew Rojecki, *The Entman-Rojecki Index of Race and Media* (2000), http://www.press.uchicago.edu/Misc/Chicago/210758. html (last visited Nov. 15, 2006).
29. Elizabeth Grauerholz and Bernice A. Pescosolido, *Gender Representation in Children's Literature: 1900–1984,* 3 Gender and Soc'y 113, 118 (1989).
30. Meg James, "Ruling on Pooh Is a Setback for Disney," L.A. Times, May 3, 2003 at C1 ("At the peak of Winnie the Pooh's popularity in the late 1990s, it brought in more than $1 billion in revenue annually to Disney and companies it licensed to produce Pooh products").
31. As one fan explains on a Winnie-the-Pooh FAQ, available at http://www .lavasurfer.com/pooh-faq4.html (last visited Aug. 9, 2011): "every character in 'Winnie-the-Pooh,' and 'The House at Pooh Corner' are boys except Kanga. There are references to other female characters, namely some of Rabbit's friends and relations, but none of them have any speaking parts." For an image of Kanga, see http://us.penguingroup.com/static/packages/ us/yreaders/pooh75/characters/kanga.html (last visited Aug. 9, 2011). Of Kanga, the publisher of the *Winnie-the-Pooh* books explains, "She displays

many maternal attributes, such as: wanting to Count Things, making sure that there are enough watercress sandwiches to go round, telling you what to do, giving baths, and knowing how to play a joke." *Id.*

32. The self-insertion in the original is quite vivid. The stories are told to "you," as if they recount the adventures of the reader (Christopher Robin) himself in the Hundred Acre Wood. See, e.g., A. A. Milne, *Winnie the Pooh* (1924) at 2: "Was that me?" Said Christopher Robin in an awed voice, hardly daring to believe it./ "That was you."

33. Christine Schoefer, "Potter's Girl Trouble," Salon.com, Jan. 12, 2000, available at http://archive.salon.com/books/feature/2000/01/13/potter/index .html (last visited Aug. 9, 2011): "The world of everyone's favorite kid wizard is a place where boys come first."

34. Non-whites in the Harry Potter novels are specifically identified by race, while whiteness is assumed for all others. Keith Woods, "Harry Potter and the Imbalance of Race," PoynterOnline, July 15, 2005, available at *http://www.poynter.org/column.asp?id=58&aid=85445* (last visited Dec. 24, 2005).

35. Kelley Massoni, "Modeling Work: Occupational Messages in *Seventeen Magazine*," 18 Gender & Soc'y 47 (2004).

36. See, e.g., Hassan Fattah, "Comics to Battle for Truth, Justice and the Islamic Way," N.Y. Times, Jan. 22, 2006 at 8. ("For comic book readers in Arab countries, the world often looks like this: superheroes save American cities, battle beasts in Tokyo and even on occasion solve crimes in the French countryside. But few care about saving the Arab world.")

37. See Jerry Kang, "Trojan Horses of Race," 118 Harv. L. Rev. 1489, 1549–53 (2005) (describing the cognitive process of internalizing bias from violent crime news).

38. Mark Watson and Mary McMahon, "Children's Career Development: A Research Review from a Learning Perspective," 67 J. Vocational Behavior 119, 124 (2005) (citing S. L. O'Bryant and C. R. Corder-Bolz, "The Effects of Television on Children's Stereotyping of Women's Work Roles," 12 J. Vocational Behavior 233 [1978]).

39. Paul E. McGhee and Terry Frueh, "Television Viewing and the Learning of Sex-Role Stereotypes," 6 Sex Roles 179 (1980).

40. Ann Beuf, "Doctor, Lawyer, Household Drudge," 24 J. of Commc'n 142, 144 (1974).

41. Glenn D. Cordua et al., "Doctor or Nurse: Children's Perception of Sex Typed Occupations," 50 Child Dev. 590, 591 (1979).

42. Rebecca S. Bigler et al., "Race and the Workforce: Occupational Status, Aspirations, and Stereotyping Among African American Children," 39 Developmental Psychol. 572 (2003).

43. Sheila T. Murphy, *The Impact of Factual Versus Fictional Media Portrayals on Cultural Stereotypes*, 560 Annals Am. Acad. Pol. & Soc. Sci. 165 (1998).

44. Minn. Advisory Comm'n to the U.S. Comm'n on Civil Rights, Stereotyping of Minorities by the News Media in Minnesota 35 (1993), available at http://

www.usccr.gov/pubs/sac/mn1203/mn1203.pdf (last visited Aug. 9, 2011; providing 2003 update to 1993 study); see also Camille O. Cosby, *Television's Imageable Influences: the Self-Perceptions of Young African-Americans* 25 (1994).

45. Amber McGovern, "Neutralizing Media Bias Through the FCC," 12 DePaul-LCA J. Art & Ent. L. & Pol'y 217, 242 (2002), citing Carolyn A. Stroman, "Television's Role in Socialization of African-American Children and Adolescents," 60 J. Negro Educ. 314, 315 (1991).

46. Wikipedia, "Nichelle Nichols," available at http://en.wikipedia.org/wiki/Nichelle_Nichols (last visited Dec. 19, 2005).

47. See, e.g., TA Maxwell, "The Mary Sue Manual," Nov. 6, 2003, available at http://www.fictionpress.com/s/1440163/1/ (last visited Aug. 9, 2011); Melyanna, "The Trouble with Mary," TheForce.Net, July 1, 2002, available at http://fanfic.theforce.net/articles.asp?action=view&ID=33 (last visited Aug. 9, 2011). For a remarkable electronically scored personality test variant, see "The Original Fiction Mary-Sue Litmus Test," available at http://www.ponylandpress.com/ms-test.html (last visited Aug. 9, 2011).

48. Fiona Carruthers, "Fanfic Is Good for Two Things—Greasing Engines and Killing Brain Cells," 1 Particip@tions (May 2004).

49. Speaking of disciplining the consumption of texts, the French theorist Michel de Certeau observes: "By its very nature open to plural reading, the text becomes a cultural weapon, a private hunting reserve, the pretext for a law that legitimizes as 'literal' the interpretation given by socially authorized professionals and intellectuals." Michel de Certeau, *The Practice of Everyday Life* 171 (Steven Rendall, trans., 1984).

50. See generally Frantz Fanon, *The Wretched of the Earth* (1963).

51. Pflieger, "Too Good to Be True."

52. Sonia K. Katyal, "Performance, Property, and the Slashing of Gender in Fan Fiction," 14 J. Gender, Race, & Justice 463 (2006) (arguing in favor of permitting slash fan fiction in order to allow recoding of texts).

53. Shoshanna Green et al., "Normal Female Interest in Men Bonking: Selections from *The Terra Nostra Underground* and *Strange Bedfellows*," in *Theorizing Fandom: Fans, Subculture and Identity* 41, 42 (Cheryl Harris and Alison Alexander, eds., 1998).

54. Neva Chonin, "If You're an Obsessed Harry Potter Fan, Voldemort Isn't the Problem. It's Hermione Versus Ginny," S.F. Chron., Aug. 3, 2005 at E1.

55. "Potter Translations Withdrawn," May 1, 2003, http://www.news24.com/News24/Entertainment/Abroad/0,2–1225–1243_1354257,00.html (last visited Dec. 18, 2005). See also Pogrebin, "Dissipate," available at http://www.fictionalley.org/authors/pogrebin/dissipate01.html (last visited Aug. 9, 2011; two minor South Asian female characters from *Harry Potter* visit India).

56. Manjira Majumdar, "When Harry Met Kali," Outlook (India), July 7, 2003, available at http://www.outlookindia.com/article.aspx?220651 (last visited

Dec. 29, 2010). The fictional characters include Professor Shanku, a protagonist in science-fiction stories by Satyajit Ray. See Wikipedia, "Professor Shanku," available at http://en.wikipedia.org/wiki/Professor_Shanku (last visited Dec. 27, 2010). Potter also meets historical figures, such as Satyajit Ray's father. Priyanjali Mitra, "Bengali Babu," Indian Express, Apr. 20, 2003, available at http://www.indianexpress.com/full_story.php?content _id=22323 (last visited Dec. 27, 2010).

57. The letter asserted copyright, character merchandise, trademark, and fraud claims. Urmi A. Goswami, "Illegally Cashing in on Harry Potter," Economic Times (India), Apr. 3, 2003. The book included stills from the film *Harry Potter and the Sorcerer's Stone.*

58. See Judge Posner's list of cartoon characters in *Gaiman v. McFarlane,* 360 F.3d 644, 660 (7th Cir. 2004); *DC Comics Inc. v. Reel Fantasy, Inc.,* 696 F.2d 24, 25, 28 (2d Cir. 1982) (assuming Batman to be copyrightable); *Walt Disney Prods. v. Air Pirates,* 581 F.2d 751, 753–55 (9th Cir. 1978) (Mickey Mouse et al.); *Detective Comics v. Bruns Publ'ns,* 111 F.2d 432, 433–34 (2d Cir. 1940) (Superman); *Fleischer Studios, Inc. v. Ralph A. Freundlich, Inc.,* 73 F.2d 276, 278 (2d Cir. 1934), cert. denied, 294 U.S. 717 (1934) (Betty Boop). Cartoon characters seem to have received greater protections than literary characters; see Leslie A. Kurtz, "The Independent Legal Lives of Fictional Characters," 1986 Wis. L. Rev. 429, 451 (1986). Even the setting—the world created by a writer devoid of its specific characters—will likely be subject to copyright. Thus, pupiling Hogwarts with newly invented characters is not enough to escape Rowling's copyright claim.

59. 17 U.S.C. § 106(2) (2002).

60. 17 U.S.C. § 107 (1978).

61. *Campbell v. Acuff-Rose Music, Inc.,* 510 U.S. 569, 583 (1994).

62. *Id.* at n.6B.

63. *Id.* at 593–94.

64. *Suntrust Bank v. Houghton Mifflin Co.,* 268 F.3d 1257, 1259 (11th Cir. 2001).

65. *Id.* at 1270.

66. *Id.* at 1281.

67. *Id.* at 1270.

68. *Id.* at 1271.

69. *Mattel Inc v. Walking Mt. Prods.,* 353 F.3d 792, 801 (9th Cir. 2003).

70. *Leibovitz v. Paramount Pictures Corp.,* 137 F.3d 109, 115 (2nd Cir. 1998).

71. *Campbell,* 510 U.S. at 580–81 n.14.

72. *Id.* at 581.

73. *Id.* at 579 ("[T]he more transformative the new work, the less will be the significance of other factors, like commercialism, that may weigh against a finding of fair use"); *Leibovitz v. Paramount Pictures Corp.,* 137 F.3d 109, 110 (2d Cir. 1998) (noting that commercial use weighed against fair use, but nonetheless holding that the advertisement at issue was fair use). A popular misconception holds that noncommercial use is legally *required.* While

not required, noncommercial use is a factor weighing in favor of fair use. *Cf.* Rebecca Tushnet, *Legal Fictions: Copyright, Fan Fiction, and a New Common Law*, 17 Loy. L.A. Ent. L.J. 651, 654 (1997) ("Fan fiction should fall under the fair use exception to copyright restrictions because fan fiction involves the productive addition of creative labor to a copyright holder's characters, it is noncommercial, and it does not act as an economic substitute for the original copyrighted work"). Furthermore, copyright owners might be less likely to sue authors of noncommercial fan fiction.

74. Paul Goldstein, *Goldstein on Copyright* §12.2.1.1(a), 12:38 (3d ed. 2005) ("by far the great bulk of decisions finding fair use have involved commercial, rather than noncommercial, uses").

75. *Campbell,* 510 U.S. at 579.

76. Writing fan fiction helps many amateur writers to develop their craft, occasionally leading to commercial success through book contracts for original stories. John Jurgensen, "Rewriting the Rules of Fiction," Wall St. J., Sept. 16, 2006, at P1, available at http://online.wsj.com/public/article/SB115836001321164886-GZsZGW_ngbeAjqwMADJDX2wofrg_20070916.html (last visited Dec. 29, 2010).

77. *Campbell,* 510 U.S. at 591.

78. William F. Patry and Richard A. Posner, *Fair Use and Statutory Reform in the Wake of Eldred,* 92 Calif. L. Rev. 1639, 1644–45 (2004) (complaining that this factor "fails to distinguish between a use that impairs the potential market for the copyrighted work by criticizing it from a use that impairs the copyrighted work's market or value by free riding on the work").

79. *Campbell,* 510 U.S. at 581.

80. See *Berlin v. E.C. Publ'ns Inc.,* 329 F.2d 541, 545 (2d Cir.), *cert. denied,* 379 U.S. 822 (1964) (holding that the amount copied should be no more than necessary to conjure up the original).

81. Rebecca Tushnet, "Legal Fictions: Copyright, Fan Fiction, and a New Common Law," 17 Loy. L.A. Ent. L.J. 651, 680 (1997) (describing disclaimers in fan fiction as "[r]itual").

82. *Campbell,* 510 U.S. at 580.

83. AnneRice.com, available at http://www.annerice.com/fa_writing_archive.htm (last visited Sept. 30, 2006). (Emphasis added.)

84. Goldstein, *Goldstein on Copyright* at §12.2.1.1(b), 12:31. Others are optimistic that there are alternatives for the bulk of intellectual properties, but this seems more far-reaching than Goldstein, who after all limits his claim to satire, as that term has come to be understood in law. See, e.g., Justin Hughes, "'Recoding' Intellectual Property and Overlooked Audience Interests," 77 Tex. L. Rev. 923, 969–72 (1999).

85. Henry Louis Gates, Jr., Decl. at 1, *SunTrust Bank v. Houghton Mifflin Co.,* 136 F. Supp. 2d 1357 (N.D. Ga. 2001) (No. 1:01 CV-701-CAP).

86. Toni Morrison, Decl. at 1, *SunTrust Bank v. Houghton Mifflin Co.,* 136 F. Supp. 2d 1357, (N.D. Ga. 2001) (No. 1:01 CV-701-CAP).

87. Henry Louis Gates, Jr., Decl. at 1, *SunTrust Bank v. Houghton Mifflin Co.*, 136 F. Supp. 2d 1357 CAP (N.D. Ga. 2001) (No. 1:01 CV-701).

88. Keith Aoki, *Adrift in the Intertext: Authorship and Audience "Recoding" Rights*, 68 Chi.-Kent L. Rev. 805, 836 (1993). (Emphasis added.)

89. Rosemary J. Coombe, "Objects of Property and Subjects of Politics: Intellectual Property Laws and Democratic Dialogue," 69 Tex. L. Rev. 1853, 1879 (1991).

90. Paul Goldstein, *Derivative Rights and Derivative Works in Copyright*, 30 J. Copyright Soc'y U.S.A. 209, 218 (1983) (*"all* works are to some extent based on works that precede them"). (Emphasis in original.)

91. See Henry Louis Gates, Jr., *The Signifying Monkey* 52 (1988); Henry Louis Gates, Jr., *Figures in Black: Words, Signs, and the "Racial" Self* 236 (1987) (describing the black writer as "he who dwells at the margins of discourse, ever punning, ever troping, ever embodying the ambiguities of language" and engaged in "repetition and revision . . . repeating and reversing simultaneously . . . in one deft discursive act").

92. Henry Jenkins, *Textual Poachers: Television Fans and Participatory Culture* 35 (1992).

93. Gates, *Figures in Black* at 240.

94. De Certeau, *The Practice of Everyday Life* at 29.

95. Constance Penley, *Brownian Motion: Women, Tactics, and Technology, in Technoculture* 135, 155 (Constance Penley and Andrew Ross, eds., 1991).

96. See Madhavi Sunder, "Cultural Dissent," 54 Stan. L. Rev. 495, 555–67 (2001).

97. Jane Austen, *Persuasion* 162–63 (Bantam Classic ed. 1984).

98. Anupam Chander and Madhavi Sunder, "The Romance of the Public Domain," 92 Calif. L. Rev. 1331, 1351–52 (2004) (explaining why few corporations based in developing countries have successfully commercialized traditional knowledge for a global consumer market).

99. Kelley Massoni, "Modeling Work: Occupational Messages in *Seventeen Magazine*," 18 Gender & Soc'y 47, 50. To take another well-known example, BET (Black Entertainment Television) emerged as a music television alternative to MTV and VH1, only to be bought by MTV's and VH1's owner, Viacom. Lynette Clemetson, "Chief of BET Plans to Broaden Programming Appeal," N.Y. Times, Jan. 10, 2006 at E1.

100. USPTO registration #1179067 purports to give Marvel and DC exclusive rights to the name in the marketing of "publications, particularly comic books and magazines and stories in illustrated form." Todd Verbeek, "Super-Heroes® a Trademark of DC and Marvel," available at *http://briefs .toddverbeek.com/archives/SuperHeroes_a_Trademark_of_DC_and_Marvel .html* (Jan. 30, 2004); Editorial, Set Our Super Heroes (trademark symbol) Free, L. A. Times, Mar. 26, 2006 at M4.

101. See 74 Am. Jur. 2d *Trademarks and Tradenames* § 31 (2005).

102. *Campbell*, 510 U.S. at 592. The Court bolstered the point with literary sup-

port: "'People ask . . . for criticism, but they only want praise.' S. Maugham, *Of Human Bondage* 241 (Penguin ed. 1992)."

103. Bruce P. Keller and Rebecca Tushnet, "Even More Parodic Than the Real Thing: Parody Lawsuits Revisited," 94 Trademark Rep. 979, 996 (2004).

104. The move coincides with a concerted push by leading comic book publishers to offer readers more diverse heroes. DC Comics recently introduced the new Blue Beetle, "aka Jaime Reyes, a Mexican American teenager in El Paso," and Batwoman, whose alter ego is a lipstick lesbian socialite named Kathy Kane. And Marvel celebrated the nuptials of two of its most popular black superheroes, Storm and Black Panther. George Gene Gustines, "Straight (and Not) Out of the Comics," N.Y. Times, May 28, 2006 at B25. In the meantime, new creators are stepping up to fill the void in the industry. See, e.g., Hassan M. Fattah, "Comics to Battle for Truth, Justice, and the Islamic Way," N.Y. Times, Jan. 22, 2006, at A8 (reporting the Kuwaiti publisher Teshkeel Media's plans to publish "'The 99,' a series of comic books based on superhero characters who battle injustice and fight evil, with each character personifying one of the 99 qualities that Muslims believe God embodies"); Virgin Comics, available at http://www.facebook .com/pages/Virgin-Comics/12117873474 (last visited Aug. 9, 2011; introducing a Bangalore-based comics series seeking to "tap into the vast library of mythology and re-invent the rich indigenous narratives of Asia").

105. See Siddharth Srivastava, "When Spiderman Speaks in Hindi," *Asia Times Online,* June 23, 2004, available at http://www.atimes.com/atimes/South _Asia/FF23Df03.html (last visited Dec. 29, 2010).

106. BBC News, "New-Look Pooh 'Has Girl Friend,'" Dec. 9, 2005, available at http://news.bbc.co.uk/go/pr/fr/-/2/hi/entertainment/4512770.stm (last visited Dec. 29, 2010).

107. Will Pavia, "My, Christopher Robin, You've Changed," The Times (Britain), Dec. 9, 2005, at 5.

108. Marco R. della Cava, "Disney Lets Girl into Winnie's World," USA Today, Dec. 7, 2005 at 1D.

109. Susan Dominus, "A Girly-Girl Joins the 'Sesame' Boys," N.Y. Times, Aug. 6, 2006 at B1. ("The feminist-minded parent might not only applaud the decision to make a more high-profile female character, but wonder why on earth it took so long").

110. *SunTrust Bank v. Houghton Mifflin Co.,* 268 F.3d 1257, 1282 (11th Cir. 2001) (Marcus, J., concurring).

111. "'Gay Batman' Artist Gets 'Cease & Desist,'" Artnet.com, Aug. 18, 2005, available at *http://www.artnet.com/magazineus/news/artnetnews/artnetnews8 –18–05.asp* (last visited Dec. 29, 2010).

112. Justin Hughes, "'Recoding' Intellectual Property and Overlooked Audience Interests," 77 Tex. L. Rev. 923, 940–66 (1999). See also William M. Landes and Richard A. Posner, "Indefinitely Renewable Copyright," 70 U. Chi. L. Rev. 471, 486–88 (2003) (arguing that the value of a copyrighted work may

decrease if individuals were free to create derivatives of the copyrighted material, but conceding that the works of Shakespeare, for example, do not seem to suffer from the proliferation of derivative works).

113. See, e.g., Frank Miller, *Batman: The Dark Knight Returns* (1986).

114. James Clifford, *Routes: Travel and Translation in the Late Twentieth Century* 43 (1997); Sunder, *Cultural Dissent* at 519.

CHAPTER 5. CAN INTELLECTUAL PROPERTY HELP THE POOR?

1. Interview with V. C. Vivekanandan, Professor, Nalsar Univ. of Law, in Hyderabad, India (Dec. 28, 2004).

2. Interview with V. K. Unni, Professor, Nalsar Univ. of Law, in Hyderabad, India (Dec. 30, 2004).

3. *Id.*

4. The Geographical Indications of Goods (Registration and Protection) Act, No. 48, Acts of Parliament, 1999 (India), hereinafter GI Act. The GI Act became effective in 2003; see also *id.*

5. Agreement on Trade-Related Aspects of Intellectual Property Rights, Apr. 15, 1994, Marrakesh Agreement Establishing the World Trade Organization, Annex 1C, Legal Instruments—Results of the Uruguay Round, Arts. 22–24, 1869 U.N.T.S. 299, 33 I.L.M. 1197 (2004), hereinafter TRIPS.

6. See "Pochampally Paves the Way for Local IP Protection," Econ. Times, Dec. 19, 2004.

7. See Anupam Chander, "The New, New Property," 81 Tex. L. Rev. 715 (2003) (discussing the allocation of property rights in Internet domain names).

8. James Boyle, *Shamans, Software, and Spleens: Law and the Construction of the Information Society* xiv (1996).

9. James Boyle, "The Second Enclosure Movement and the Construction of the Public Domain," 66 Law & Contemp. Probs. 33, 69 (Winter/Spring 2003).

10. See generally James Boyle, "Foreword: The Opposite of Property?," 66 L. & Contemp. Probs. 1 (Winter/Spring 2003).

11. See generally *Poor People's Knowledge: Promoting Intellectual Property in Developing Countries* (J. Michael Finger and Philip Schuler, eds., 2004).

12. *Id.* at back cover.

13. Boyle, "Foreword" at 1.

14. See, e.g., Kal Raustiala, "Density and Conflict in International Intellectual Property Law," 40 U.C. Davis L. Rev. 1021, 1036 (2007) (commenting that protections for geographical indications in the global South may "exacerbate an already troubling erosion of the public domain").

15. James Boyle, "Foucault in Cyberspace: Surveillance, Sovereignty, and Hardwired Censors," 66 U. Cin. L. Rev. 177 (1997).

16. Boyle, *Shamans, Software, and Spleens* at xii.

17. *Id.* at 142 ("If one has the slightest concern for distributional justice in one's criteria for property regimes, this regime must surely fail").

18. *Id.* at xiv.

19. James Boyle, "A Politics of Intellectual Property: Environmentalism for the Net?," 47 Duke L.J. 87, 114 (1997). In *Shamans, Software, and Spleens* at 127, Boyle wrote: "Whether I am right or wrong about the distributional effects, I think it can be convincingly demonstrated that an exclusively author-centered regime will have negative effects on efficiency. In many ways, this may be the more important point to make. To condemn a system as unfair is one thing; to argue that it does not work, that it may sometimes actually *impede* innovation, is another." (Emphasis in original.)

20. James Boyle, "A Manifesto on WIPO and the Future of Intellectual Property," 2004 Duke L. & Tech. Rev. 0009, 11, available at http://www.law .duke.edu/journals/dltr/articles/PDF/2004DLTR0009.pdf (last visited Aug. 9, 2011).

21. Boyle, *Shamans, Software, and Spleens* at xiv.

22. Boyle, "A Politics of Intellectual Property" at 115.

23. See World Intellectual Property Organization, *Geneva Declaration on the Future of the World Intellectual Property Organization* (Oct. 4, 2004), available at http://www.cptech.org/ip/wipo/futureofwipodeclaration.pdf (last visited September 14, 2011). The Geneva Declaration states that intellectual property law's mandate should "not only be to promote efficient protection and harmonization, but also to promote fairness, development and innovation." The WIPO General Assembly responded to the call, voting that same month to incorporate a "development agenda" into its intellectual property law and policy. World Intellectual Property Organization, "Proposal by Argentina and Brazil for the Establishment of a Development Agenda for WIPO," WO/GA/31/11, (Aug. 27, 2004), available at http://www.wipo.int/ edocs/mdocs/govbody/en/wo_ga_31/wo_ga_31_11.pdf (last visited September 14, 2011). The proposal was joined by a group of ten other countries, which called themselves the "Friends for Development." World Intellectual Property Organization, "Proposal to Establish a Development Agenda for WIPO: An Elaboration of Issues Raised in Document WO/GA/31/11," IIM/1/4 (Apr. 11–13, 2005), available at http://www.wipo.int/ edocs/mdocs/ mdocs/en/iim_1/iim_1_4.pdf (hereinafter *Elaboration of Issues*). The countries were Bolivia, Cuba, the Dominican Republic, Ecuador, Iran, Kenya, Sierra Leone, South Africa, Tanzania, and Venezuela.

24. Boyle, *Shamans, Software, and Spleens* at 128. For other helpful analyses of the rosy periwinkle controversy see Shayana Kadidal, "Plants, Poverty, and Pharmaceutical Patents," 103 Yale L.J. 223, 224 (1993); Srividhya Ragavan, "Protection of Traditional Knowledge," 2 Minn. Intell. Prop. Rev. 1, 8 (2001).

25. See generally Boyle, *Shamans, Software, and Spleens* at 128.

26. *Id.* at 126 (emphasis omitted).

27. *Id.* at 142 (emphasis added).

28. *Id.* at 128.

29. *Id.* at 128–29.
30. Boyle, "The Second Enclosure Movement and the Construction of the Public Domain" at 52.
31. Darrell A. Posey, *Indigenous Knowledge and Ethics: A Darrell Posey Reader* 161 (Kristina Plenderleith, ed., 2004); see also United Nations Conference on Environment and Development, Rio de Janeiro, Braz., Rio Declaration on Environment and Development, Principle 22, U.N. Doc A/CONF.151/26 (Aug. 12, 1992) ("Indigenous peoples and their communities, and other local communities, have a vital role in environmental management and development because of their knowledge and traditional practices. States should recognize and duly support their identity, culture, and interests and enable their effective participation in the achievement of sustainable development").
32. Treaty on Access to Knowledge 2, May 9, 2005, available at http://www .cptech.org/a2k/a2k_treaty_may9.pdf (last visited Aug. 9, 2011).
33. *Id.* at art. 4(1)(b)(iii).
34. See Michael F. Brown, *Who Owns Native Culture?* 55 (2003) (observing that many indigenous "lawyers and activists believe that intellectual property holds the key to heritage protection"). See generally Madhavi Sunder, "Property in Personhood," in *Rethinking Commodification* 164 (Martha M. Ertman and Joan C. Williams, eds., 2005).
35. See Brown, *Who Owns Native Culture?*, at 43–68 (chronicling efforts by Australian aboriginals to assert collective copyright in native designs); *id.* at 69–94 (describing efforts to use trademark and the right of publicity to combat perceived misuse of traditional symbols, such as the image of the revered Indian leader Crazy Horse on malt liquor); *id.* at 95–143 (noting indigenous responses to ethnobotany patents).
36. Anupam Chander and Madhavi Sunder, "The Romance of the Public Domain," 92 Cal. L. Rev. 1331, 1335 (2004).
37. See, e.g., Brown, *Who Owns Native Culture?*, at 8 ("The readiness of some social critics to champion new forms of silencing and surveillance in the name of cultural protection should trouble anyone committed to the free exchange of ideas").
38. Chander and Sunder, "The Romance of the Public Domain" (discussing how "the romance of the public domain" works to the detriment of poor communities).
39. *Id.* at 1335.
40. *Id.* at 1332.
41. *Id.* at 1354.
42. Boyle, *Shamans, Software, and Spleens* at 119.
43. See, e.g., *id.* at xiii (bemoaning intellectual property ownership by corporations that is "so expansive that they make it much harder for future independent creators to actually create"); and at 142 (citing "the utilitarian failures of the current regime").

44. Vandana Shiva, *Protect or Plunder? Understanding Intellectual Property Rights* 47 (2001).
45. William Cronon, *Changes in the Land: Indians, Colonists, and the Ecology of New England* 127 (1983).
46. *Id.* at 164.
47. Shiva, *Protect or Plunder?* at 50.
48. This is the subtitle to Boyle's *Shamans, Software, and Spleens* (emphasis added).
49. Shiva, *Protect or Plunder?* at 49 (emphasis added). Shiva writes: "*Terra nullius* has its contemporary equivalent in 'Bio-Nullius'—treating biodiversity knowledge as empty of prior creativity and prior rights, and hence available for 'ownership' through the claim to 'invention.'"
50. *Id.* at 50.
51. *Id.* at 64.
52. Maureen Leibl and Tirthankar Roy, "Handmade in India: Traditional Craft Skills in a Changing World," in *Poor People's Knowledge* at 69.
53. J. Michael Finger, "Introduction and Overview," in *Poor People's Knowledge* at 1, 30.
54. *Id.*
55. World Intellectual Property Organization, "Intellectual Property and Traditional Knowledge" 6, available at http://www.wipo.org/freepublications/en/tk/920/wipo_pub_920.pdf (last visited Feb. 24, 2006).
56. *Id.* (emphasis added).
57. Aruna Chandaraju, "Modern MYSURU," The Hindu, Mar. 3, 2005, available at http://www.hindu.com/mp/2005/03/05/stories/2005030500860100.htm (last visited September 14, 2011).
58. *Id.*
59. *Id.*
60. For a more detailed account of the couple's efforts see "Peace Industry," available at http://www.peaceindustry.com/about.html (last visited Mar. 5, 2007).
61. Finger, "Introduction and Overview" at 31.
62. *Id.*
63. Liebl and Roy, "Handmade in India" at 70.
64. *Id.* at 67.
65. Pedro Echeverria, Letter to the Editor, Fin. Times, July 5, 2004 at 10 ("Better protecting geographical indications would allow for the localization of productions in the framework of trade globalization."); see also Rosemary J. Coombe, "Legal Claims to Culture in and Against the Market: Neoliberalism and the Global Proliferation of Meaningful Difference," 1 L., Culture & Human. 35, 46 (2005) (warning that geographical indications may be unduly used to limit competition and exacerbate existing inequalities within groups).
66. See, e.g., Liebl and Roy, "Handmade in India" at 56 ("The full potential of

the role craft traditions can play in the development process, and specifically in the generation of income . . . has only recently begun to be appreciated").

67. Graham Dutfield argues that "estimating the full value of [traditional knowledge] in monetary terms is difficult if not impossible" because it "is often an essential component in the development of other products"; many products derived from traditional knowledge never enter modern markets and thus are not included in GNP calculations; the replacement cost of traditional knowledge would be "quite high"; and the spiritual value of some traditional knowledge cannot be quantified. Graham Dutfield, *Developing and Implementing National Systems for Protecting Traditional Knowledge: A Review of Experiences in Selected Developing Countries* 7 (2000). *Cf.* Graham Dutfield, "Legal and Economic Aspects of Traditional Knowledge," in *International Public Goods and Transfer of Technology under a Globalized Intellectual Property Regime* 504–5 (Keith E. Maskus and Jerome H. Reichman, eds., 2005) (suggesting that "the global value added to rice yields by use of [Indian] landraces can be estimated at $400 million per year"), with Stephen B. Brush, "Farmers' Rights and Protection of Traditional Agricultural Knowledge" 17 (Int'l Food Policy Research Inst., Working Paper no. 36, 2005) (noting there is "no estimate of value or widely accepted method to estimate the value of crop genetic resources developed by farmers").

68. Liebl and Roy, "Handmade in India" at 56 ("Crafts show tremendous potential in terms of employment generation and poverty alleviation in India. Handicrafts provide a livelihood, albeit modest, to large numbers of poor people in India, and especially to the rural poor"). A recent United Nations Educational, Scientific, and Cultural Organization (UNESCO) symposium concluded, for example, "the industries of the imagination, content, knowledge, innovation and creation clearly are the industries of the future . . . they are also important contributory factors to employment and economic growth." *Id.* at 53.

69. Coenraad J. Visser, "Making Intellectual Property Laws Work for Traditional Knowledge," in *Poor People's Knowledge* at 213.

70. Finger, "Introduction and Overview" at 35.

71. *Id.* at 19.

72. See Jasper Vikas George, "Geographical Indications and India," IMC India (Apr. 3, 2005, 7:24 PM), available at http://india.indymedia.org/en/2005/03/210197.shtml (last visited Aug. 9, 2011; urging Indians to seek GI protection of traditional knowledge).

73. TRIPS at art. 22(1).

74. *Id.* at art. 22(2).

75. *Id.* at art. 23.

76. *Id.* at art. 23(1) (prohibiting use of the GI when the product does not originate "in the place indicated by the geographical indication . . . even where the true origin of the goods is indicated or the geographical indication is

used in translation or accompanied by expressions such as 'kind,' 'type,' 'style,' 'imitation' or the like"). The designation "Napa Valley Champagne," for example, even when truthful as to the indication of the product's origin, would be impermissible under the heightened level of protection mandated by TRIPS for wines and spirits.

77. A handful of India's submissions in the WTO relating to TRIPS since 2000 show this. See, e.g., Council for Trade-Related Aspects of Intellectual Property Rights, *Communication from Bulgaria, Cuba, Cyprus, the Czech Republic, the European Communities and Their Member States, Georgia, Hungary, Iceland, India, Kenya, Liechtenstein, Malta, Mauritius, Pakistan, Romania, The Slovak Republic, Slovenia, Sri Lanka, Switzerland, Thailand and Turkey,* IP/C/W/353 (June 24, 2002) (focusing on "protecting all geographical indications equally"); Council for Trade-Related Aspects of Intellectual Property Rights, *Proposal from Bulgaria, Cuba, the Czech Republic, Egypt, Iceland, India, Jamaica, Kenya, Liechtenstein, Mauritius, Nigeria, Pakistan, Slovenia, Sri Lanka, Switzerland, Turkey and Venezuela,* IP/C/W/247/ Rev.1 (May 17, 2001) ("The TRIPS Agreement does not provide sufficient protection for geographical indications of products other than wines and spirits"); Council for Trade-Related Aspects of Intellectual Property Rights, *Communication from India* IP/C/W/196 (July 12, 2000) (proposing that "additional protection for geographical indications must be extended for products other than wines and spirits").

78. GI status for basmati rice is controversial because its production is not limited to any particular geographical region in India. Countrywide recognition may also qualify, however. The European Patent and Trademark Office, for example, upheld Greece's GI in feta cheese after a decadelong battle with other European countries. Stéphanie Bodon, "The EU Feta Debate Concludes," Managing Intellectual Property, MIP Week, Oct. 31, 2005, available at *http://www.managingip.com/Article/1258169/Search/ The-EU-Feta-debate-concludes.html?Home=true&Keywords=feta&Brand =Site* (last visited Aug. 9, 2011). India and Pakistan jointly agreed in 2008 to register together for a GI in basmati. See "India, Pakistan to Protect Basmati Right Together," Business Standard, Nov. 10, 2008, available at http://www.business-standard.com/india/news/india-pakistan-to-protect -basmati-right-together/339640 (last visited Sept. 14, 2011).

79. The Indian GI Act defines "geographical indication" in relation to goods as an "indication which identifies such goods as agricultural goods, natural goods or manufactured goods as originating, or manufactured in the territory of a country, or a region or locality in that territory, where a given quality, reputation or other characteristic of such goods is essentially attributable to its geographical origin and in case where such goods are manufactured goods one of the activities of either the production or of processing or preparation of the goods concerned takes place in such territory, region or locality, as the case may be." Geographical Indications of

Goods (Registration and Protection) Act § I-2(1)(e), No. 48, Acts of Parliament, 1999.

80. The cost to renew a GI is 3,000 rupees. The Geographical Indications of Goods (Registration and Protection) Rules, 2002, The First Schedule, 4A. Once approved, GIs and all producers and authorized users of the GIs are listed in a national register. Geographical Indications of Goods Act § II-5–6. Registration lasts for ten years and is renewable "from time to time" for periods of an additional 10 years. *Id.* § III-18.

81. *Id.* § III-11(2)(a).

82. Geographical Indications of Goods Rules § Form GI-1, available at http://www.ipindia.nic.in/girindia/Form_GI1.pdf (last visited Aug. 9, 2011).

83. Geographical Indications of Goods Act § IV-21(1-b).

84. *Id.* § IV-24.

85. See Liebl and Roy, "Handmade in India" at 65 (asking "[a]nd what happens when a weaver from another part of India moves to Kanjeevaram," famous for its silk sarees?).

86. See Coombe, "Legal Claims to Culture, in and Against the Market." See also, e.g., Madhavi Sunder, "Cultural Dissent," 54 Stan. L. Rev. 495, 504 (2001) (urging assurance that "legal efforts to counter globalization and modernization do not buttress the hegemony of cultural elites and suppress efforts by cultural dissenters to gain autonomy and equality within their cultural context"); Madhavi Sunder, "Intellectual Property and Identity Politics: Playing with Fire," 4 J. Gender, Race & Just. 69, 70 (2000) (discussing "the new centrality of struggles over discursive power—the right to create, and control, cultural meanings").

87. See Elizabeth Povinelli, "At Home in the Violence of Recognition," in *Property in Question: Value Transformation in the Global Economy* 185, 185–206 (Katherine Verdery and Caroline Humphrey, eds., 2004) (describing pressure on indigenous peoples to present their communities as "a synchronic structure" that comports to legal requirements for land based on colonial notions of authentic difference). See generally Rosemary J. Coombe et al., "Bearing Cultural Distinction: Informational Capitalism and New Expectations for Intellectual Property," in *Intellectual Property Law: Articles on Crossing Borders Between Traditional and Actual* 193, 193–213 (F. Willem Grosheide and Jan J. Brinkhof, eds., 2005); Cristina Grasseni, "Packaging Skills: Calibrating Cheese to the Global Market," in *Commodifying Everything: Relationships of the Market* 259–286 (Susan Strasser, ed., 2003) (describing commodification of tradition in the context of local cheese production in Europe).

88. Comm'n on Intellectual Property Rights, Integrating Intellectual Property Rights and Development Policy 90 (2002). *Cf.* Kal Raustiala and Chris Sprigman, "Eat, Drink and Be Wary: Why the U.S. Should Oppose the WTO's Extending Stringent Intellectual Property Protection of Wine and Spirit Names to Other Products," Findlaw, Dec. 12, 2002, available

at http://writ.news.findlaw.com/commentary/20021212_sprigman.html (last visited Aug. 9, 2011; highlighting free-speech concerns posed by heightened GI protection).

89. See Duncan Kennedy, *A Critique of Adjudication* 334 (1997) (describing his own "loss of faith" in rights as always producing positive outcomes for the disempowered). In this work, Kennedy advocates a critical stance toward the discourse of rights but does not abandon rights altogether. *Cf.* Daria Roithmayr, "Left Over Rights," 22 Cardozo L. Rev. 1113, 1113–34 (2001) (arguing for pragmatic use of rights arguments by communities of color).

90. See Douglas A. Kysar, "Preferences for Processes: The Process/Product Distinction and the Regulation of Consumer Choice," 118 Harv. L. Rev. 525, 529 (2004) (noting that "consumer preferences may be heavily influenced by information regarding the manner in which goods are produced").

91. Finger, "Introduction and Overview" at 3.

92. See generally "Light Years IP," available at http://www.lightyearsip.net (last visited Mar. 5, 2007) (recognizing that "within the last two decades, intellectual property has rapidly become the central means to create wealth in almost all industries," and that "[t]here is an urgent need to increase knowledge and capability in developing country producers, exporters and government managers in the tasks of assessing intangible value opportunities, identifying IP solutions and implementing them").

93. Jennifer Allen, "Superflex: Rooseum—Reviews: Amsterdam—Bjornstjerne Reuter Christiansen, Jakob Fenger, and Rasmus Nielsen," Artforum (Feb. 2003), available at http://www.findarticles.com/p/articles/mi_m0268/is_6_41/ai_98123170 (last visited Feb. 24, 2006).

94. See, generally, Anupam Chander, "Illegal Art? The Artists' Group Superflex Co-Opts Global Trademarks," Findlaw (May 13, 2004), available at http://writ.news.findlaw.com/commentary/20040513_chander.html (last visited Aug. 9, 2011).

95. Amartya Sen, *Development as Freedom* 7 (1999).

CHAPTER 6. BOLLYWOOD/HOLLYWOOD

1. Satyajit Ray, "Ordeals of the Alien," Calcutta Statesman, Oct. 4, 1980, available at http://www.satyajitrayworld.com/raysfilmography/unmaderay2 (last visited December 16, 2009).

2. *Id.*

3. *Id.*

4. Andrew Robinson, *Satyajit Ray: The Inner Eye* 292 (1989).

5. *Pather Panchali* (Government of West Bengal, 1955).

6. See generally Michael Sragow, "An Art Wedded to Truth," available at http://satyajitray.ucsc.edu/articles/sragow.html (last visited Dec. 29, 2010).

7. *E.T.: The Extra-Terrestrial* (Universal Pictures, 1982).

8. Robinson, *Satyajit Ray* 294 (1989).

9. *Id.*
10. *Id.*
11. Obaidur Rahman, "Satyajit Ray and *The Alien!*" Daily Star Weekend Mag., May 22, 2009, available at http://www.thedailystar.net/magazine/2009/ 05/04/perceptions.htm (last visited Aug. 9, 2011).
12. Paul Gilroy, *The Black Atlantic* at xi (1993).
13. See generally *Mrs. Doubtfire* (Twentieth Century Fox, 1993); *My Cousin Vinny* (Palo Vista Productions, 1992).
14. See generally *The Lion King* (Disney, 1995); *Kimba the White Lion* (Tezuka Productions).
15. *Id.*
16. See Madhavi Sunder, "The Invention of Traditional Knowledge," 70 L. & Contemp. Probs. 95 (Spring 2007).
17. On the Romantic origins of the concept of "authorship" and the related notions of "originality" and "individualism" in Britain and Germany during the eighteenth century, see Peter Jaszi, "Toward a Theory of Copyright: The Metamorphoses of 'Authorship,'" 1991 Duke L.J. 455 (1991).
18. My vision of culture as a critically important sphere for fulfilling individual self-realization and mutual recognition echoes Hegel's more elaborate social theory set out in *Philosophy of Right*. Arguing against Kant, Hegel emphasized that individual freedom could only be realized through mutual recognition by and of others in social relations or projects. See generally Axel Honneth, *The Pathologies of Individual Freedom: Hegel's Social Theory* (2001).
19. John Dewey, *Art as Experience* 332 (1934).
20. *Slumdog Millionaire* (Warner Independent Pictures, 2008).
21. Martha C. Nussbaum, *Not for Profit: Why Democracy Needs the Humanities* 102 (2010).
22. Robinson, *Satyajit Ray* 360 (quoting Scorsese).
23. See TheOscarSite.com, Satyajit Ray (1921–1992), available at http://theoscar site.com/whoswho7/ray_s.htm (last visited June 14, 2010).
24. Robinson, *Satyajit Ray* at 361 (quoting Ray).
25. *Id.* at 360 (quoting Ray).
26. As the Indian actress Shabana Azmi describes, women in Bollywood films in the 1960s were often portrayed stereotypically as "the forgiving mother, the all-suffering wife, the large-hearted sister, the sacrificing wife, etc." Recently women have been cast as what Azmi calls the "two-in-one heroine," a "sultry sexy siren before marriage and then . . . the chaste wife after." Women are objectified, subjecting themselves to "the male gaze." As filmmakers emphasize "a heaving bosom, a bare midriff, a shaking hip," says Azmi, "the woman is really losing all autonomy over her whole body." Tejaswini Ganti, *Bollywood: A Guidebook to Popular Hindi Cinema* 189–90 (2004) (citing Azmi).
27. Margaret Mitchell, *Gone with the Wind* (Pocket Books, 2008).

28. *The Party* (Mirisch Corporation, 1968).
29. Satyajit Ray, *The Alien* (1967).
30. *The Millionairess* (Dimitri De Grunwald Production, 1960).
31. Robinson, *Satyajit Ray* at 291 (quoting Ray).
32. *Id.*
33. *The Party.*
34. Ray, "Ordeals of the Alien."
35. *Pather Panchali.*
36. Robinson, *Satyajit Ray* at 294 (quoting Ray).
37. *The Lion King.*
38. See Sharon LaFraniere, "In the Jungle, the Unjust Jungle, a Small Victory," N.Y. Times, Mar. 22, 2006 at A6. See also generally Rian Malan, *In the Jungle* 3 (2003), available at http://www.coldtype.net/Assets.08/pdfs/0808 .Jungle.pdf (last visited Dec. 29, 2010).
39. *Kimba the White Lion.*
40. The *San Francisco Chronicle* broke the story. See Charles Burress, "Uproar over *The Lion King*, Disney Film Similar to Work from Japan," S.F. Chronicle, July 11, 1994 at A1, available at http://articles.chicagotribune.com/1994 –07–11/news/9407110111_1_kimba-tv-series-evil-japanese-lion-respects -humans-play-key-roles (last visited Dec. 29, 2010); see also Robert W. Welkos, "A *Kimba* Surprise for Disney," L.A. Times, July 13, 1994 at F1.
41. *Jungle Emperor* (Tezuka Productions Ltd., 1997).
42. See Fred Patten, "Simba Versus Kimba: The Pride of Lions," in *The Illusion of Life 2: More Essays on Animation* 275, 285–89 (Alan Cholodenko, ed., 2007); Shinobu Price, "Cartoons from Another Planet: Japanese Animation as Cross-Cultural Communication," 24 J. Am. & Comp. Cultures 153, 162 (Spring 2001).
43. Sean Leonard, "Progress Against the Law: Anime and Fandom, with the Key to the Globalization of Culture," 8 Int'l J. Cultural Stud. 281, 284–85 (2005).
44. Yasue Kuwahara, "Japanese Culture and Popular Consciousness: Disney's *The Lion King* vs. Tezuka's *Jungle Emperor*," 31 J. Popular Culture 37, 41 (1997).
45. *Id.*
46. See, e.g., Price, "Cartoons from Another Planet" ("Unlike US comics, which are read mostly by boys and young men . . . Japanese comics account for nearly 1/3 of all books and magazines issued in Japan and are stocked in regular book stores and magazine stands").
47. See Burress, "Uproar over *The Lion King*" (quoting the president of Tezuka Productions: "If Disney took hints from 'The Jungle Emperor,' our founder, the late Osamu Tezuka, would be very pleased by it").
48. For a fuller comparison, see Patten, "Simba Versus Kimba" at 291–96.
49. See generally *Jungle Emperor.*
50. See generally "Kimba the White Lion vs Lion King," available at http://

www.youtube.com/watch?v=-SonnCTlcIM (last visited Aug. 9, 2011);
"Lion King–An Overview on Kimba and Interesting Facts," available at
http://www.youtube.com/watch?v=72AVvgRNf2Q (last visited Aug. 9,
2011).

51. "The Simpsons: Round Springfield" (Fox Broadcasting Co., Apr. 30, 1995).
52. See Burress, "Uproar over *The Lion King*."
53. *Id.*
54. See Kuwahara, "Japanese Culture and Popular Consciousness" at 45
    ("[A] majority of published opinions supported the protest").
55. Welkos, "A *Kimba* Surprise for Disney."
56. See Burress, "Uproar over *The Lion King*" ("Disney has promoted the film
    as its first cartoon feature since 1970 not taken from an existing story").
57. Richard Corliss and Jeffrey Ressner, "The Mouse Roars," Time, June 20,
    1994 at 59 (quoting Katzenberg).
58. *The Lion King: Platinum Edition,* disc 2: *Origins* (Walt Disney Home Enter-
    tainment 1994).
59. See, e.g., Patten, "Simba Versus Kimba" at 298–99.
60. *Id.* at 299.
61. *Id.* at 303.
62. *Id.* at 310.
63. *Id.* at 306.
64. *Bambi* (Walt Disney Productions, 1942).
65. Kuwahara, "Japanese Culture and Popular Consciousness" at 42.
66. Patten, "Simba Versus Kimba" at 281.
67. Matthew Roth, "Man Is in the Forest: Humans and Nature in *Bambi* and
    Lion King," Invisible Culture 9 (2005), available at http://www.rochester.
    edu/in_visible_culture/Issue_9/issue9_roth.pdf (last visited Aug. 9, 2011).
    Roth recounts: "[T]he similarities [between *Bambi* and *The Lion King*] are
    numerous. Both films are inhabited entirely by animals: humans, though
    consequential, are on the periphery of *Bambi;* there is no indication of
    humans in *The Lion King.* Pride Rock, the Lion King's 'throne' overlooking
    the Pridelands, is a rocky ledge that resembles the outcropping that Bam-
    bi's father stands on. A parent dies in both movies, though it is a father in
    The Lion King. Simba, the hero of *The Lion King,* has an adult romance with
    a childhood friend. Finally, both stories climax with a threatening pack of
    predators (dogs or hyenas), a fire, and the ultimate triumph over physical
    danger."
68. *Dastar Corp. v. Twentieth Century Fox Film Corp.,* 539 U.S. 23, 36 (2003).
69. Patten, "Simba Versus Kimba" at 277.
70. Michael J. Ybarra, "Anime Instinct: Osamu Tezuka Has Been Called Ja-
    pan's Walt Disney, But His Drawings Aren't Happy Fantasies," L.A. Times,
    June 6, 2007 at A2.
71. Michelle Faul, *Lion Sleeps Tonight* Deal Likely to Boost Poor Musicians,
    Chi. Trib., Mar. 23, 2006 at 14.

72. Rick Lyman, "Akira Kurosawa, Film Director, Is Dead at 88," N.Y. Times, Sept. 7, 1998 at A1.

73. *Seven Samurai* (Toho Company, 1954).

74. *The Magnificent Seven* (Mirisch Corporation, 1960).

75. See "Akira Kurosawa: Influences and Influence Part I," a video interview with Yul Brynner, available at http://www.youtube.com/watch?v=G1STFM3 9vJ4&feature=PlayList&p=A8AFAF545CE1F135&playnext_from=PL&play next=1&index=31 (last visited Aug. 9, 2011).

76. *Yojimbo* (Kurosawa Production Co., 1961).

77. *A Fistful of Dollars* (Constantin Film Produktion, 1964).

78. See John Tottenham, "Yojimbo, A Fistful of Dollars: A Spaghetti-Western Classic and Its Samurai Inspiration Return to the Big Screen," L.A. Weekly, Mar. 6, 2008, available at http://www.laweekly.com/2008–03–06/ film-tv/men-with-no-names/ (last visited Aug. 9, 2011).

79. Vikramdeep Johal, "Plagiarism as an Art-form," The Tribune (India), Nov. 8, 1998, available at http://www.tribuneindia.com/1998/98nov08/sunday/ bolywood.htm.

80. Eva Hemmungs Wirtén, *Terms of Use: Negotiating the Jungle of the Intellectual Commons* 120–21 (2008).

81. *The Jungle Book* (Walt Disney Productions, 1967).

82. Wirtén, *Terms of Use* at 120–22.

83. Abena Dove Osseo-Asare, "Bioprospecting and Resistance: A View from West Africa," Remarks at A2K2 Conference, Yale Law School (Apr. 28, 2007). See generally Abena Dove Osseo-Asare, "Bioprospecting and Resistance: Transforming Poisoned Arrows into Strophanthin Pills in Colonial Gold Coast, 1885–1922," 21 Soc. Hist. Med. 269 (2008).

84. Daniel Kahneman et al., "Fairness and the Assumptions of Economics," 59 J. Bus. S285, S299 (1986) ("A realistic description of transactors should include the following traits. [1] They care about being treated fairly and treating others fairly. [2] They are willing to resist unfair firms even at a positive cost. [3] They have systematic implicit rules that specify which actions of firms are considered unfair").

85. See, e.g., Seana Valentine Shiffrin, "Intellectual Property," in *A Companion to Contemporary Political Philosophy* 661 (Robert Goodin et al., eds., 2007) ("[O]nce a work is created . . . it is often relatively easy and inexpensive for others to copy and use the work. This makes it easy for competitors (and consumers) to 'steal' a work and undercut the creator's price. This *vulnerability* may deter creators from generating intellectual works."). (Emphasis added.)

86. Priti H. Doshi, "Copyright Problems in India Affecting Hollywood and 'Bollywood,'" 26 Suffolk Transnat'l L. Rev. 295, 314 (2003).

87. Nasreen Munni Kabir, *Bollywood: The Indian Cinema Story* 1 (2001).

88. *Id.*

89. In contrast, Hollywood rakes in more than $50 billion annually. Susan P.

Crawford, "The Biology of the Broadcast Flag," 25 Hastings Comm. & Ent L.J. 603, 652 n.4 (2003) ("By 2006, movie theater admissions and the movie aftermarket [DVD sales, rentals, TV] will be generating more than $50 billion in North America, according to PricewaterhouseCoopers").

90. "60 Minutes: The World's Most Beautiful Woman?" (CBS News Jan. 2, 2005).

91. Manjeet Kripalani, "Bollywood: Can New Money Create a World-Class Film Industry in India?," Bus. Wk., Dec. 2, 2002, available at http://www .businessweek.com/magazine/content/02_48/b3810013.htm (last visited Aug. 9, 2011).

92. Ganti, *Bollywood* at 6 (quoting a *Times of India* article dated July 7, 1986).

93. *Id.* at 8–9.

94. *Id.* at 9.

95. *Id.*

96. *Raja Harishchandra* (Phalke Films, 1913).

97. Ganti, *Bollywood* at 10.

98. See Sushil Arora, *Cyclopaedia of Indian Cinema*, vol. 1 (2004).

99. The Copyright (Amendment) Act, No. 49, Acts of Parliament, 1999 (India).

100. Agreement on Trade-Related Aspects of Intellectual Property Rights, Apr. 15, 1994, Marrakesh Agreement Establishing the World Trade Organization, Annex 1C, 1869 U.N.T.S. 299; 33 I.L.M. 1197 (1994).

101. Kripalani, "Bollywood." An Indian film industry official estimated that the industry loses about $360 million annually from piracy. Doshi, "Copyright Problems in India Affecting Hollywood and 'Bollywood'" at 297.

102. Doshi, "Copyright Problems in India Affecting Hollywood and 'Bollywood'" at 307–10.

103. Kripalani, "Bollywood."

104. Emily Wax, "Hollywood Finally Challenging India's Booming Bollywood Over Knockoffs," Wash. Post, Aug. 26, 2009, available at http://www.wash ingtonpost.com/wp-dyn/content/article/2009/08/25/AR2009082503104 .html.

105. *Id.*

106. In sharp contrast, Hollywood dominates 80–90 percent of the European film market. See Tyler Cowen, "Why Hollywood Rules the World, and Whether We Should Care," in *Creative Destruction: How Globalization Is Changing the World's Culture* 75 (2002); Carl Bromley, "The House That Jack Built: How Valenti Brought Hollywood to the World," The Nation, Apr. 3, 2000, available at http://www.thenation.com/archive/house-jack-built -how-valenti-brought-hollywood-world (last visited Aug. 9, 2011).

107. Hindi-language films produced by Warner Bros. and Disney have "bombed at the Indian box office." See Rama Lakshmi, "Bollywood, Hollywood Tightening Ties," Overseas Indian, Mar. 7, 2009 at para. 12, available at http://www.overseasindian.in/2009/mar/news/20091003–045918.shtml (last visited December 16, 2009).

108. Ganti, *Bollywood* at 182–83 (quoting an email to the author written by Bollywood writer Anjum Rajabali on Apr. 9, 1998).

109. *Chandni Chowk to China* (Warner Bros. Pictures, 2009).

110. Joe Leahy, "Bollywood Dreams On," Fin. Times, May 27, 2009, at 38, 39, available at http://www.ft.com/cms/s/0/3ddea8d6–4ac1–11de-87c2 –00144feabdc0,dwp_uuid=1d202fd8-c061–11dd-9559–000077b07658 .html#axzz19vGe0jzT.

111. See rediff.com, "*Chandni Chowk to China* Is a Disaster," Jan. 19, 2009, available at http://specials.rediff.com/movies/2009/jan/19box.htm (last visited Aug. 9, 2011).

112. Leahy, "Bollywood Dreams On" at 40.

113. *Monsoon Wedding* (IFC Productions, 2001).

114. *Lagaan* (Aamir Khan Productions, 2001).

115. *Deewana* (Mayank Arts, 1992).

116. *Sleeping with the Enemy* (Twentieth Century Fox Film Corporation, 1991).

117. *Akele Hum Akele Tum* (United Seven Combines, 1995).

118. *Sleepless in Seattle* (TriStar Pictures, 1993).

119. *Chachi 420* (Eros Entertainment, 1997).

120. *Aunty No. 1* (Lata Films, 1998).

121. *Ghajini* (Gita Arts, 2008).

122. *Memento* (Newmarket Capital Group, 2000).

123. Ganti, *Bollywood* at 182–83.

124. See Nandini Lakshman, "*Slumdog* Oscars Boost India Film Industry," Bus. Wk., Feb. 23, 2009, available at http://www.businessweek.com/globalbiz/ content/feb2009/gb20090223_810139.htm (last visited Dec. 21, 2010).

125. Wax, "Paying the Price for Hollywood Remakes" at para. 5.

126. *Paa* (Amitabh Bachchan Corporation Ltd., 2009); *The Curious Case of Benjamin Button* (Warner Bros. Pictures, 2008).

127. *Hari Puttar: A Comedy of Terrors* (Mirchi Movies, 2009).

128. *Warner Bros. Entm't v. Kohli,* IA No.9600/2008 in CS(OS) 1607/2008, para. 33 (India Sept. 22, 2008), available at http://indiankanoon.org/ doc/395839 (last visited Aug. 9, 2011).

129. *Id.* at para. 33.

130. *Banda Yeh Bindaas Hai* (BR Films, 2010).

131. *My Cousin Vinny* (Palo Vista Productions, 1992).

132. *Wedding Crashers* (New Line Cinema, 2005).

133. ApunKaChoice.com, "*Wedding Crashers* to Be Officially Remade in Bollywood," May 4, 2008 at para. 2, available at http://www.apunkachoice.com/ scoop/bollywood/20080504-3.html (last visited Sept. 14, 2011).

134. "*Krazzy 4* Case Highlights Bollywood's Copyright Woes," available at http://movies.sulekha.com/hindi/krazzy-4/news/krazzy-4-case-highlights -bollywood-s-copyright-woes.htm (last visited Apr. 15, 2008).

135. *Race* (Tips Films Pvt. Ltd., 2008).

136. *Goodbye Lover* (Regency Enterprises, 1998).

137. *Singh Is King* (Blockbuster Movie Entertainers, 2008); *Race* (Ashutosh Gowarikar Productions Pvt. Ltd., 2008).
138. Ganti, *Bollywood* at 144–72. See also *Devdas* (Mega Bollywood, 2002); *Mother India* (Mehboob Productions, 1957); *Guide* (Navketan International Films, 1965); *Sholay* (United Producers, 1975); *Lagaan* (Aamir Khan Productions, 2001).
139. *The Departed* (Warner Bros. Pictures, 2006); *Mou Gaan Dou* (Media Asia Films, 2002).
140. *The Ring* (DreamWorks SKG, 2002); *Ring* (Omega Project, 1998).
141. Lawrence Liang, "Piracy, Creativity, and Infrastructure: Rethinking Access to Culture" 2 (July 20, 2009), unpublished manuscript available at http://ssrn.com/abstract=1436229 (last visited Aug. 9, 2011).
142. *Id.* at 1.
143. *Id.*
144. *Id.* at 2.
145. *Id.*
146. *Id.* at 15.
147. Ganti, *Bollywood* at 182 (quoting Rajabali).
148. Wax, "Paying the Price for Hollywood Remakes" at para. 17 (quoting Anshi Bansal, a university student in New Delhi).
149. Anupam Chander and Madhavi Sunder, "Everyone's a Superhero: A Cultural Theory of 'Mary Sue' Fan Fiction as Fair Use," 95 Cal. L. Rev. 597 (2007).
150. Liang, "Piracy, Creativity, and Infrastructure" at 22.
151. *Id.* at 24.
152. A similar idea motivates cultural protectionism in the European film industry. See generally Sean A. Pager, "Catching a Korean Wave from Bollywood to Nollywood: Promoting Diversity in Filmmaking Through a Decentralized, Market-Based, Trade-Friendly Cultural Protectionism," 64–66 (2010), unpublished manuscript, on file with author. Pager quotes François Mitterand, former president of France, saying, "A society that surrenders to others the means to depict itself would soon be an enslaved society" (at 1).
153. William P. Alford, *To Steal a Book Is an Elegant Offense* 19–20 (1995).
154. *Id.* at 20.
155. *Id.* at 27.
156. *Id.* at 28 (emphasis added).
157. *Id.* at 29 (emphasis added).
158. *Id.*
159. See Sen, "Human Rights and Asian Values" at 36.
160. *Id.* at 40.
161. See Charles R. Stone, "What Plagiarism Was Not: Some Preliminary Observations on Classical Chinese Attitudes Toward What the West Calls Intellectual Property," 92 Marq. L. Rev. 199, 202 (Fall 2008) (concluding that

"although the influence of Confucianism in its various incarnations is unmistakable, the influence that Buddhism exerted [on copyright], and continues to exert, is still relevant and therefore deserving of further study").

162. Justin O'Connor and Gu Xin, "A New Modernity? The Arrival of 'Creative
Industries' in China," 9 Int'l J. Cultural Stud. 271, 279 (2006).

163. Belinda Luscombe, "Zynga Harvests the Cyberfarmer: The Meteoric and
Controversial Rise of the Company Whose Games You Play on Facebook,"
Time, Nov. 30, 2009 at 60.

164. Hiroko Tabuchi, "Paris, Milan, Tokyo. Tokyo?," N.Y. Times, Jan. 2, 2010 at
B1 (concluding that "[i]n that business model, there is little financial gain
for Japan").

165. Gilroy, *The Black Atlantic* at 19.

CHAPTER 7. AN ISSUE OF LIFE OR DEATH

1. World Health Organization, *Antiretroviral Therapy for HIV Infection in
Adults and Adolescents: Recommendations for a Public Health Approach* 72
(2006).

2. Doctors Without Borders, available at https://doctorswithoutborders.org/
publications/alert/article.cfm?id=3969&cat=alert-article (last visited Dec.
30, 2010).

3. E. Richard Gold et al., "Are Patents Impeding Medical Care and Innovation?," PLoS Medicine, Jan. 2009 at 1 ("In all countries, existing patents
make research and development more expensive for the simple reason that
researchers and companies must clear patent rights to do their work").

4. Reuters, quoted by IP Heath (Dec. 30, 2004).

5. See "Investing in Global Health Research: Government Should Play a
Larger Role; A Global Health Initiative Fact Sheet" (Feb. 2007), available
at http://www.familiesusa.org/issues/global-health/government-funding
.PDF (last visited Aug. 9, 2011).

6. See *id.*

7. See *id.*; also "Drugs for Neglected Diseases initiative (DNDi)," available at
http://www.dndi.org/index.php/global.html?ids=5 (last visited on Dec. 30,
2010).

8. World Health Organization, *Report of the Commission on Intellectual Property Rights, Innovation, and Public Health, Public Health Innovation and
Intellectual Property Rights* 85 (2006).

9. *Id.*

10. *Id.* at 22.

11. Doctors Without Borders, "MSF to EU: Stop the Spin, Backdoor Policies
and Closed-door Negotiations That Threaten Access to Affordable Medicines," available at http://www.doctorswithoutborders.org/press/release.
cfm?id=4841&cat=press-release (Nov. 8, 2010).

12. Amartya Sen, "Foreword: Understanding the Challenge of AIDS," in *AIDS
Sutra: Untold Stories from India* 8 (2008).

13. Jan Fagerberg et al., *The Oxford Handbook of Innovation* 270–71 (2006).
14. N. Rajagopala Ayyangar, "Report on the Revision of the Patent Law," Government of India (1959).
15. See *id.* at 307.
16. Vandana Shiva, *Protect or Plunder? Understanding Intellectual Property Rights* 137 (2001).
17. Chan Park and Arjun Jayadev, "Access to Medicines in India: A Review of Recent Concerns" 9, unpublished manuscript, available at http://papers .ssrn.com/sol3/papers.cfm?abstract_id=1436732.
18. Tanuja V. Garde, "India's Intellectual Property Regime: A Counterbalance to Market Liberalization" 9, 11 (Freemon Spogli Institute for International Studies, Working Paper no. 99, 2009), available at http://iis-db.stanford .edu/pubs/22419/No_99_Garde_Indiasintellectualproperty.pdf (last visited Aug. 9, 2011).
19. Shiva, *Protect or Plunder?* at 86.
20. *Novartis v. Union of India*, (2007) 4 MLJ 1153, para. 19; see also *Roche v. Cipla*, IA No. 642/2008 in CS(OS) 89/2008 (India Mar. 19, 2008), available at http://www.delhidistrictcourts.nic.in/Mar08/F.%20Hoffmann%20 Vs.%20Cipla%20Ltd.pdf (last visited Aug. 9, 2011; upholding the Indian Constitution's Article 21 recognizing a "Right to Life" in rejecting Roche's request for a preliminary injunction to stop Cipla from distributing generic lung cancer medication).
21. *State v. Shack*, 277 A.2d 369, 372 (N.J. 1971).
22. *Id.*
23. *Id.*
24. World Health Organization, Declaration on the TRIPS Agreement and Public Health, para. 1 (2001), (hereinafter Doha Declaration), available at http://www.wto.org/english/thewto_e/minist_e/min01_e/mindecl_ trips_e.htm (last visited Aug. 9, 2011).
25. *Id.* at para. 4.
26. *Id.*
27. *Id.* at para. 5(b).
28. *Id.* at para. 6.
29. See generally, World Trade Organization, "Members OK Amendment to Make Health Flexibility Permanent," Dec. 6, 2005, available at http://www .wto.org/english/news_e/pres05_3/pr426_e.htm (last visited Sept. 14, 2011).
30. Jagdish Bhagwati, *In Defense of Globalization* 184 (2004).
31. Doha Declaration, para. 5(b).
32. World Trade Organization, TRIPS: Agreement on Trade-Related Aspects of Intellectual Property Rights, art. 31(b) (hereinafter TRIPS agreement), available at http://www.wto.org/english/tratop_e/trips_e/t_agm3_e.htm (last visited Aug. 9, 2011).
33. See *id.*

34. Doha Declaration, para. 4.

35. See Park and Jayadev, "Access to Medicines in India" at 12.

36. James Love, "Pogge and Hollis on the Trade-off Between Access and Incentives," Knowledge Ecology International, available at http://keionline.org/blogs/2008/11/27/trade-off-innov-access (last visited Aug. 9, 2011).

37. *Id.*

38. See TRIPS agreement, art. 31(f).

39. See generally Park and Jayadev, "Access to Medicines in India" at 17 (citing *INP+ v. Boehringer Ingelheim*).

40. The United States pressured Cambodia to recognize patents in medicines as early as 2007, nine years before they are required to under the Doha Declaration. See Doctors Without Borders, "Doha Derailed: A Progress Report on TRIPS and Access to Medicines," available at http://doctorswith outborders.org/publications/reports/2003/cancun_report.pdf (last visited Aug. 9, 2011).

41. See Why Universities Matter: The Importance of Universities to the Future of Drug R&D, available at http://academicsforaccess.org/index.php/why universities/ (last visited Sept. 14, 2011).

42. See Park and Jayadev, "Access to Medicines in India" at 11.

43. William W. Fisher and Talha Syed, *A Prize System as a Partial Solution to the Health Crisis in the Developing World* 84–85 (2007).

44. See Seana V. Shiffrin, "The Incentives Argument for Intellectual Property Protection," in *Intellectual Property and Theories of Justice* (Axel Gosseries et al., eds., 2009), available at www.law.ucla.edu/docs/shiffrin-incentives argumentintellectualproperty.pdf (last visited Aug. 9, 2011).

45. Letter from Thomas Jefferson to Isaac McPherson (August 13, 1813), available at http://press-pubs.uchicago.edu/founders/documents/a1_8_8s12 .html (last visited Sept. 14, 2011).

INDEX

Vander Ark, Steve, 97, 119
videocasting, 60–61, 72

Warner Bros., 33, 34, 97, 114, 164
*Warner Bros. Entertainment, Inc. and
    J. K. Rowling v. RDR Books,* 119
Web 2.0, 47, 74, 95
Weber, Max, 50
Wikipedia, 60, 70–71
"Wimoweh," 2, 82, 87
Winnicott, David, 75
Winnie the Pooh (fict.), 109–10, 123–24
Wirtén, Eva Hemmungs, 158
women, empowerment of, 11, 108–11, 121
World Bank, 95

World Health Organization, 174, 176, 177,
    184, 190, 196–97
World Intellectual Property Organization
    (WIPO), 138, 140, 193; development
    agenda, 4, 84
World Trade Organization (WTO): and
    medicines, 177, 182, 186; and TRIPS, 4,
    96, 98, 126, 182–83, 186–88, 189, 192,
    194–95
World Wide Web, emergence of, 106–7
Wright Brothers, 191

Young, Iris Marion, 91
YouTube, 10, 14, 33, 35, 38, 39, 47, 56–57,
    61, 65, 67, 72–73, 75, 78, 89